IMAGES
of America

JEWISH COMMUNITY OF SOLANO COUNTY

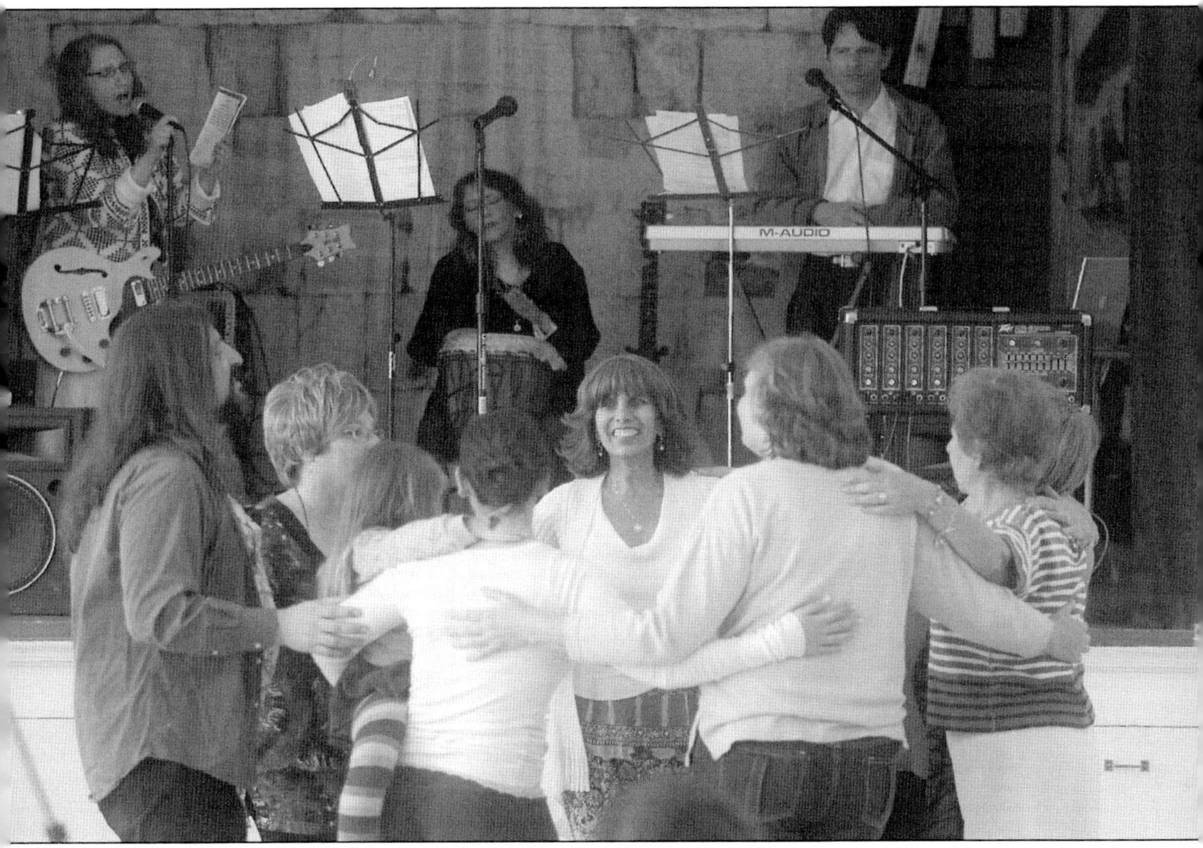

Seen here during Israel Independence Day at Congregation B'nai Israel, Fahni Pierce (center) lost her decade-long battle with breast cancer during this book's production. Before dying too soon, she touched the lives of many hundreds of Solano and Napa County Jewish families by teaching Hebrew, Sunday school, and Bar/Bat Mitzvah preparation, and she made hundreds smile through her love of Israeli folk and belly dancing. Born in Morocco and raised in Israel, Fahni came to Congregation B'nai Israel through her husband, Ralph Pierce—grandson of Solano County Jewish pioneer Raphael Pizante—and together they raised two children, Steven and Angelic. Fahni lived long enough to meet her grandson, Amari. (Courtesy of the *Vallejo Times-Herald*.)

ON THE COVER: Sol Levee and employees pose in front of Vallejo's first department store, Levee's, around 1898. Pictured are John Nelson, Gertrude Kiene, Sol Levee, Mrs. Levee, Alice Pennell, Mabel Williamson, Lewis Williamson, Percy Bernheim, Albert Bernheim, James Loudin, and a person identified as a window draper. (Courtesy of the Vallejo Naval and Historical Museum.)

IMAGES
of America

JEWISH COMMUNITY OF SOLANO COUNTY

Rachel Raskin-Zrihen,
Rachel Rae Moncharsh-Lessem
and Shoshana Deutscher-Nurik

ARCADIA
PUBLISHING

ISBN 978-1-4671-3208-4

Published by Arcadia Publishing
Charleston, South Carolina

Printed in the United States of America

Library of Congress Control Number: 2014930170

For all general information, please contact Arcadia Publishing:
Telephone 843-853-2070
Fax 843-853-0044
E-mail sales@arcadiapublishing.com
For customer service and orders:
Toll-Free 1-888-313-2665

Visit us on the Internet at www.arcadiapublishing.com

Dedicated to Solano County's sometimes-hidden Jews, and to those that follow. May they never feel a need to hide.

Contents

ACKNOWLEDGMENTS

This book would not have been possible without the research done by those who came before us, and we're especially indebted to the late Harry Gray—upon whose work we relied heavily. Help for this effort came from many quarters, though, and we offer special recognition to the following:

Donna Plantz, who made her electronic equipment and expertise available to us; Jim Kern, executive director of the Vallejo Naval and Historical Museum, for his advice, for his vast knowledge of Vallejo history, and for allowing us unlimited access to the museum's treasures; Brian Irwin of the Vacaville Historical Council for his tireless effort in finding the pioneers in northern Solano County; Elizabeth d'Huart, Jim Lessinger, Bob Kvasnicka, and especially Beverly Phelan of the Benicia Historical Museum, whose support, knowledge, and research of Benicia's history also proved invaluable; and a special shout-out to the Benicia Public Library staff. We also thank photographer Mike Jory, of the *Vallejo Times-Herald*, for helping us track down some photographs and information; Pearl Rothman, Ralph Pierce, Bernard Monetta, Raymond and Terry Prather, Ken Ross, David and Beryl Cohen, Molly Leavitt, and Rabbi Chaim Zaklos for their photographs and their memories; and Congregation B'nai Israel for the access to its archives.

Unless otherwise noted, images appear courtesy of the following: the Vallejo Naval and Historical Museum (VHM); the *Vallejo Times-Herald* (VTH); the Benicia Historical Museum (BHM); Congregation B'nai Israel (CBI); the Vacaville Historical Council (VHC); Chabad of Solano County (Chabad); and Shoshana Deutscher-Nurik (SDN).

We also sincerely appreciate Arcadia editors Jared Nelson and Jeff Ruetsche for their patience in walking us through this unfamiliar territory.

Finally, we'd like to thank our families for sticking with us through this long and all-consuming process.

Any omissions or errors discovered in this book were inadvertent and we sincerely apologize for them.

Introduction

To be a Jew is to know that the history of our people lives on in us. To be a Jew is to be part of a story that extends across 40 centuries and almost every land on the face of the earth.

—Chief Rabbi Lord Jonathon Sacks

The story of the Jews of Solano County began early in the history of the state of California, at about the time that Sol Levy came to America from Germany to join an uncle who was already living in Vallejo. This was only some 30 years after Ole Johnson and his bride built what was believed to be the first home in Edan—the area later called Eureka and, finally, Vallejo.

But the story has its origins long before that, with the first Jews—some of them newly converted, or pretending to have converted—to arrive in America with Columbus in 1492, and also with the 23 Brazilian Jewish refugees who came seeking safe haven New Amsterdam in 1654. Those souls were not welcomed by Peter Stuyvesant, the governor of the New Amsterdam colony, and would have been turned away had officials of the Dutch West Indies Company not stepped in to block that from happening.

By 1776, there were some 2,000 Jews—mostly Sephardic Jews from Spain, Portugal, and Arab countries—living in America, contributing to the cause of independence. This contribution was recognized by Pres. George Washington when the first Jewish temple, the Touro Synagogue, opened in Newport, Rhode Island, in 1790. That synagogue was named for the same family for which Vallejo's Touro University on Mare Island is named.

Washington sent a letter to the Touro synagogue's members expressing his hope that "children of the stock of Abraham who dwell in the land continue to merit and enjoy the good will of the other inhabitants. While everyone shall sit safely under his own vine and fig tree and there shall be none to make him afraid."

That was the promise of America for the downtrodden Jews of the world. And they made their way here—at first in small clusters. Until 1820, there were only about 6,000 Jews in the United States, but that number swelled when a wave of reformed German Jews arrived in the 1830s. This was followed by a great migration of poor, oppressed Eastern European Jews in the late 1800s and early 1990s.

Between 1880 and the onset of restrictive immigration quotas in 1924, more than 2 million Jews from Russia, Austria-Hungary, and Romania poured into the country. Most of them settled in large cities like New York, Chicago, and Cleveland—where there were already large Jewish populations—but many also came west to California, where they found important centers of Jewish life in San Francisco and Los Angeles.

San Francisco was already home to a well-established German Jewish population—whose ancestors had come in the 19th century—and included important figures like Levi Strauss of blue jeans fame and with whom a Vallejo Jewish family has a tenuous connection that will be covered later in this volume. By 1853, more than 5,000 Jews had joined the thousands of people from all over the world who were drawn to California by the Gold Rush.

While most of these settlers stayed in the bigger cities, some ventured even further into the outlying areas and wound up in what is now Solano County.

Jewish pioneers with names like Blum, Salz, Koshland, Casper, and Handlery eventually became known for their philanthropy and earned regional fame, amassing fortunes through dry goods, produce, and other endeavors. It is those pioneers, and those who came after them, who will be touched on in this volume. It is their stories that we have hoped to tell, having learned what we could about them by speaking to relatives and friends, by poring through old volumes, and by perusing old photographs. It was a fascinating treasure hunt.

In the course of researching this book, we feel as though we came to know many of the characters that populate its pages as they populated the world in which they lived. In following these life stories, we found that it made sense to introduce them as they were when they first arrived, setting foot in a new country alone and barely more than children.

As these pioneers acclimated to their surroundings, they found themselves in a time of growth and change for the nation and the Solano County area in particular. Many applied the skills and courage that they had developed to help transform an unpaved, uncivilized backwater into the modern metropolis the area has become. They left their marks on the buildings they constructed, creating successful businesses and rising to prominence within the Jewish community. They often found prominence in the larger surrounding community as well, even if some of them did so while keeping their Jewish heritage secret from all but their closest friends and relatives. Nevertheless, many became important in their various fields as Jewish community members continue to do today, though not without the occasional bump in the road.

But, as much as our research was able to uncover, there is likely much more that we missed. Hopefully, this body of knowledge will be added to by those who come after us, because the story of our people lives on in our children and, hopefully, will extend across the centuries to come.

We gladly step aside to make way for those coming up behind us.

One

Pioneers

החלוצים (Hachalutzim)

די פּייאַנירז (De Piyanirz)

. . . They came with the arrival of the Gold Rush

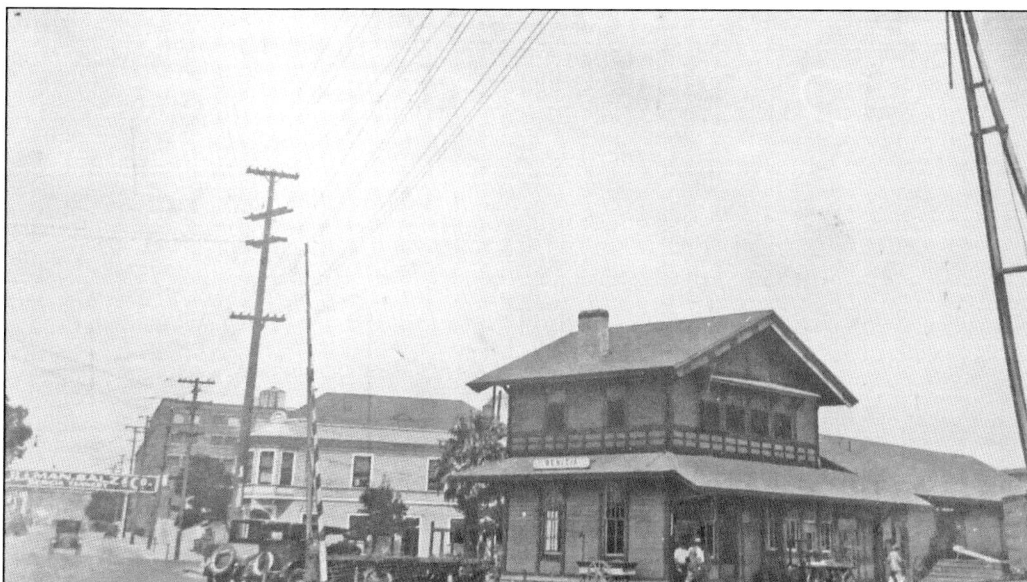

Passing through Benicia—where the discovery of gold was announced by Charles Bennett on his way to Monterey—pioneers arrived by ferry and by train (like at the Benicia Depot, pictured here in the 1800s). Benicia and Vallejo catered to the likes of Jack London and Bret Harte and saw the arrival of merchants and manufacturers such as the Levee, Dannenbaum, Kullman, and Salz families. (BHM.)

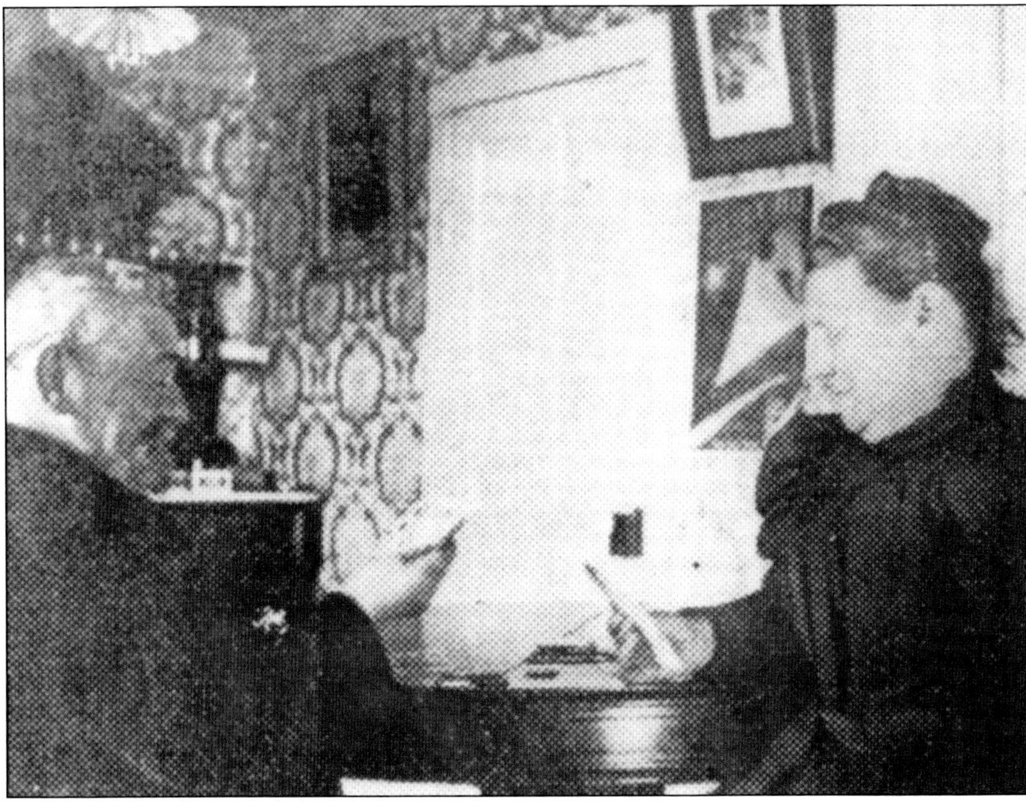

In 1849, at age 23, Moses Blum (left) left the pogroms of Alsace, France, for America, arriving in Vacaville with his brothers by 1853. Moses met and married German émigré Bertha Koshland—who was 17 at the time—and they opened a store downtown. The railroad came in 1868, and Moses was among the prominent citizens elected as directors of the Vaca Valley Railroad Company in 1869. By 1884, he had also been elected the mayor of Vacaville. (VHC.)

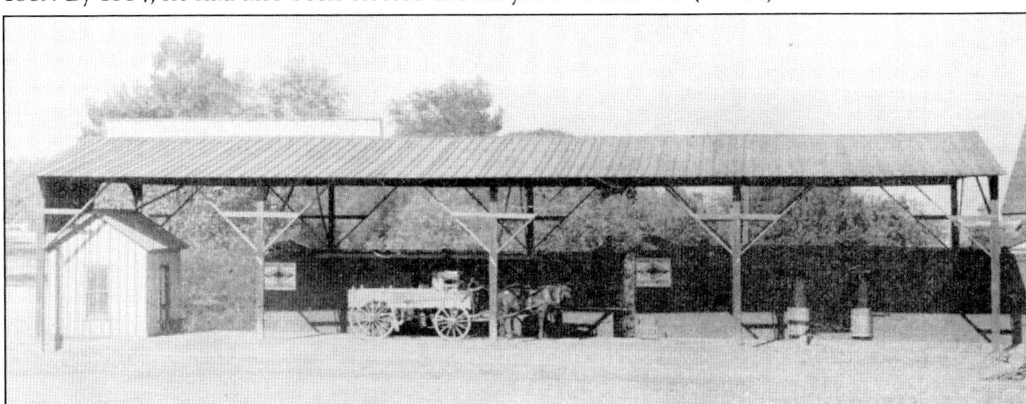

Moses opened a store in a stone building on downtown Vacaville's block 20 where credit and loans were offered to cattle ranchers and fruit growers. His ads became a staple in the *Vacaville Reporter*. The Blum family handled fresh and dried fruit for local growers and later established a shipping business. Jacob and Moses Blum were among 28 affluent merchants and farmers, or nabobs, with incomes exceeding $10,000 as listed in the Suisun City paper between 1863 and 1874. (VHC.)

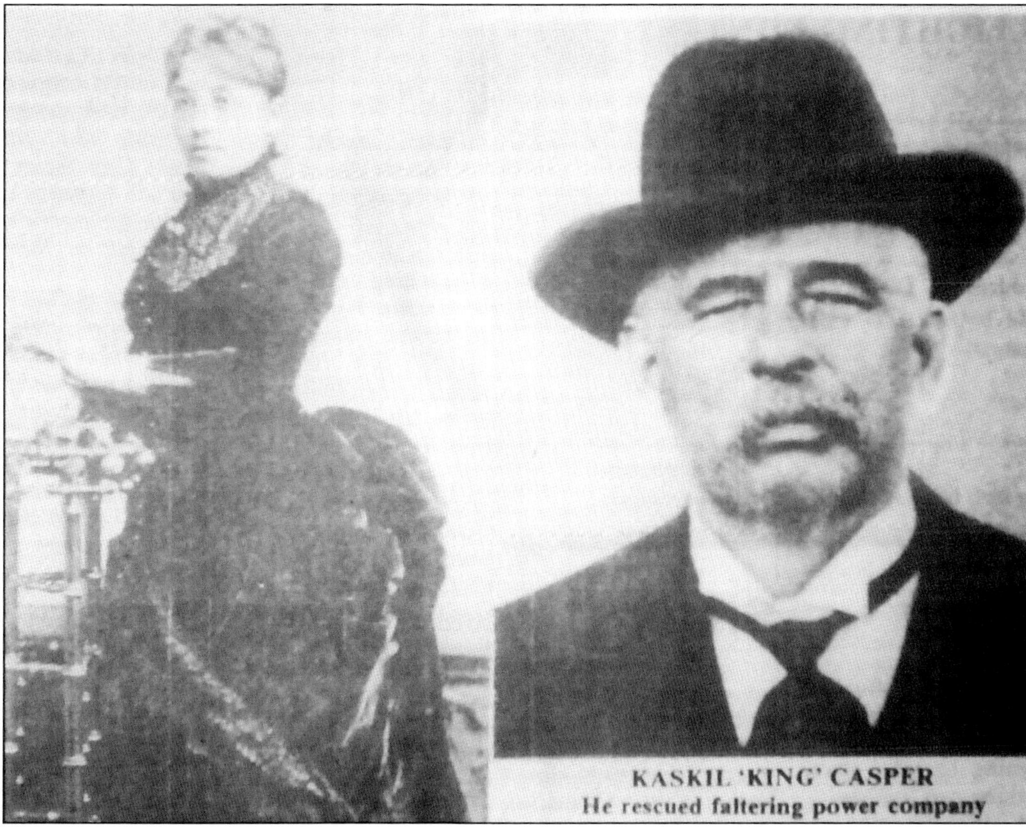

Kaskill "King" Casper arrived in New York in 1853 with his parents, Samuel and Mary Blumenthal, before striking out on his own at 17 in 1863. Working as a Nevada City, California, haberdasher for 23 years, Casper married the 22-year-old Sophie Newman in 1879, and the couple had four children. Another son, Melville—who was likely from a previous relationship—died in 1879, at age 14, and was buried in Nevada City's Jewish cemetery. Later, Casper moved to Vallejo, where he continued mining and promoting electric lighting. He rescued a fledgling power company, pictured below, taking the city from gas lamps to electric lights. Kaskill Casper died in 1911 and was buried in San Francisco's Hills of Eternity Jewish cemetery. A *macher* even in death, he shares space in the cemetery—now located in Colma—with Levi Strauss, Wyatt Earp, and Earp's Jewish wife Josephine Sarah Marcus Earp. (Both, VHM.)

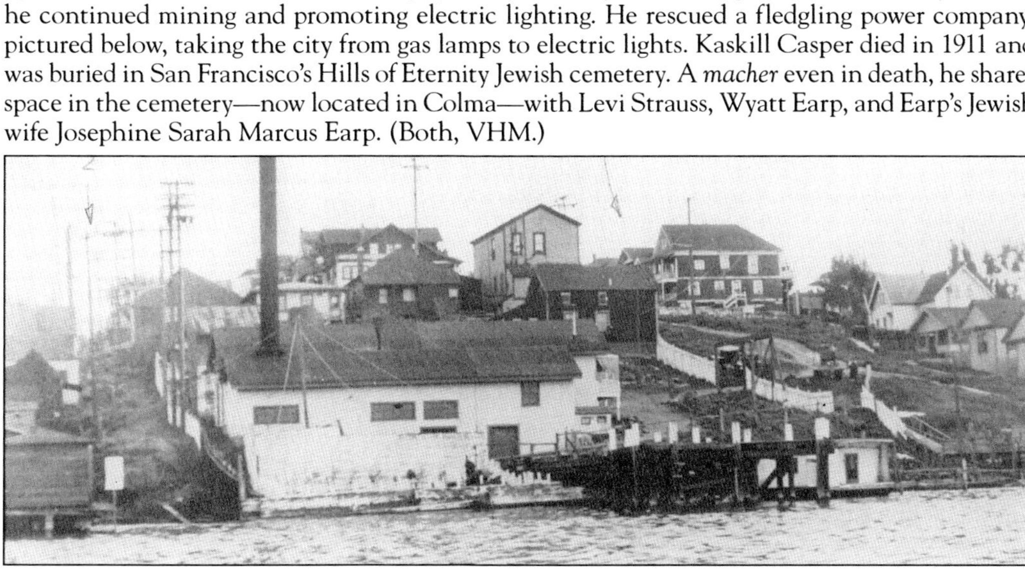

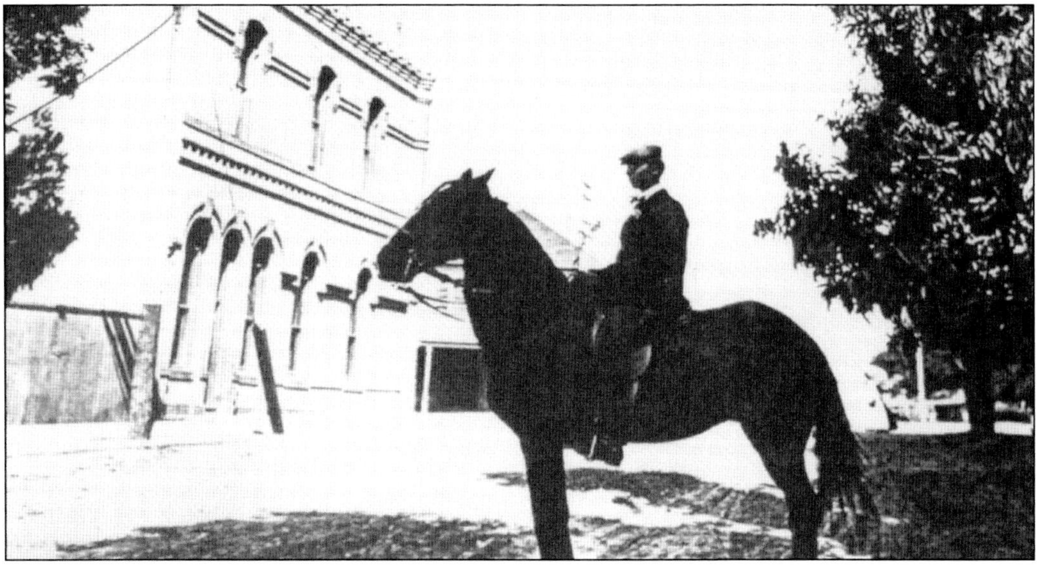

Ansley Salz, a violinist and art collector, inherited the Kullman-Salz Tannery from his father. After the Benicia Tannery fire, he bought and ran a tannery in Santa Cruz. Following in the footsteps of his uncle Herbert Kullman, he became president of the Benicia Water Supply Company. He and his wife, Helen, entertained artists and musicians and donated money to Jewish causes like Hadassah and the Jewish War Veterans. (BHM.)

I. Dannenbaum,

The wholesale merchant of this city, who believes there is virtue in printer's

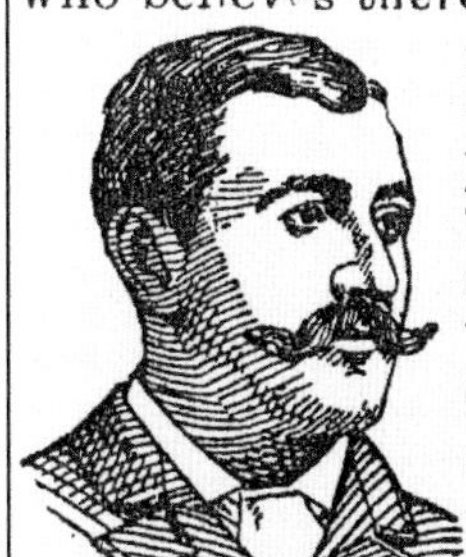

ink, and who, in a brief time, has built up for himself a substantial business, was born October 1, 1861, in Westfalia, Germany. There he went to school up to 1879, after which he served one year in the army, and ever since has been engaged in mercentile business. He came to America first on a pleasure trip in 1882, but returned in 1887 to make this free country his home for good. His success in business is partly due to his frank nature and liberality. His store is located in what is known to old Vallejoites as the Frost Building, in the center of the business houses in the city, and even without his genial smile, it is handsome and attractive at any time. The finest brands of cigars and liqueuers can be had here in quantities to suit.

Brothers Joseph and Sal Dannenbaum came to California from Germany in 1855 and founded a men's store in Vallejo. They eventually brought their cousin Sol Levy (later Levee) to Vallejo and taught him the trade. Sal Dannenbaum was a Mason and a Vallejo Naval Lodge member. Another cousin, John Rothschild, also worked in the Dannenbaums' store before starting his own business in San Francisco and becoming a founder of the San Francisco Music Association. He remained connected to Vallejo. (VHM.)

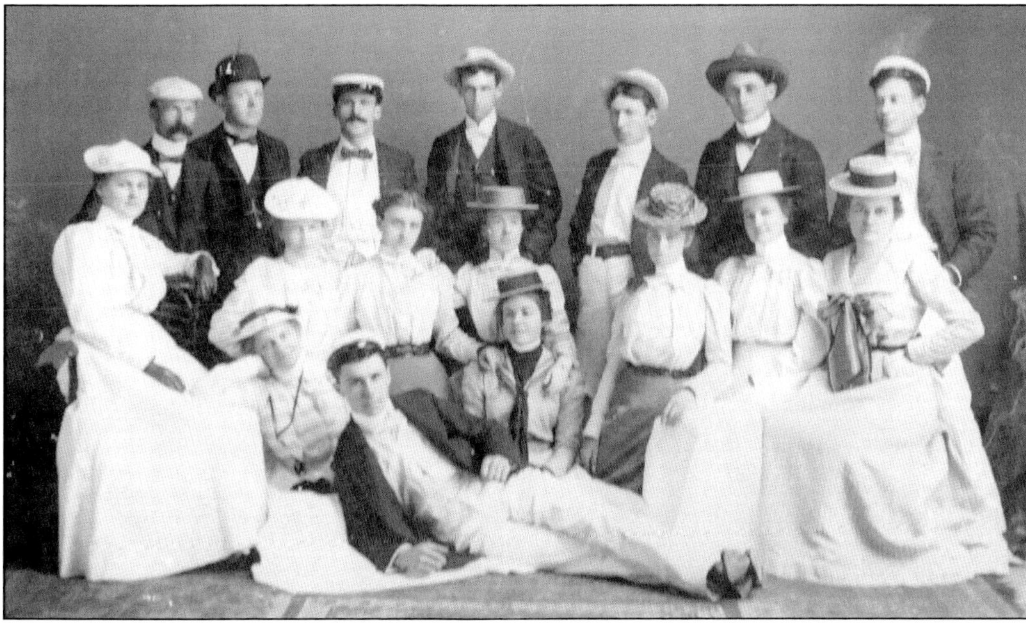

Sol Levy was brought from Germany at age 13 by his older brother, Simon, and their uncle S. Dannenbaum in 1878. Levy first worked in his uncle's menswear store for $10 per month. Five years later, he was manager of the dry goods department and then, three years after that, of the whole store. Changing his name to S.W. Levee, Sol opened Vallejo's first department store on Georgia Street in 1888, when he was 23 years old. Levee's became a great success, boasting the first escalator in town. Levee also built two apartment buildings in Vallejo, one being the Seevel—"Levees" backwards. A brother, Jonas Levee, left Vallejo to start his own business in San Francisco that was still operating in 1948. Levee's in Vallejo closed in the early 1980s. (Both, VHM.)

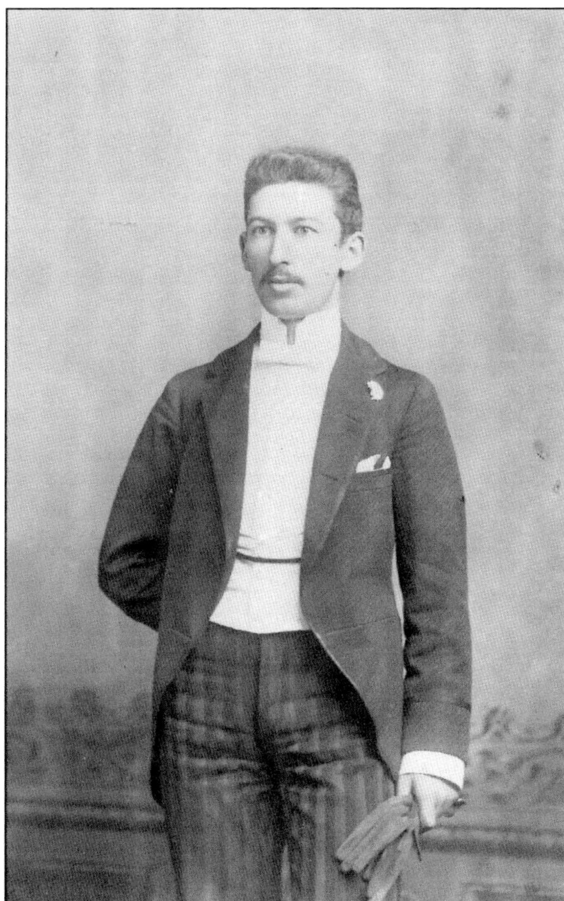

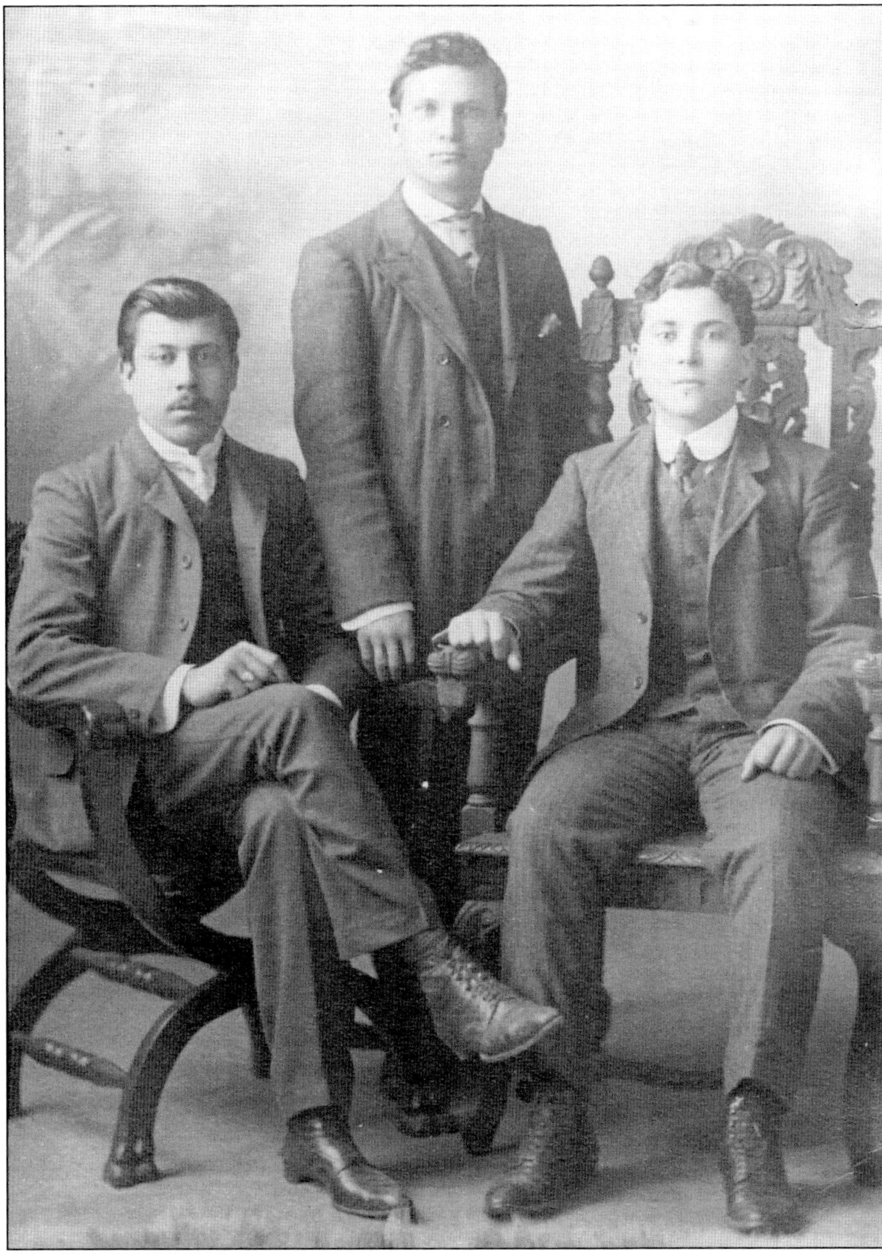

Raphael "Ralph" Pizante, pictured at center and flanked by his brothers, Asher (left) and Rahamin (Victor, right), emigrated from Rhodes' Jewish Quarter in 1907, having earned his fare by selling cigarettes to Turkish miners. Speaking Hebrew, Ladino, and some English, he made his way west from New York, washing dishes for room and board as he moved from synagogue to synagogue. Once in Vallejo, he opened a store, slept in the back, and rented the rooms above to "working girls." An observant Jew, Pizante offered shelter to brothers and friends who followed him west, providing financial support until they could stand on their own. A marriage to Fortunee Abouaf, also from Rhodes, was arranged when Pizante was 30. Together, the couple raised a family and helped establish what is still, in 2014, Solano County's only synagogue. Three days before his death, Pizante proudly carried the Torah during the Simchat Torah. (Courtesy of Ralph Pierce.)

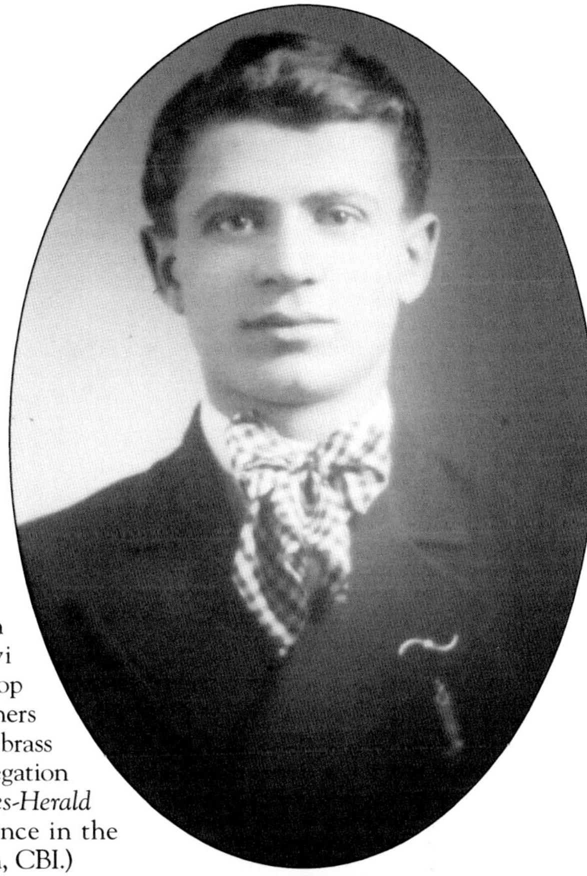

Meyer Liberman came to San Francisco in August 1906 to work rebuilding the city in the aftermath of the earthquake. He later came to Vallejo as a tailor in the employ of Nathan Epstein. As a tailor specializing in naval wear in a Navy town, Liberman had a built-in customer base. A contemporary of Levi Strauss, Liberman later went on to develop a type of work trousers especially for miners called "Ironwear"—corduroy pants with a brass button. He was a past president of Congregation B'nai Israel, and the large size of the *Times-Herald* headline indicated Liberman's importance in the community when he died in 1935. (Both, CBI.)

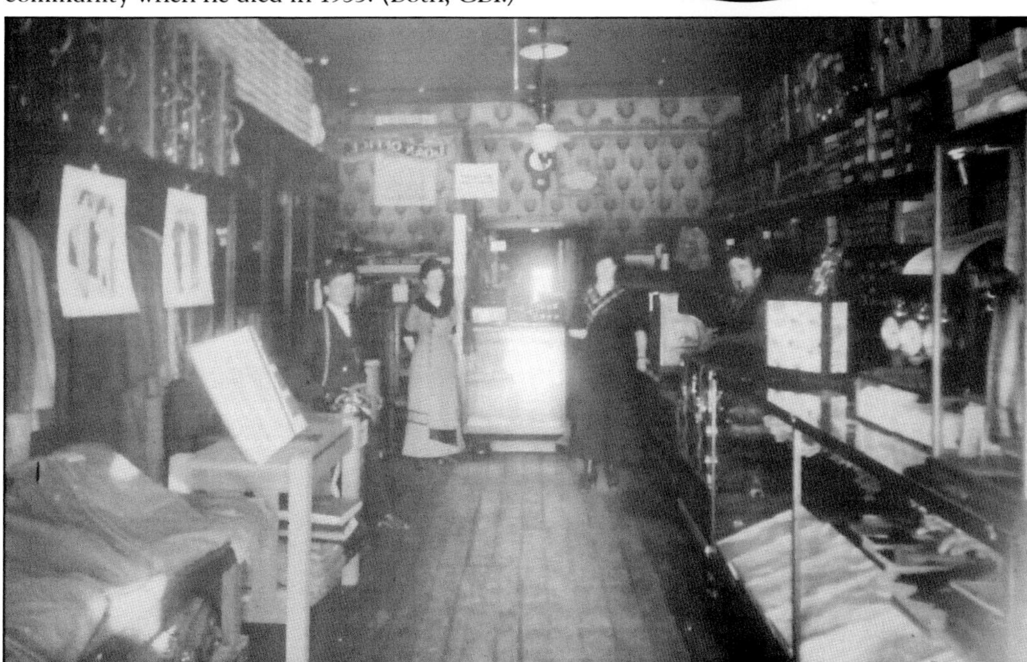

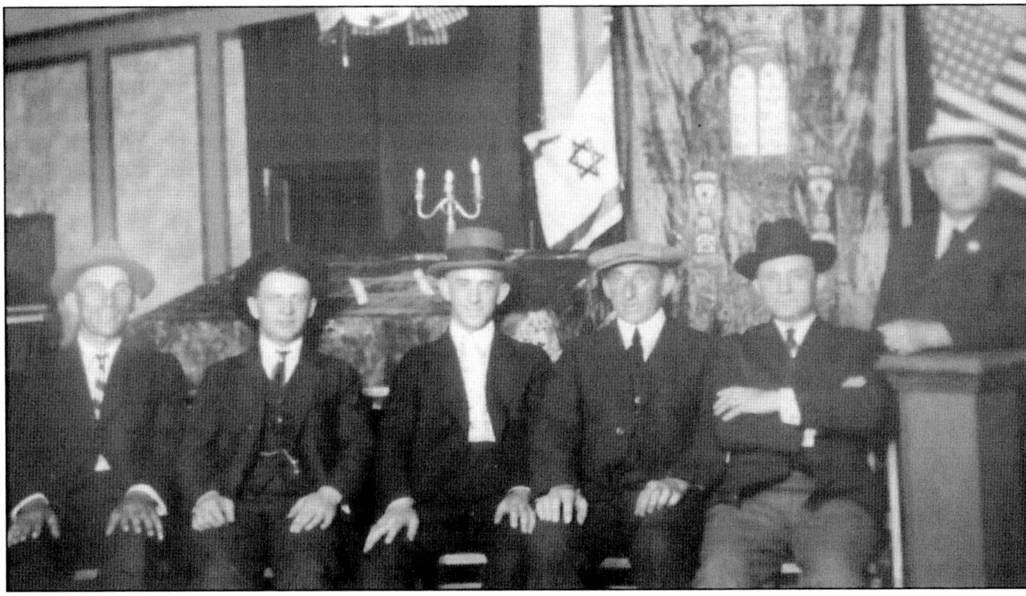

The c. 1922 photograph above shows prominent members of the Sons and Daughters of Israel—which became Congregation B'nai Israel (Children of Israel)—inside the York Street synagogue. The building, Solano County's first dedicated synagogue, was purchased in 1920. The mortgage was redeemed in 1925 and a mortgage-burning party held on March 7 that year. These men are members of the congregation's first board of directors. From left to right, they are Harry Dubnoff, Meyer Liberman, Isadore Meyer, Morris Symonds, Heine Bercu, and Nathan Fink. Several of these men were businessmen, including Meyer, a jeweler; Liberman, a tailor; and Bercu, who owned a grocery store. Pictured below is the event held in 1935 celebrating an officers' installation. (Both, CBI.)

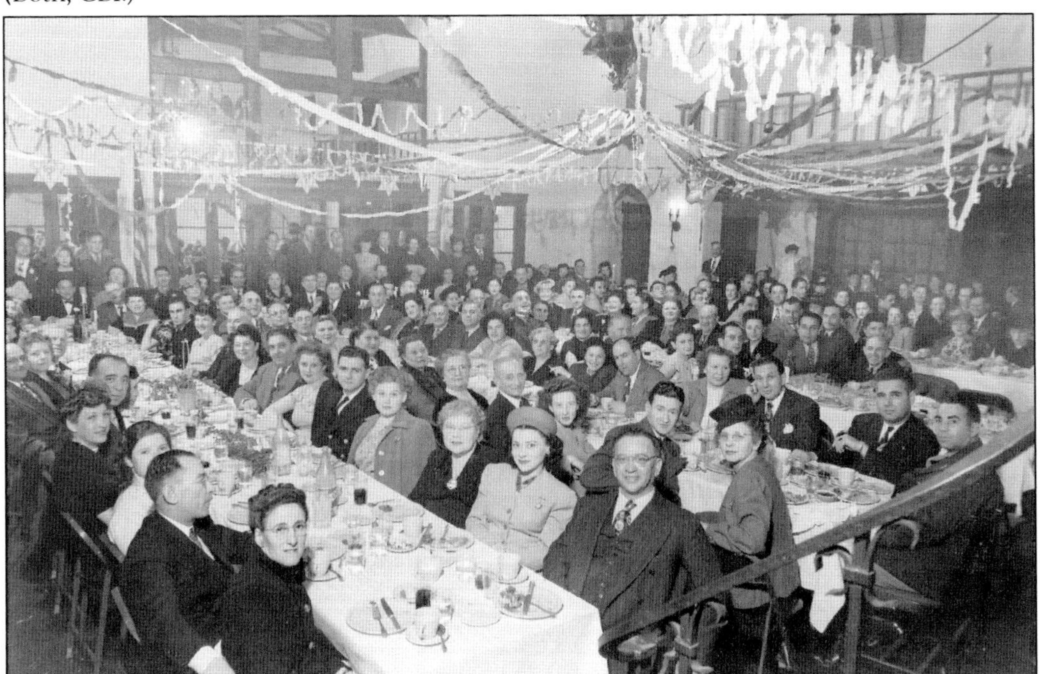

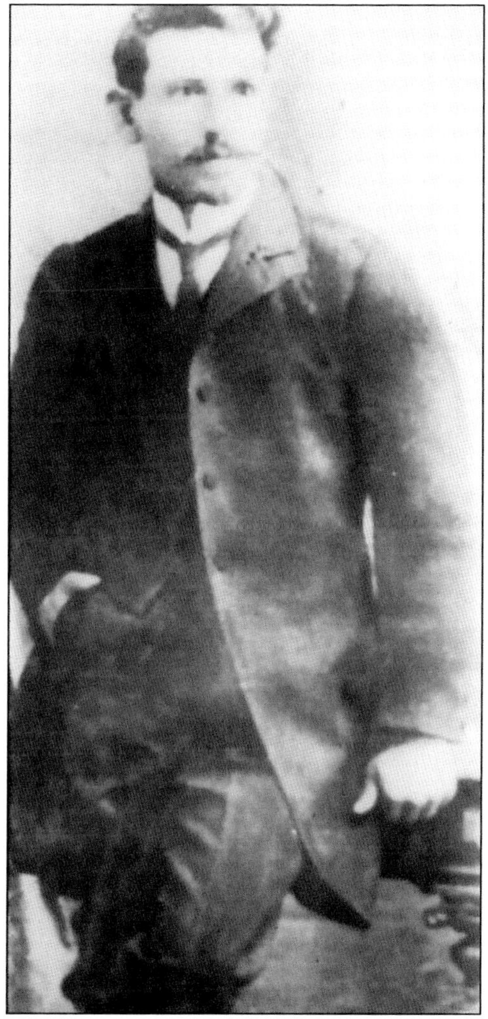

These c. 1908 photographs show Rebitzen Rebecca Gray and Rabbi Abbe Gray, who were among the fledgling Vallejo Jewish community's first rabbis and led services in Solano County's first official synagogue on York Street. The York Street shul was a residence the congregation remodeled into a temple. Bernie Manetta recalled that services were held on the ground floor, with social events upstairs. He also recalled that there was a table on the right as one entered the building that held a plate for making donations. The high-backed chairs first used there are still in use in the Congregation B'nai Israel sanctuary in 2014. (Both, CBI.)

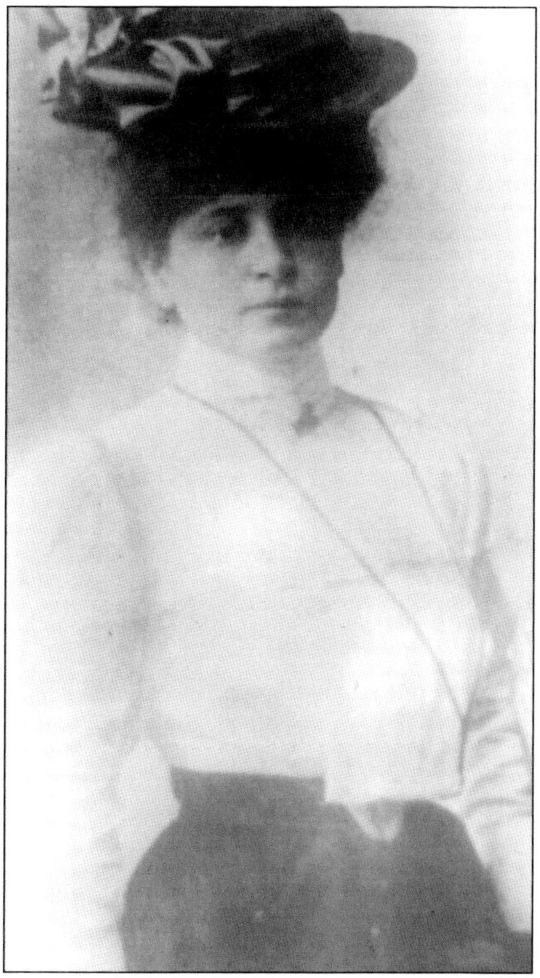

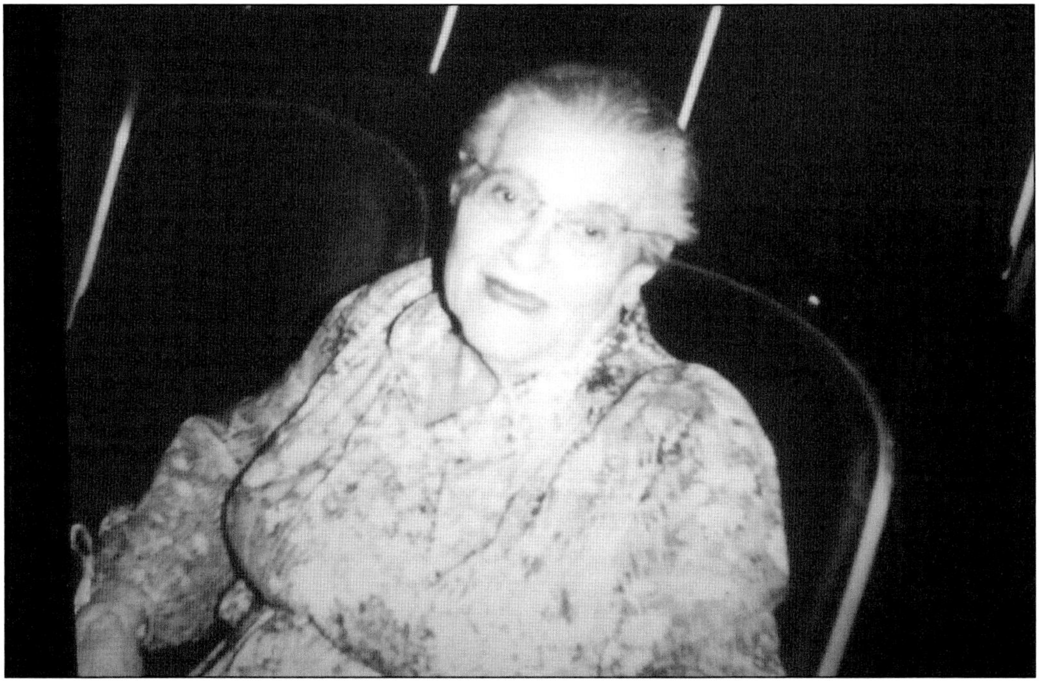

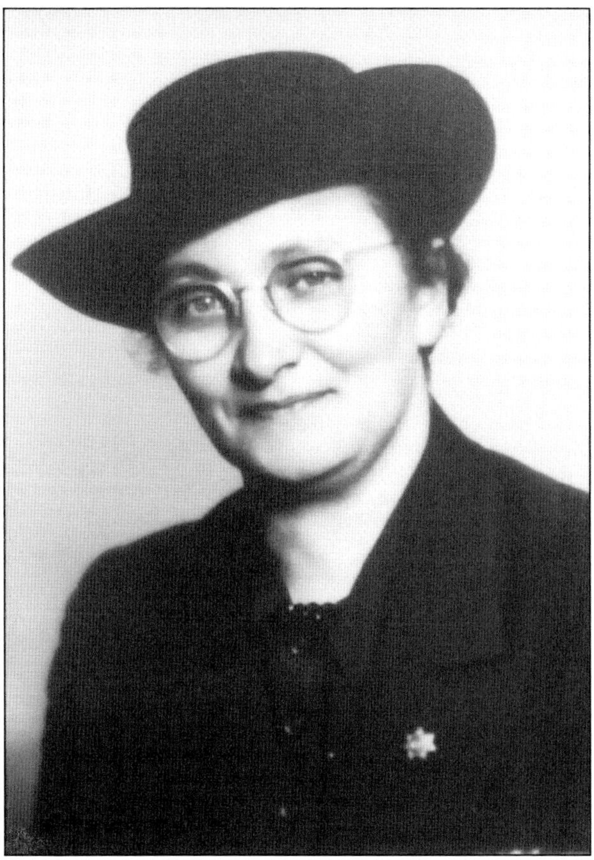

The daughter of Isaac Harris—one of the county's earliest Jews—Celia Barsky was living in Vallejo in 1906. She recalled sitting on her Florida Street porch and watching the fiery skies over San Francisco after the earthquake. Her parents welcomed many refugees afterwards, and mattresses covered the floors and porch. In 1914, "Babe" Harris married Morris Barsky, and their home hosted some of the county's earliest Jewish religious services. (CBI.)

Born in 1889, Rose Rachel Milestein became Vallejo's first female police officer after leaving Romania and the pogroms in which her grandparents were killed. She worked for 40 years with the Salvation Army, was a Mare Island fitter's helper during World War II, and knitted 500 pairs of socks for soldiers in her spare time. As a police matron, she patrolled Vallejo's waterfront on foot alone and at night after the war and won many awards for her volunteer work. (VHM.)

Two

BUILDINGS

בניינים (BINYANIM)

בנינים (BINYOH'NIM)

. . . With few options, they advertised with signs

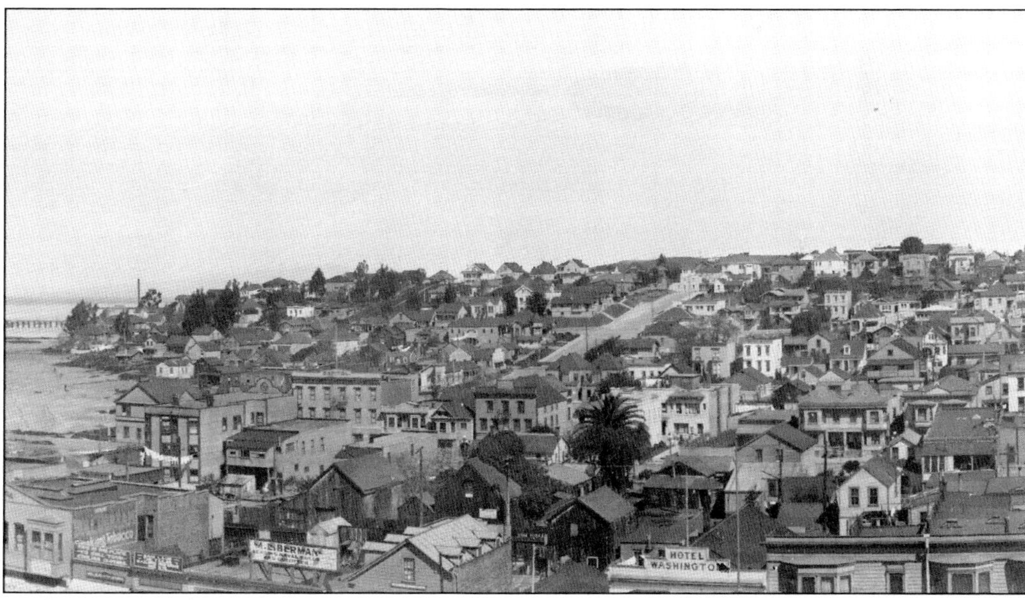

In this 1850s Vallejo scene, signs advertising naval tailors Meyer Liberman and Sam Laub can be seen in the lower left corner—conveniently located across the strait from the Mare Island Naval Shipyard. By 1867, a city directory listed at least two Jewish firms in town: Levy, a general merchandise store, and M. Cohen, a Wells Fargo and Company agent. By 1870, more had appeared, including L. Cohn's variety store, Louis and Solomon Stationers, and G. Abrams Clothing. (VHM.)

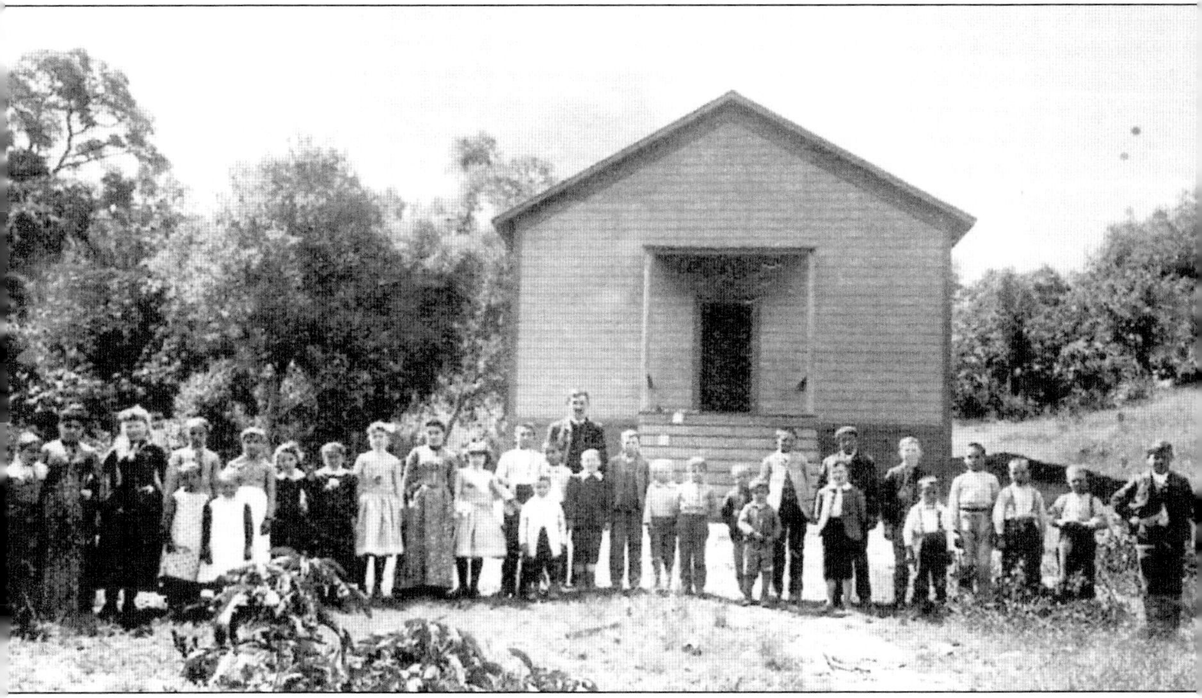

Vacaville's Milzner School was named for Austrian immigrant Morris Milzner (1834–1896), who moved to Suisun City, and then to Vacaville, around 1878. He owned the Morgenstern and Milzner general store and warehouse, which was built by the Independent Order of Odd Fellows Vacaville Lodge No. 83. The Odd Fellows, a fraternal organization that came to Vacaville in 1859, was founded in England in the 1700s on the belief that common laboring men should associate together for social unity and fellowship and for mutual aid. This was so different from the popular attitudes of the time that they became known as peculiar or odd. Milzner married Betsey (1837–1918), an emigrant from Baden, Germany, became a member of B'nai Brith, and was so active in the Vacaville community that it named a school district after him. He and his wife are buried at Salem Memorial Park in Colma, California. (VHC.)

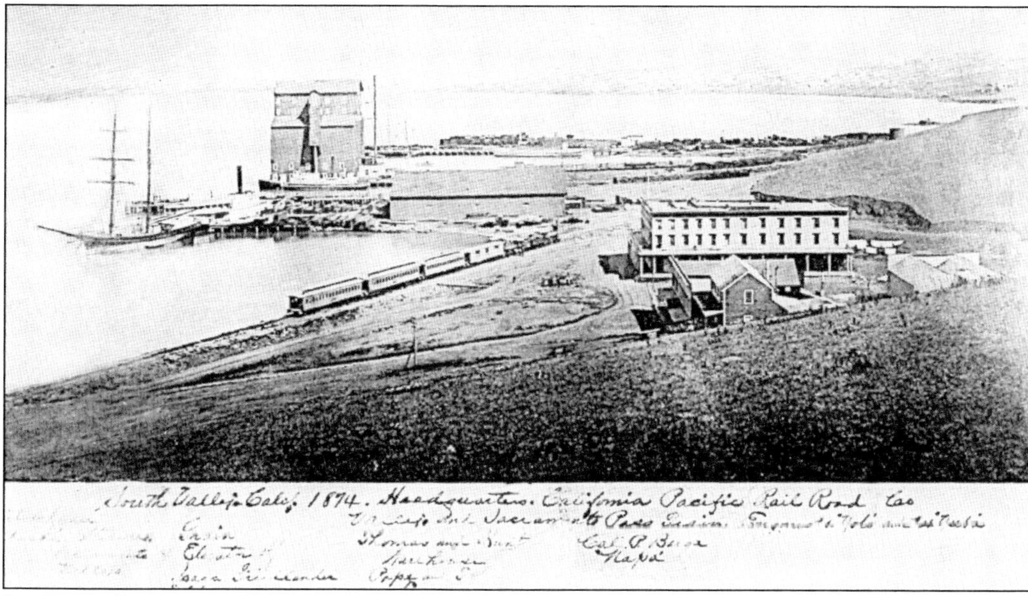

In the early 1860s, German immigrant Isaac "Grain King" Friedlander built the Starr Mills grain elevator—the first grain elevator west of the Missouri River and "the pride and hope of Vallejo"—in partnership with John Frisbee. The venture failed over fear of abandoning sack-based grain-moving techniques. Friedlander served on the University of California, Berkeley board of regents and helped transition the area's economy from one based on the quest for gold to one driven by agriculture. (VHM.)

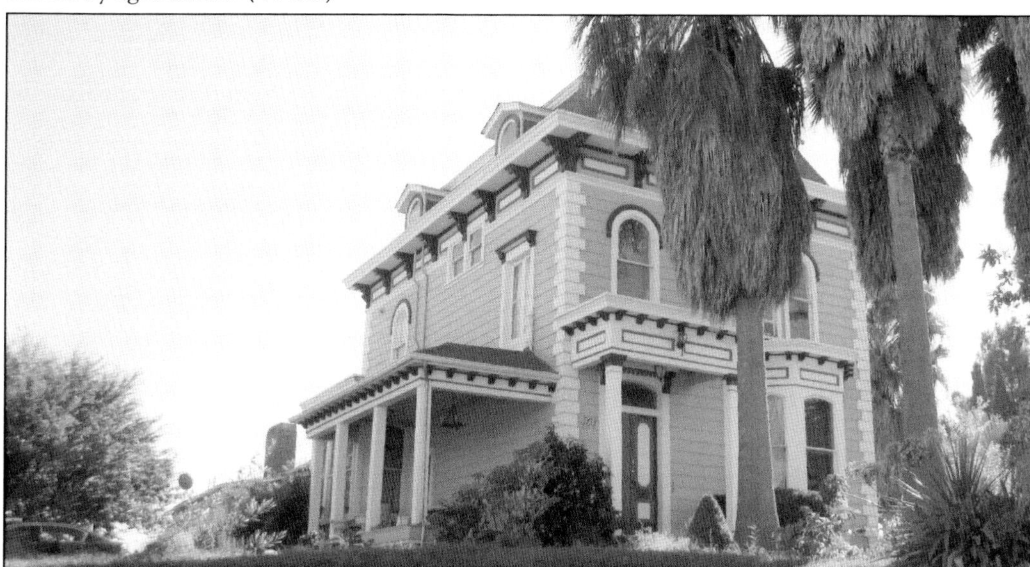

Built in 1869 by grain mill founder Abraham Dubois Starr, the dilapidated Starr Mansion was sold in 1933 to German Jewish immigrant Clarence Rothschild—an amateur pilot, Mare Island pipe fitter, and ventriloquist and magician. After Rothschild's death and 25 years of neglect, the house was renovated into Vallejo's first bed-and-breakfast and run by Jamaica-born Paula Roche Reilly, who was born to a Huguenot father and a Jewish mother whose family fled the Portuguese Inquisition. (SDN.)

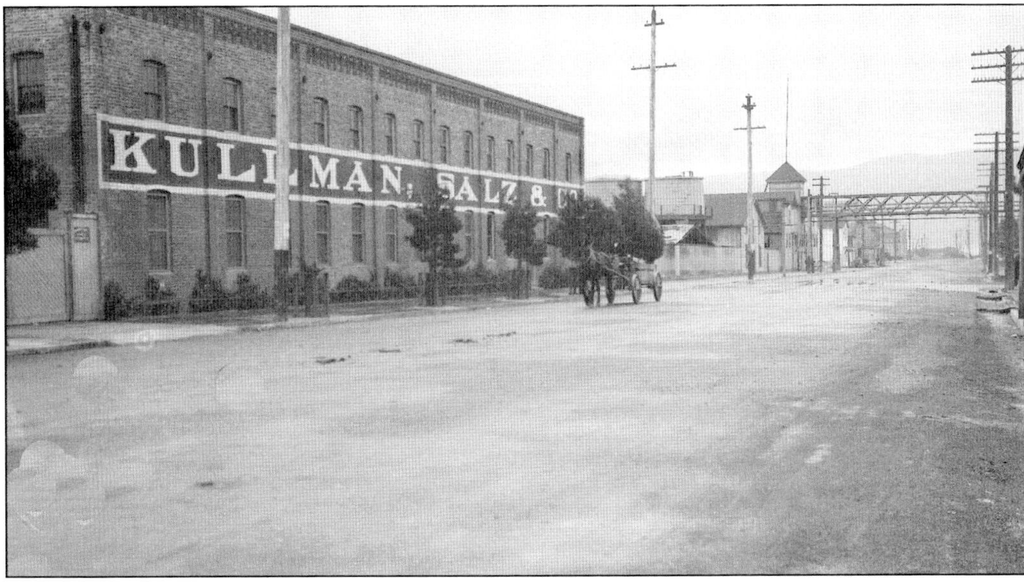

On March 24, 1881, Edward Danforth, Charles Moore, and Francis Cummings sold the Benicia Tannery, including "two horses with harnesses, machinery, vats, liquors, extracts, oil and tools together with one steam engine and two boilers" to the mercantile firm of Kullman, Salz & Co. for $25,000. This led to Benicia becoming a major West Coast tanning industry player. In the early 20th century, at the height of production, this First Street enterprise was among the state's largest tanneries, with more than 300 workers and other plants in Santa Cruz and San Francisco. The story began some 30 years earlier, when Moses Kullman came to Stockton in 1853 and partnered with a Mr. Wagner in a tannery. He was engaged to Sarah Kallisher in 1869. Kallisher's brother Herman partnered with Jacob Salz, which appears to be the association's genesis. (Both, BHM.)

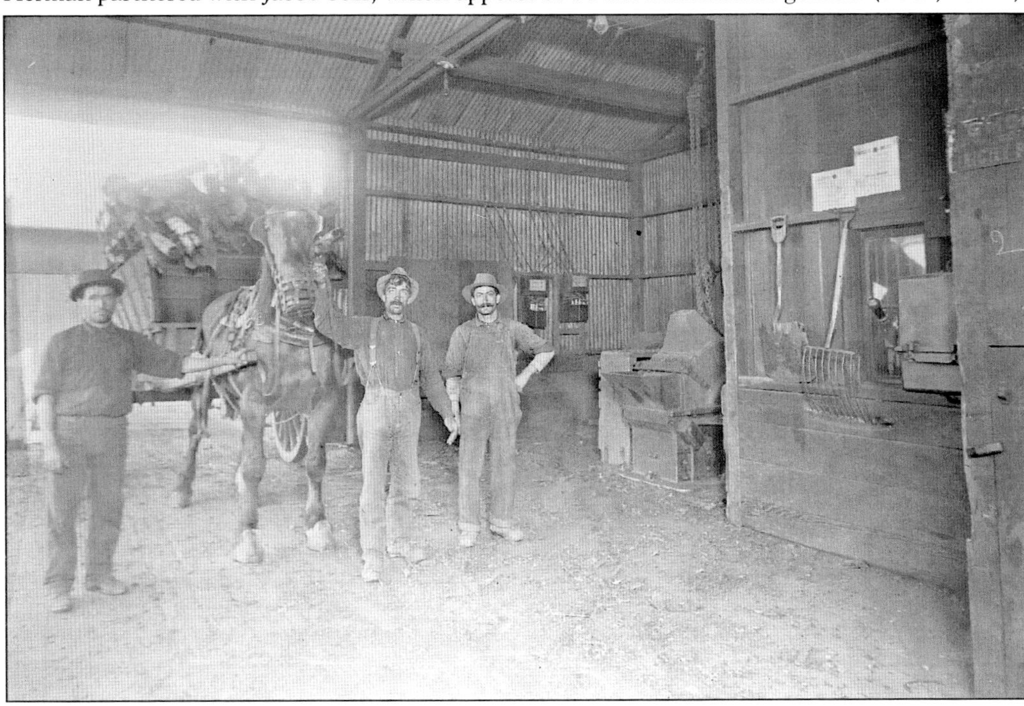

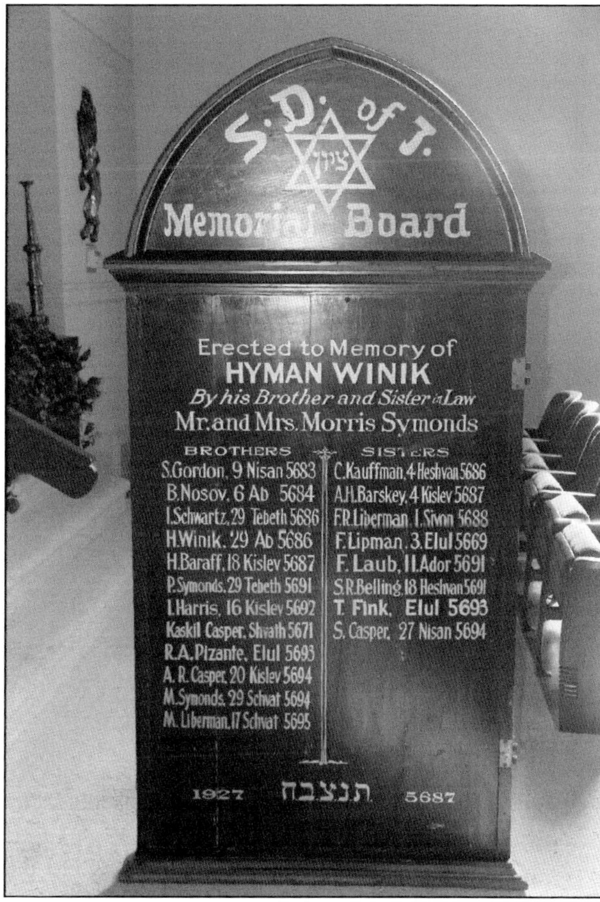

Discovered buried in a CBI closet in 2013, this memorial board appears to be among the few surviving relics of the Sons and Daughters of Israel's first synagogue on Vallejo's York Street. It contains the names of some of the city's most important early personages who, outside of the Jewish community, kept their Jewish roots secret. Names like K. and S. Casper, M. Symonds, and A.H. Barskey appear to have been painstakingly applied in gold paint to the S.&D. of I. Memorial plaque. Services in Vallejo were first held in people's homes until funds were raised to buy the two-story York Street residence. The high-backed chairs seen below are in use on the CBI bimah in 2014. (Left, courtesy of Donna Plantz; below, CBI.)

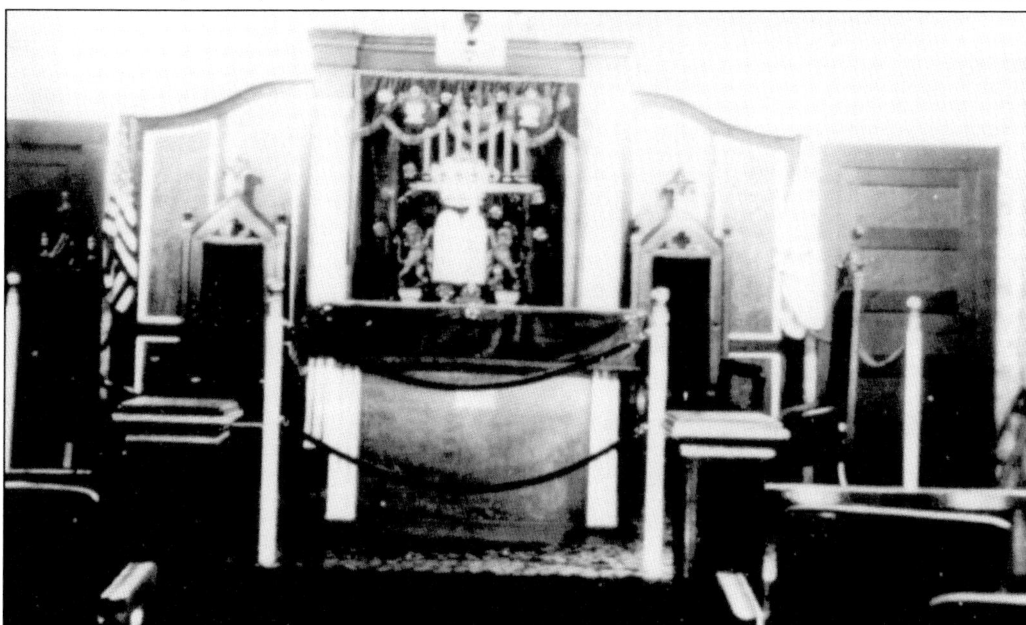

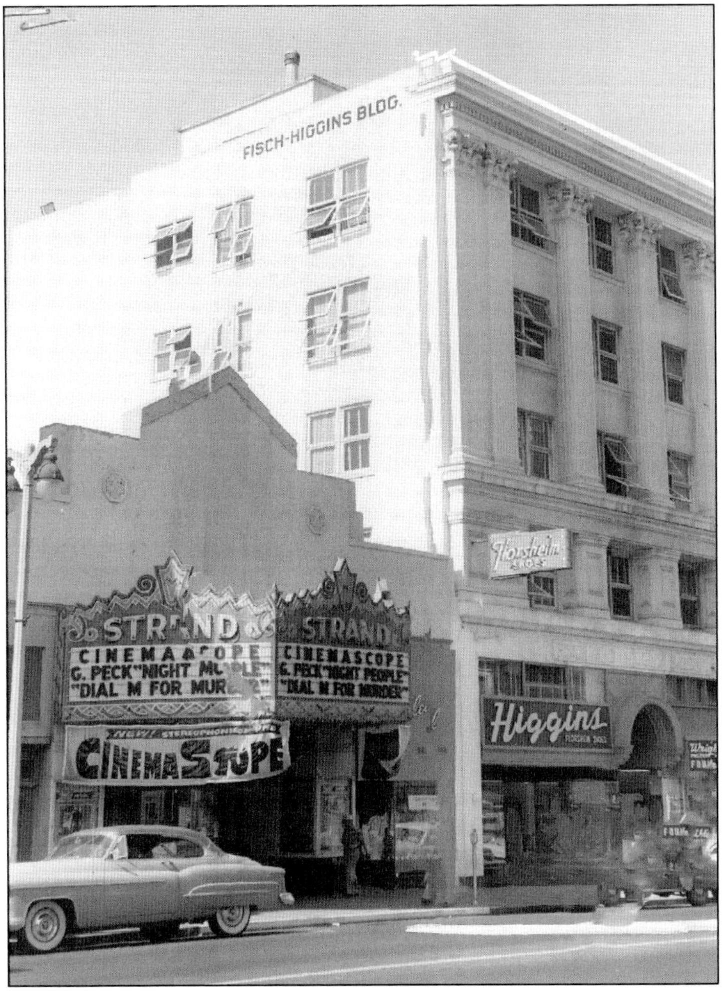

According to his daughter, Kristin Delaplane, Fred Fisch learned tailoring in his native Austria-Hungary. He came to New York at 17 and eventually made his way to Vallejo, where he set up shop in Levee's basement. He soon opened a Georgia Street store making officers' uniforms and selling men's furnishings. He met his wife when she was a Levee's cashier and built the family home in 1911. Delaplane also described attending the four-room, wooden Dewey School at Maine and Alameda Streets and recalled "Circus Day's" big parade through the streets. Fisch and a Mr. Higgins built the Fisch-Higgins Building, visible at left, which contained Fisch's shop and Higgins's shoe store. Levee owned a nearby apartment building, visible below, which he named Seveel. (Both, VTH.)

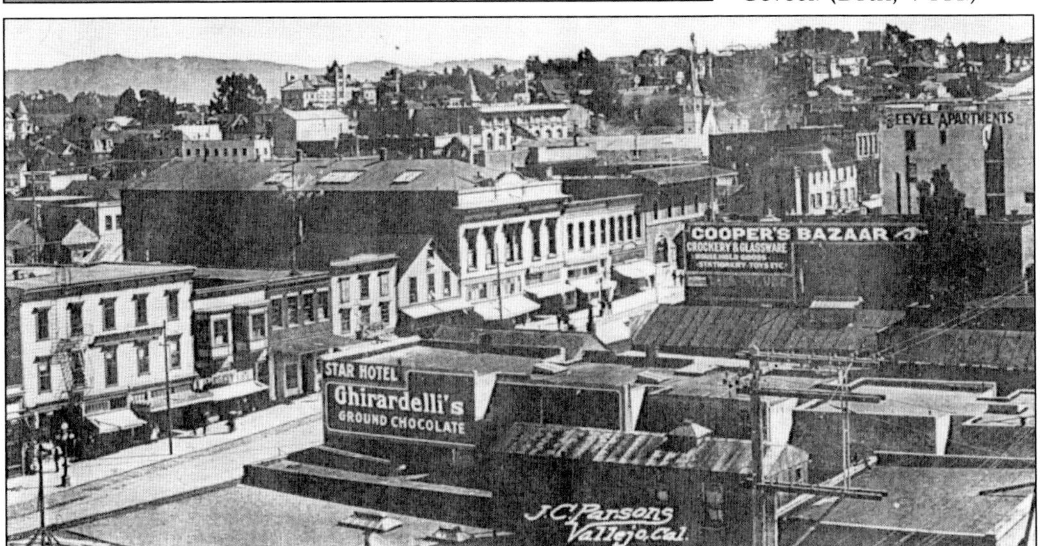

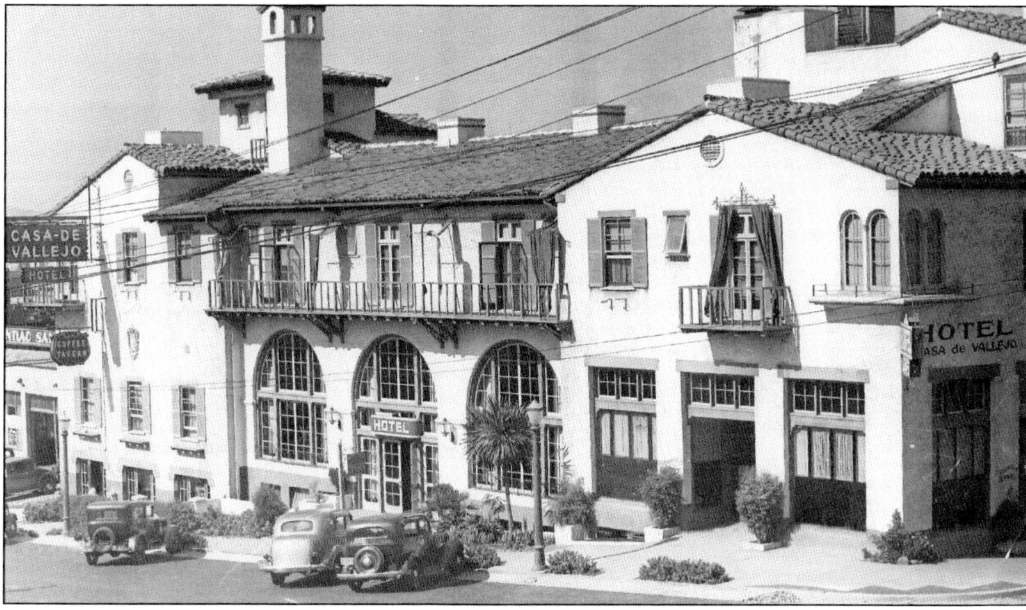

The Casa de Vallejo, pictured here in 1936, was a hotel where the top big bands played through the 1940s. Built as an industrial YMCA in 1919, it was bought by Russian-Jewish immigrant Harry Handlery in 1928. Handlery, along with Isadore Meyer, then transformed it into a 165-room hotel. With it, Handlery started a multimillion-dollar hotel chain that, by 1965, was California's largest family-owned hotel system. The building has since become a low income seniors' residence. (VHM.)

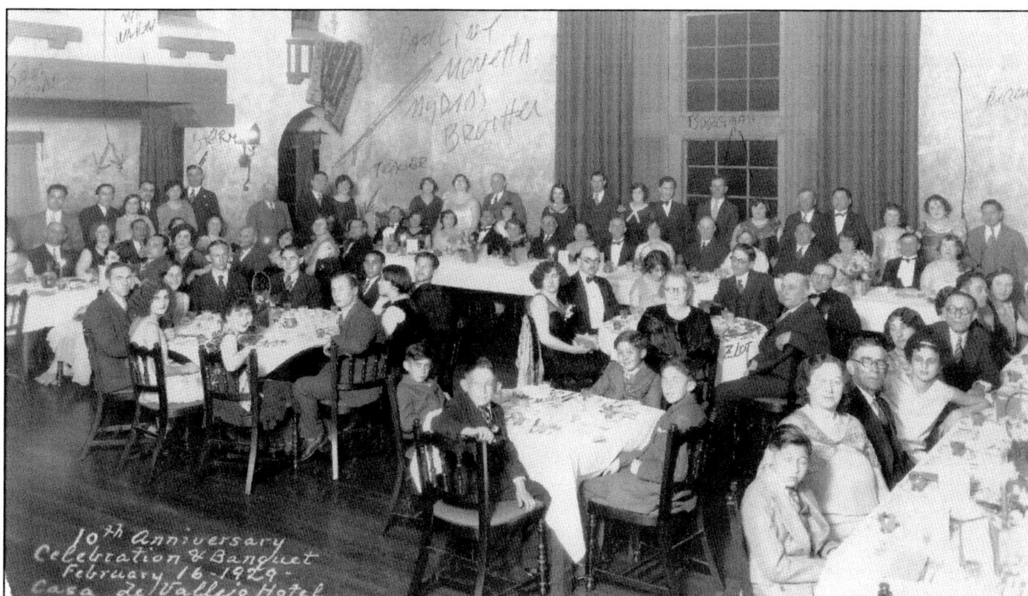

This photograph shows the 10th-anniversary celebration of the Sons and Daughters of Israel's incorporation inside the Casa de Vallejo Hotel on February 16, 1929. It was here that a vision for building a new, modern synagogue was born. The hotel's Jewish owner, Harry Handlery, can be seen in the photograph, along with most of the pioneers who helped create a Jewish community in Solano County. (CBI.)

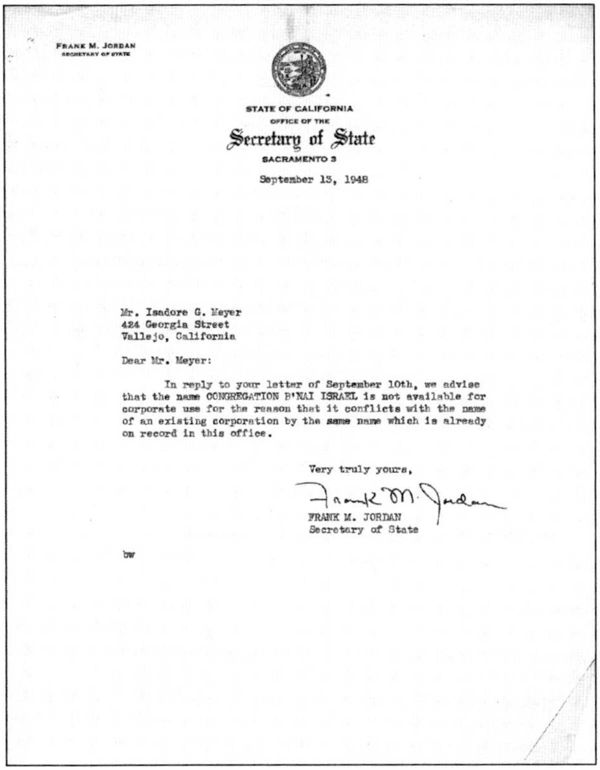

FRANK M. JORDAN
SECRETARY OF STATE

STATE OF CALIFORNIA
OFFICE OF THE
Secretary of State
SACRAMENTO 3

September 13, 1948

Mr. Isadore G. Meyer
424 Georgia Street
Vallejo, California

Dear Mr. Meyer:

In reply to your letter of September 10th, we advise that the name CONGREGATION B'NAI ISRAEL is not available for corporate use for the reason that it conflicts with the name of an existing corporation by the same name which is already on record in this office.

Very truly yours,

Frank M. Jordan
FRANK M. JORDAN
Secretary of State

bw

After years meeting in congregants' homes and, later, at a house converted into a synagogue, a lot on Vallejo's Nebraska Street was purchased on August 22, 1945. Plans for a new temple were drawn up by San Francisco architects Hyman, Appleton, and Wilford, and permits were granted by the Solano County Planning Commission by April 1947. An official letter (seen at left) denying the congregation the use of its chosen name—because it was in use elsewhere in the country—sent Isadore Meyer to Washington, DC. Meyer's success in convincing officials to see things his way got him named honorary congregation president for life. He can be seen below with the shovel at the ground-breaking ceremonies, held on April 20, 1947. The new temple was dedicated on April 11, 1948, with civic, government, and church dignitaries in attendance. (Left, CBI; below, courtesy of Bernie Monetta.)

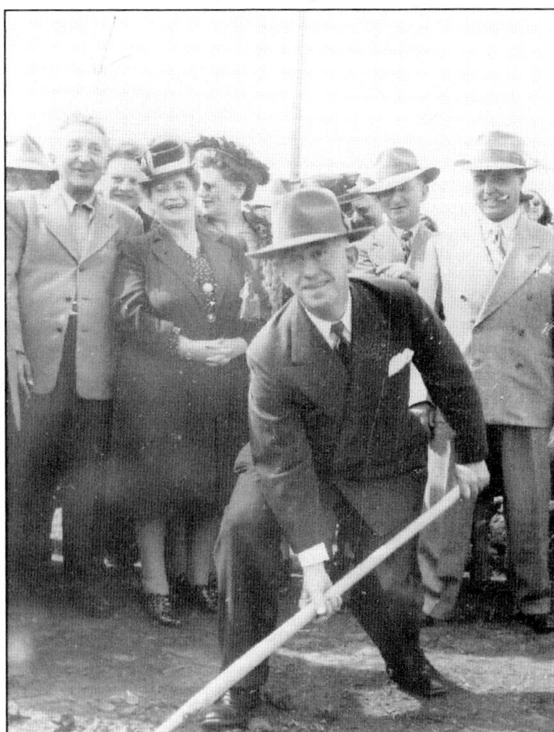

After conceiving of a new synagogue, there were some challenges to overcome. World War II was well under way when a building committee comprised of Isadore Meyer, Dr. Morris Zlot, Herman Stern, Sam Abouaf, William Monetta, Sam Moss, and Dr. Michael Wallin was selected. The Nebraska Street site was purchased on August 22, 1945, but the wartime rationing of building materials postponed the granting of permits. The contractor, James Bitcom, was finally able to break ground on April 20, 1947. Pictured at right is the Honor Roll Plaque—dedicated on December 23, 1951—on which are named the members of the building committee and those families who contributed to the erecting of the temple. Pictured below is Congregation B'nai Israel's temple as it stands today. (Both, CBI.)

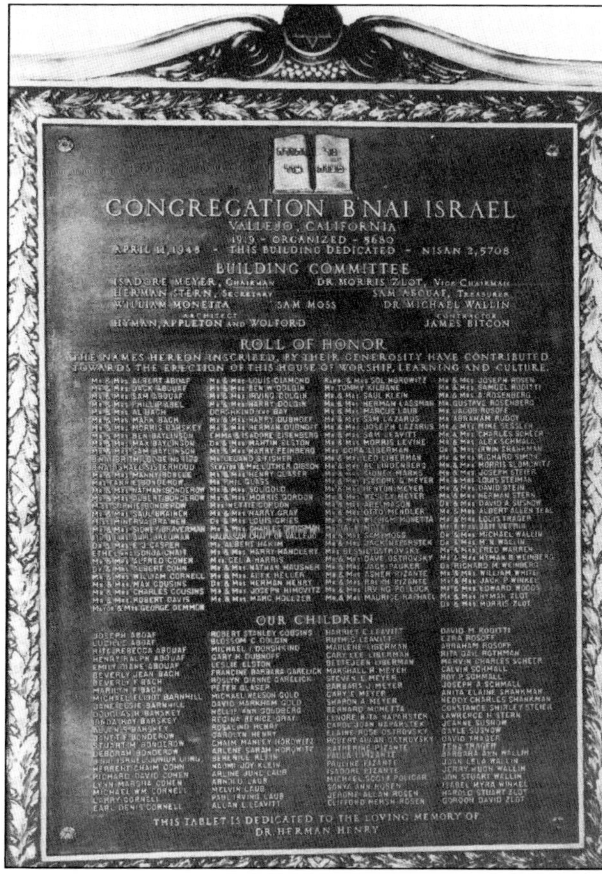

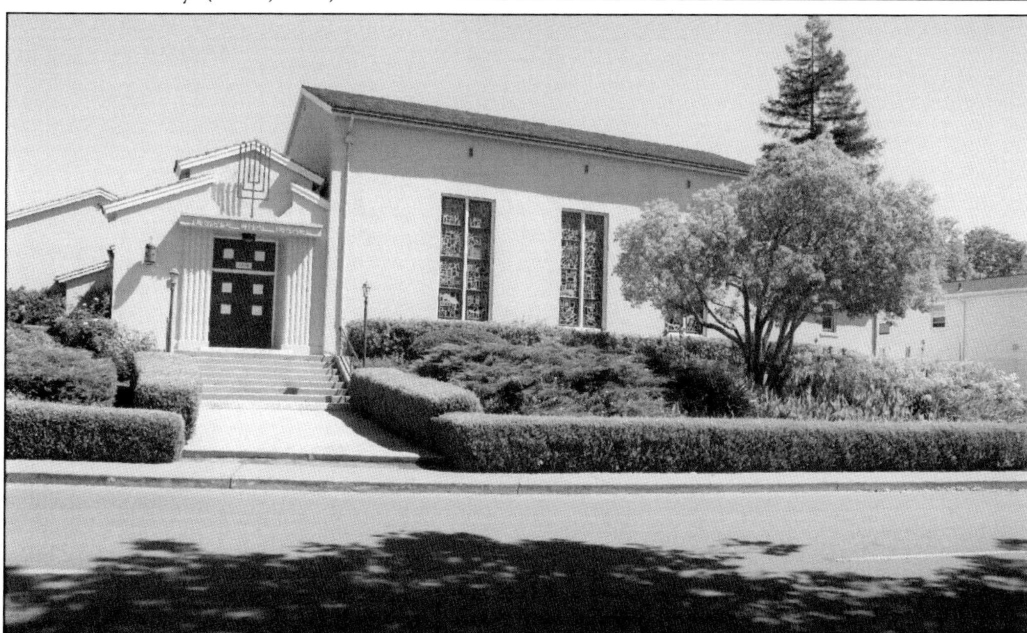

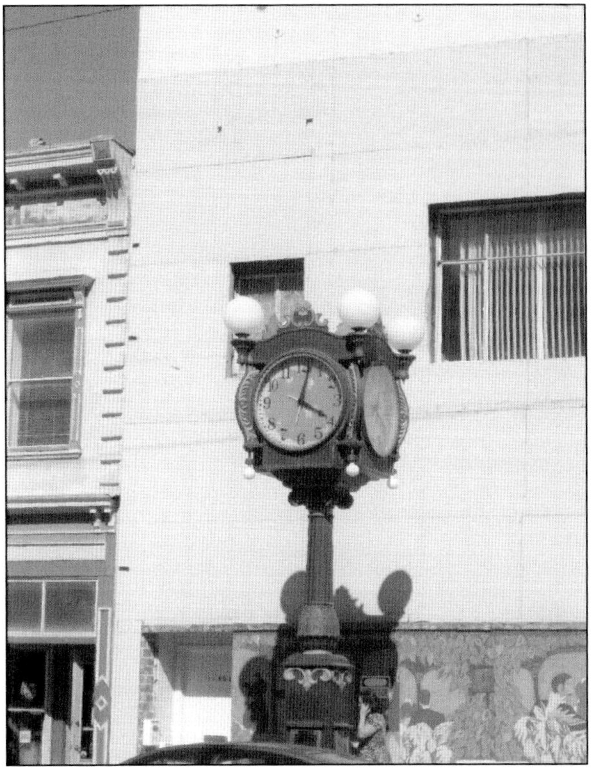

Ralph Raphael, owner of Simon's Jewelers, is seen here in front of his Georgia Street store with the so-called "Alibi Clock," which was moved to Vallejo from San Francisco's Market Street in 1932 and restored by the city in 1984. The clock got its name after a labor radical used a photograph of himself with it as an alibi when he was accused of setting off a deadly bomb in San Francisco in 1916. When Simon's closed in 1984, the City of Vallejo purchased the clock, moved it to 316 Georgia Street, and overhauled and restored it. This beautiful landmark was made possible by the generosity of Simon's Jewelers, Brown's Jewelers, the City of Vallejo, and everyone who assisted in the restoration. (Left, VTH; below, CBI.)

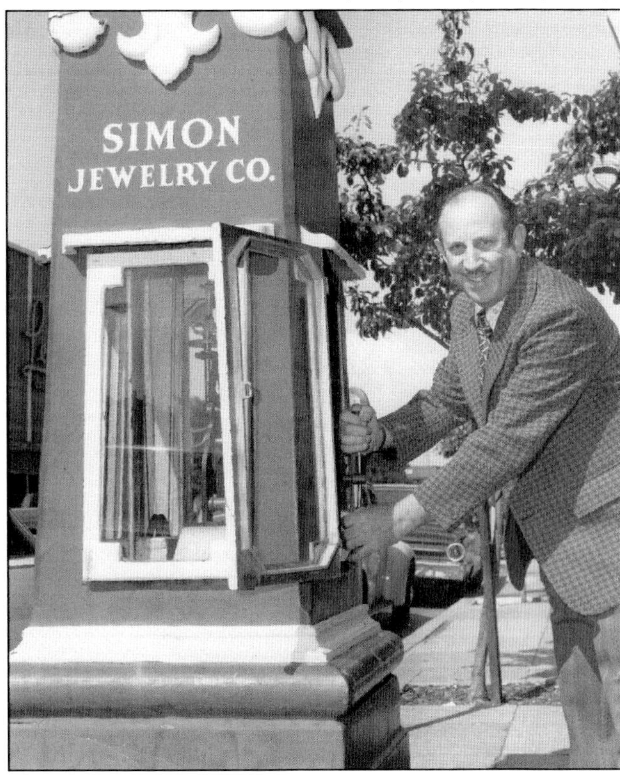

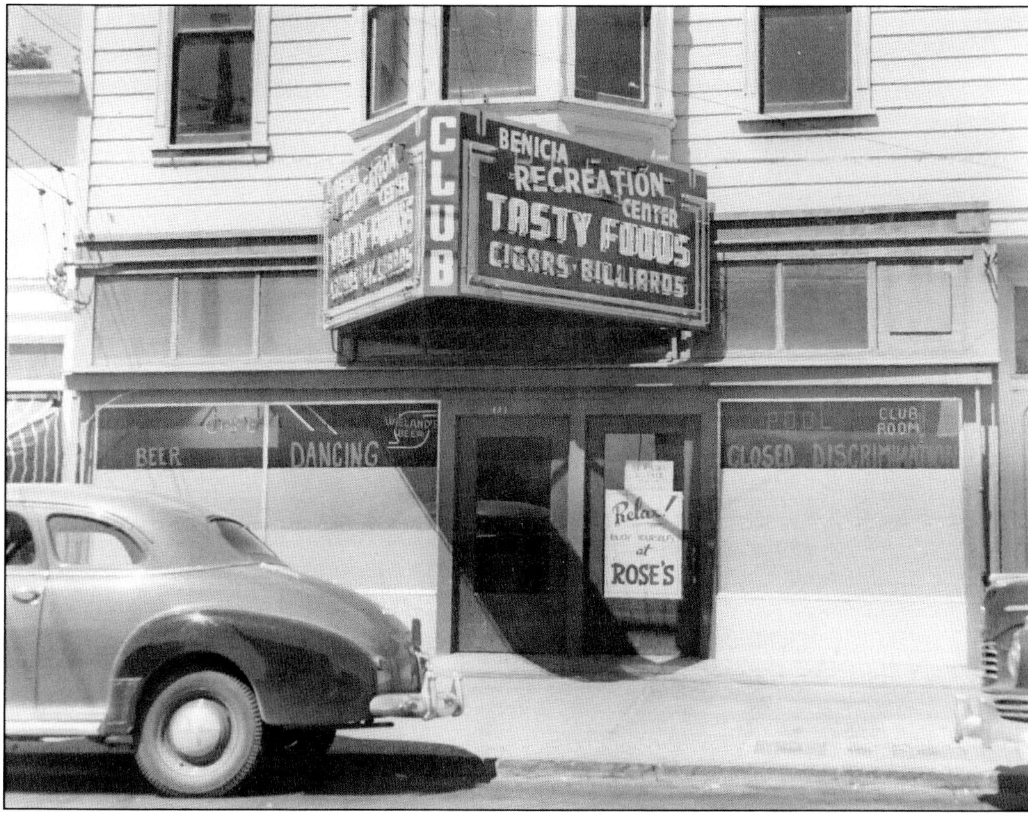

Pictured here is the Benicia pool hall and saloon of Solomon "Sol" Rose—a contentious figure through the 1940s and 1950s whose name elicited eye-rolling as late as 2014. He was arrested in a 1948 café brawl, but the charges were eventually dropped. In 1950, he called for a judge's ouster, which prompted dueling libel suits. Elected to city council in 1952, Rose was stripped of his park commission duties in 1953 after threatening to expose city government corruption. Rose was arrested twice on the day of the recall election that was demanded following his citizen's arrest of the police chief, but so were the acting police chief and a painting contractor who had had Rose arrested. Rose's letter at right responds to *Benicia Herald* editor Albert Souza's editorial about Rose's city council candidacy and alludes to Souza having gotten his education from the Burma Shave advertisements that were popular as roadside signs at the time. (Above, VTH; right, BHM.)

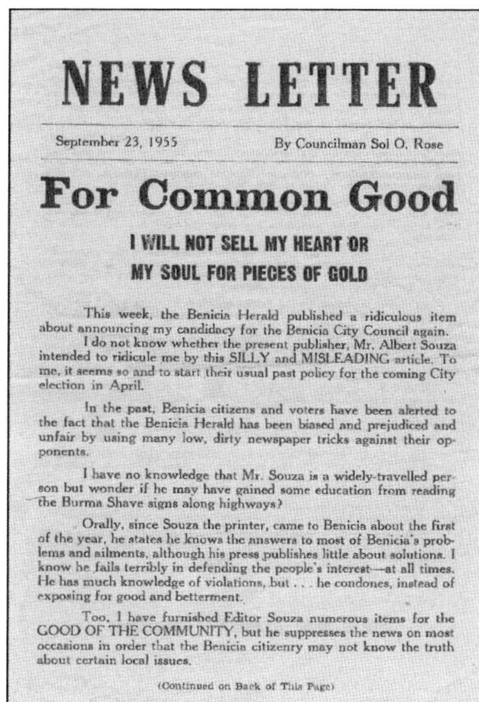

NEWS LETTER

September 23, 1955 By Councilman Sol O. Rose

For Common Good

I WILL NOT SELL MY HEART OR MY SOUL FOR PIECES OF GOLD

This week, the Benicia Herald published a ridiculous item about announcing my candidacy for the Benicia City Council again.

I do not know whether the present publisher, Mr. Albert Souza intended to ridicule me by this SILLY and MISLEADING article. To me, it seems so and to start their usual past policy for the coming City election in April.

In the past, Benicia citizens and voters have been alerted to the fact that the Benicia Herald has been biased and prejudiced and unfair by using many low, dirty newspaper tricks against their opponents.

I have no knowledge that Mr. Souza is a widely-travelled person but wonder if he may have gained some education from reading the Burma Shave signs along highways?

Orally, since Souza the printer, came to Benicia about the first of the year, he states he knows the answers to most of Benicia's problems and ailments, although his press publishes little about solutions. I know he fails terribly in defending the people's interest—at all times. He has much knowledge of violations, but . . . he condones, instead of exposing for good and betterment.

Too, I have furnished Editor Souza numerous items for the GOOD OF THE COMMUNITY, but he suppresses the news on most occasions in order that the Benicia citizenry may not know the truth about certain local issues.

(Continued on Back of This Page)

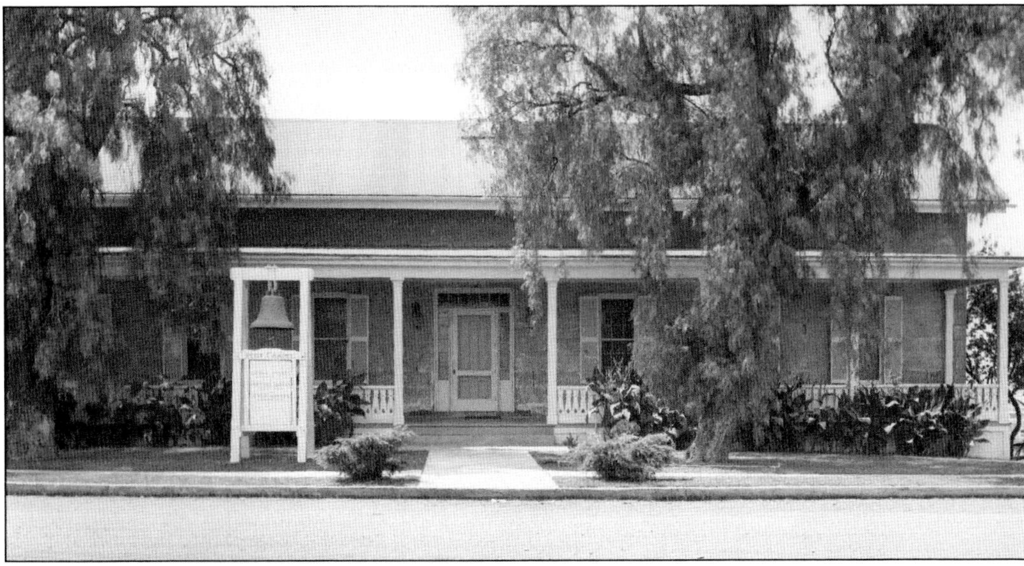

Transforming the Benicia Arsenal Post Hospital into a post chapel in 1944, the military held services there for a variety of religious denominations. There were three services offered: Jewish, Protestant, and Catholic. Jewish services, as noted on the sign outside the building, were held on Thursdays at 4:00 p.m. This photograph was taken on August 28, 1944. (BHM.)

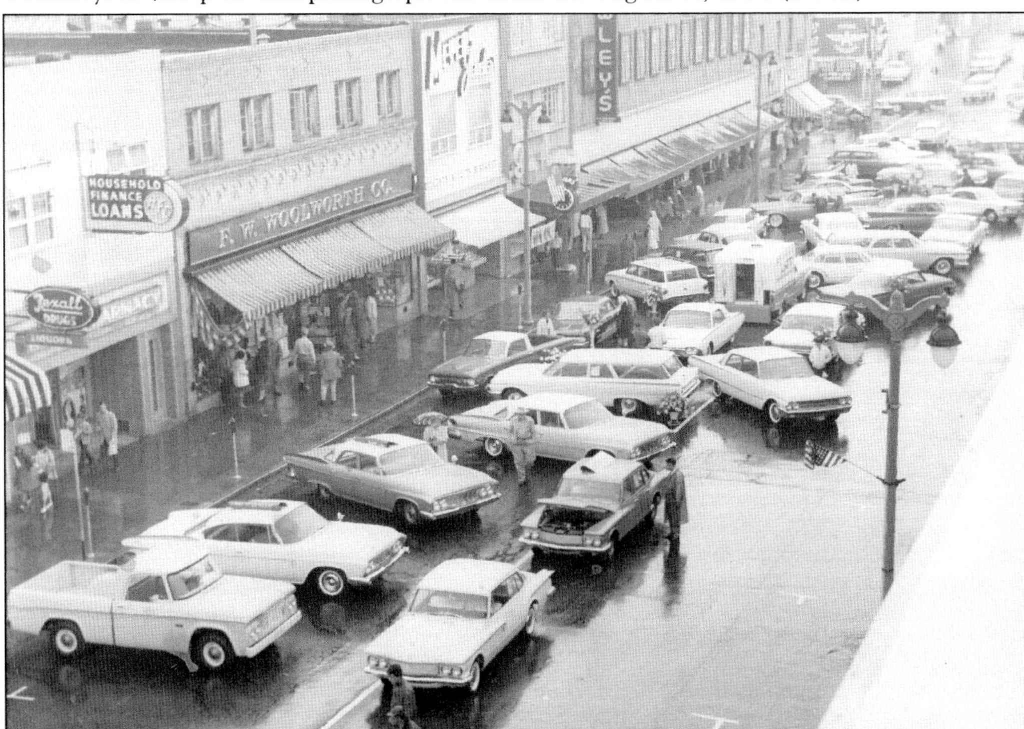

In this 1950s- or early-1960s-era photograph of Vallejo's Georgia Street, the sign for Meyer's Jewelers can be seen between Woolworth's and Crowley's. The reason for what appears to be the fairly serious traffic mess depicted here is lost to time. The jewelry store, owned by the Meyer brothers and their wives, became a Vallejo institution and moved to Sonoma Boulevard in 1979. (VHM.)

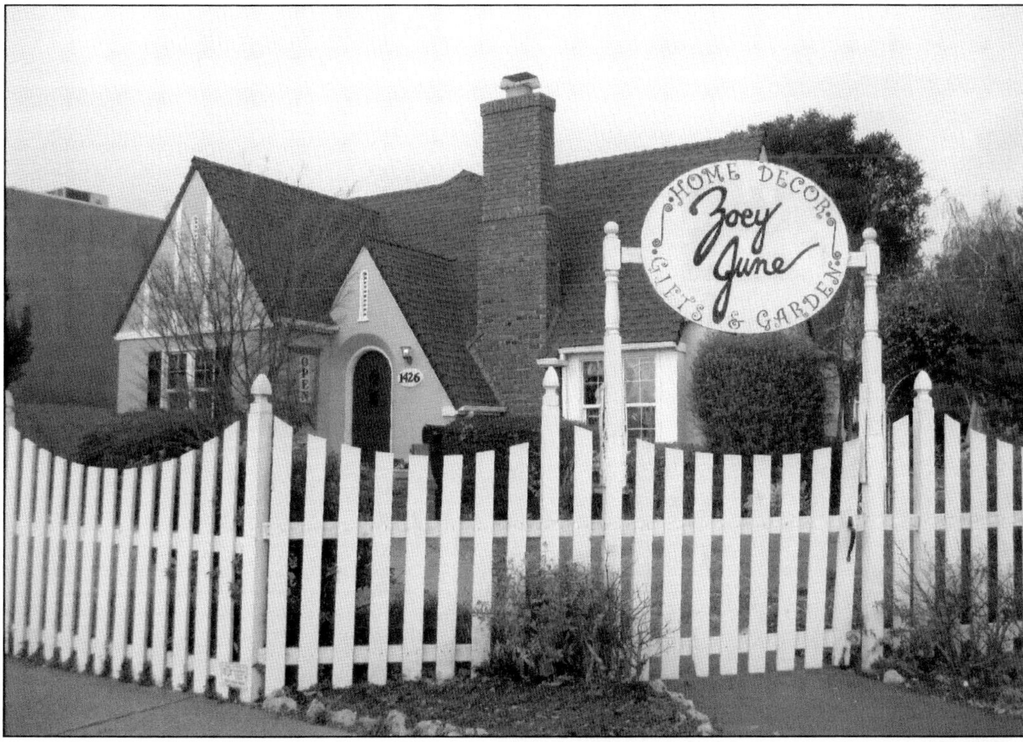

Built around 1929, this Vallejo house at Tennessee and Fresno Streets became a popular gift shop called Zoey June in 2001. But for some 50 years before that, it was the home of Tamar Abouaf and family. One often-recounted memory is of the Abouaf children decorating two spindly olive trees at Christmastime and presenting them to their father, who had planted the trees in the backyard. Today, those trees remain as huge reminders of times past. Members of the Abouaf-Pizante clan, the family was active in the York Street shul and at the synagogue on Nebraska Street. Other Abouaf relatives, the Benaroya family, owned a grocery store at Sonoma and York Streets. Tamar Abouaf, seen at right, was an artist and was active in both Hadassah and Sisterhood, and her husband, Albert, was active in the local B'nai Brith lodge. (Both, CBI.)

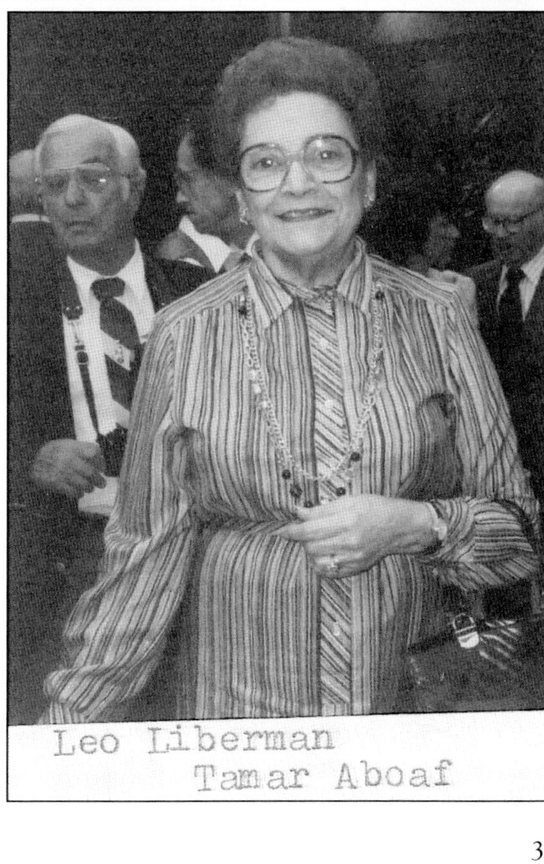

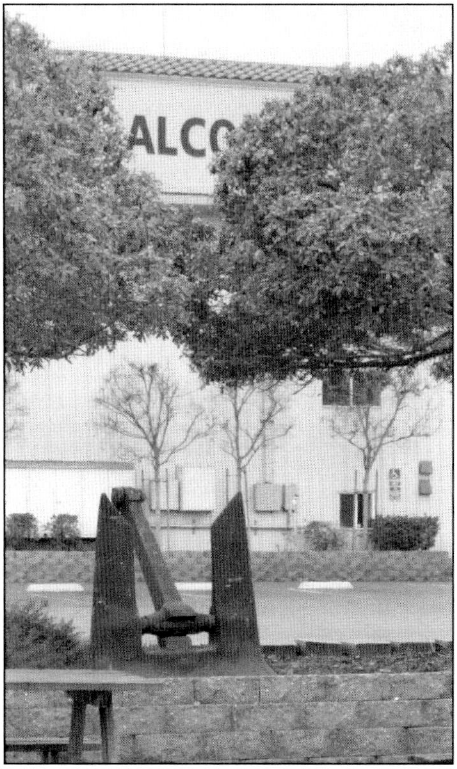

The Alco Iron and Metal Co.'s building was the second sold on the former Mare Island Naval Shipyard after the 1996 base closure. Alco's president, Kem Kantor, said that the scrap metal industry in the United States is largely Jewish. Oakland's Lakeside is owned by Kantor's cousins, and together they're known as the Bay Area's "patriarchs of scrap." Founded in 1953 by Kantor's father, the 200-plus-employee company is run by Kantor and his siblings. (SDN.)

Founded in 1995 by Ken and Dolores Zadwick, the Mare Island Historical Park Foundation created and maintains the Mare Island Museum. In 2014, Zadwick, a former rocket scientist and entrepreneur who helped develop the first Coca Cola can, still heads the organization and, with volunteers, runs the museum. Zadwick, 82, says that he takes his approach to Judaism from his father, who said if he followed the Ten Commandments, he was doing okay. (SDN.)

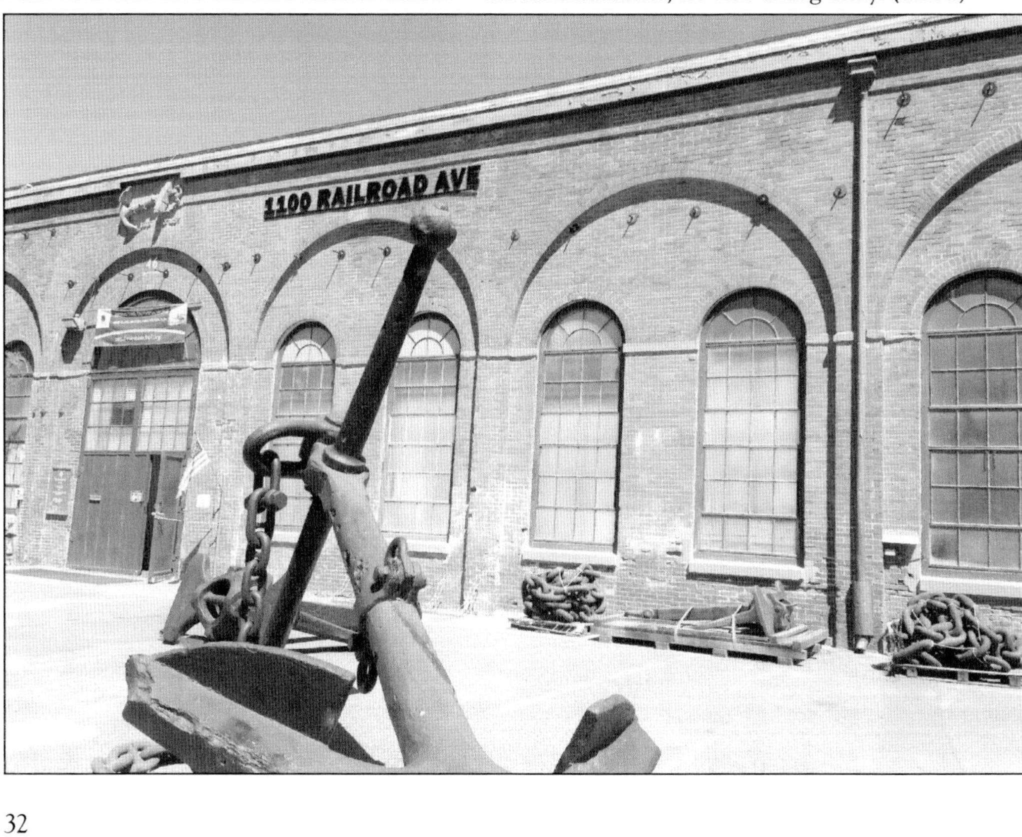

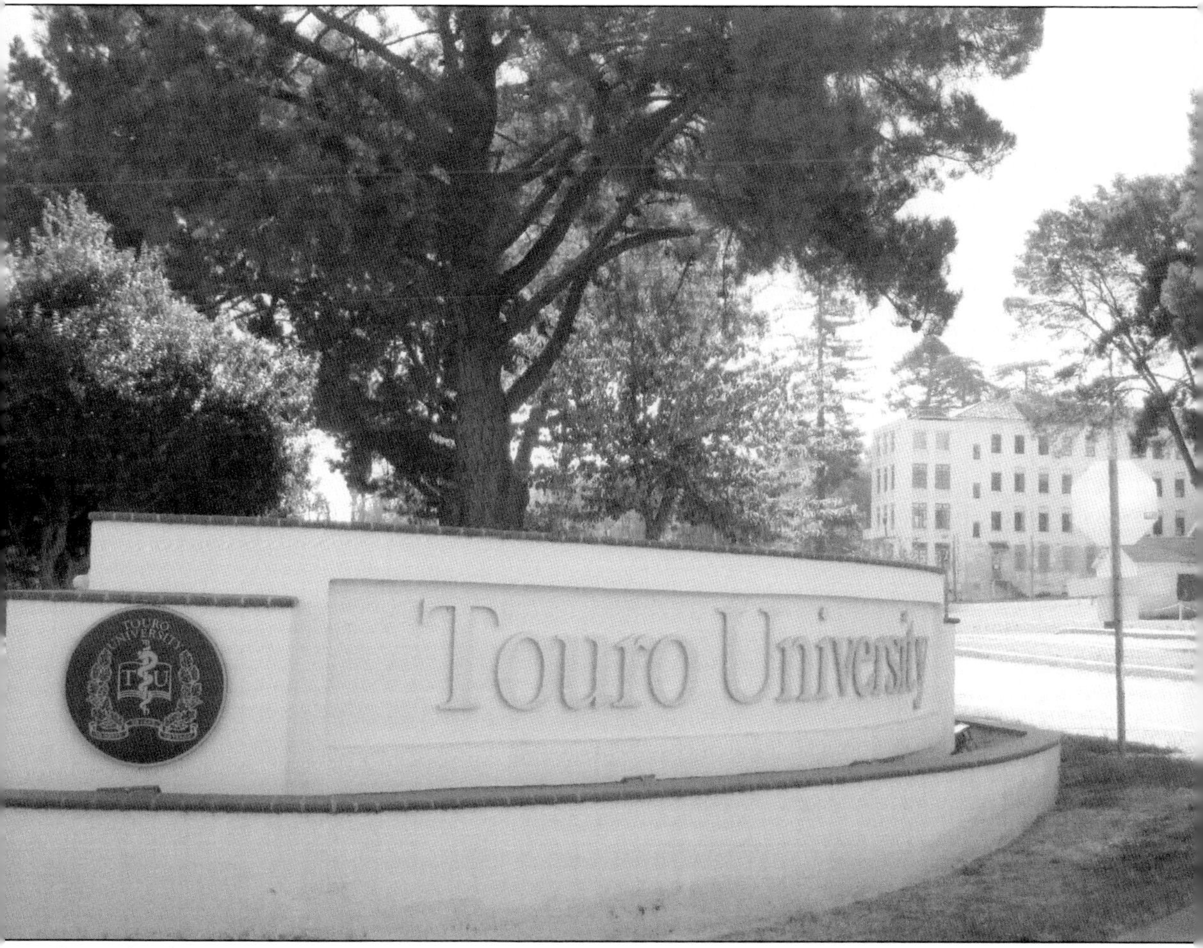

One of only 19 osteopathic medical schools in the United States, Touro University opened a 173-acre campus on the site of Mare Island's former Naval General Hospital in 1999. Founded by Bernie Lander, PhD, LHD, in New York in 1971, this Jewish-based institution of higher learning has since added schools of pharmacology, education, public health, and law. Named for colonial Americans Judah and Isaac Touro—founders of the continent's first free library for whom the country's first synagogue was named—it is based on the Jewish ideals of community service, public health care, and scholarship. Its website says that in keeping with the Jewish tradition of *tikkun olam* (repairing the world), students tutor local elementary school students and run two free health clinics. Several local Jewish community members have, or do, work there, including Bruce Silverman, Alisa Danyeur, Robin Gross, and Ralph Pierce. (SDN.)

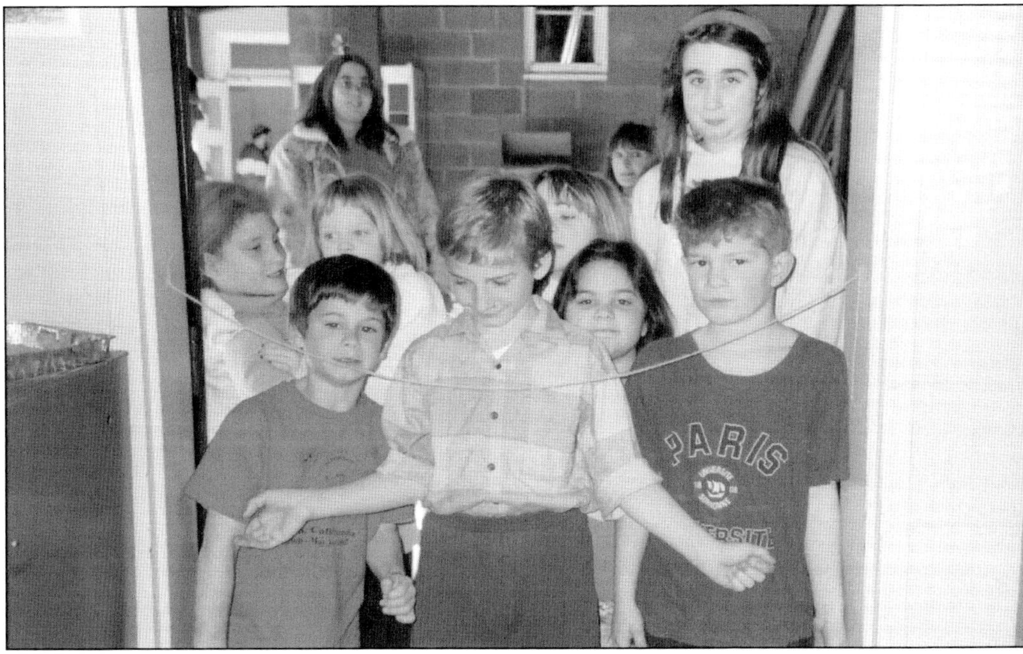

The Congregation B'nai Israel book collection is the only Jewish library in Solano County. Shoshana Deutscher-Nurik organized it by writing to publishers and receiving donations of books from them and temple members in the hope that children would read Jewish novels and nonfiction for public school book reports. The collection's bookshelves were built by John Campbell and Jack Mazer. Shown above at the "ribbon cutting" are, from left to right, (first row) Aaron and Ben Zaks, Angelic Pierce, and Oren Rosenmann; (second row) Yael Rosenmann, Hannah and Sarah Groody, and Becky Schwartz; (third row) Jennifer Schwartz and Rhea Zaks. Two time capsules are housed in the same building. One was buried at the time of the original temple dedication, and the second was added on the occasion of the 60th anniversary of the building's opening. Pictured below are longtime CBI and Sisterhood members Joyce Georgetti (left) and Donna Plantz, posing in the courtyard near both the library and the time capsules. (Both, SDN.)

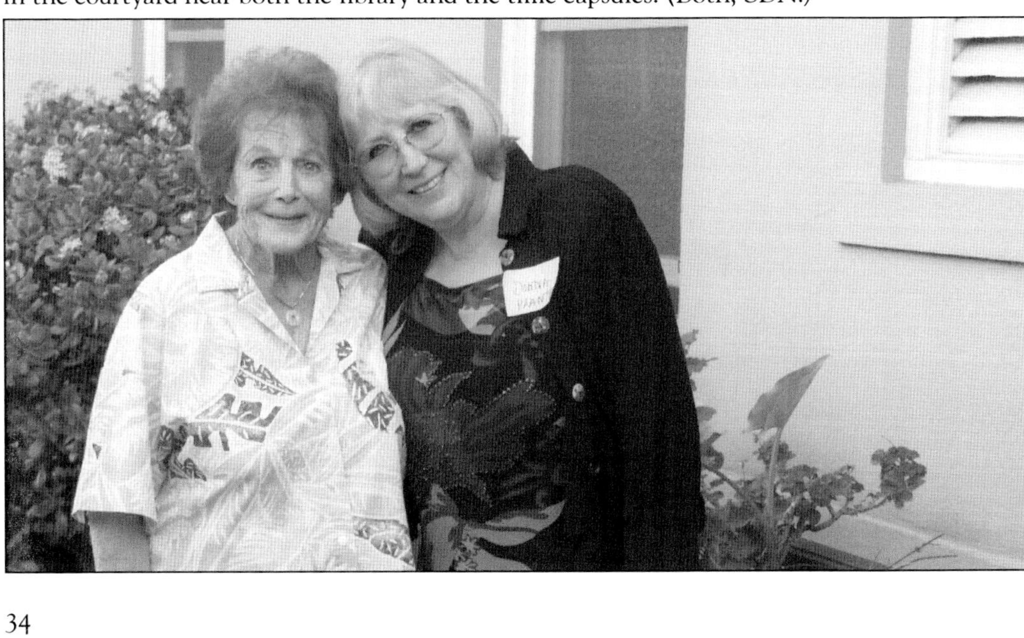

Three

Merchants

סוחרים (Socharim)

סויכערז (Soycherz)

. . . There to serve the community and make an honest living

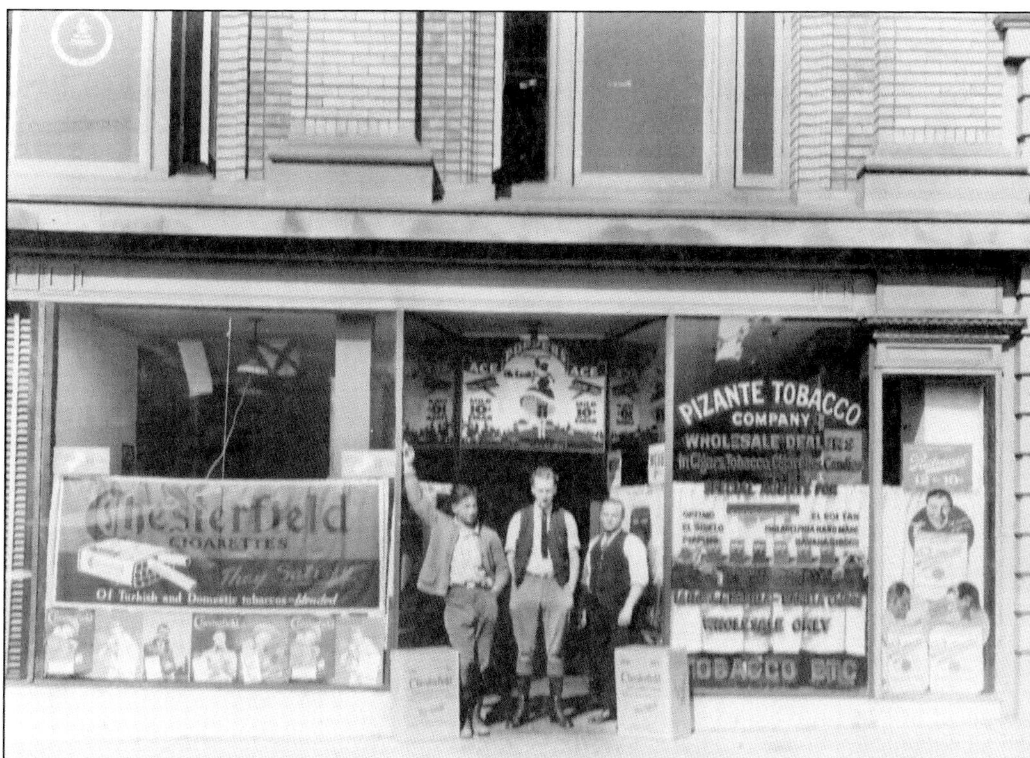

Raphael Pizante's tobacco and candy store on Virginia Street was one of a number of businesses of various types owned by Jews in Solano County. Many of the storefronts in Vallejo's downtown were lost to eminent domain in the 1960s to make way for the new civic center and John F. Kennedy Library. (Courtesy of the Pierce family.)

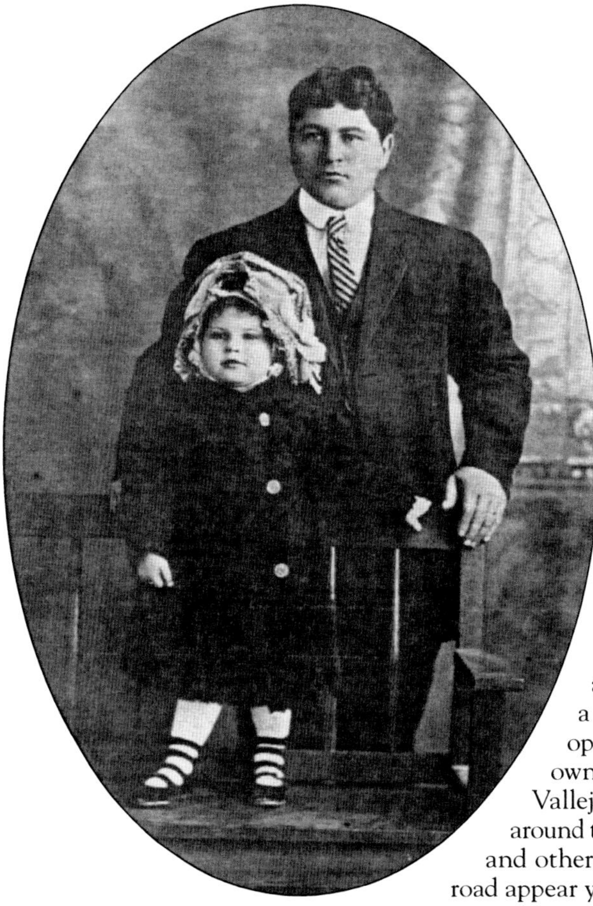

A past congregation president who was also active in Napa, Albert Kaufman—pictured here with his daughter Rosaline—worked in his father's Warsaw meat market before being conscripted into the Polish army, from which he escaped to America. He worked in a San Francisco butcher shop, married vaudeville entertainer Doris Biber after the 1906 earthquake, and was briefly a Novato cowboy. He gave all that up to open a Vallejo furniture business, which he owned from 1911 to 1939. Below is a view of Vallejo's bustling Georgia Street, looking east, around the same time period, near where Kaufman and others ran their shops and where rules of the road appear yet to be implemented. (Both, VHM.)

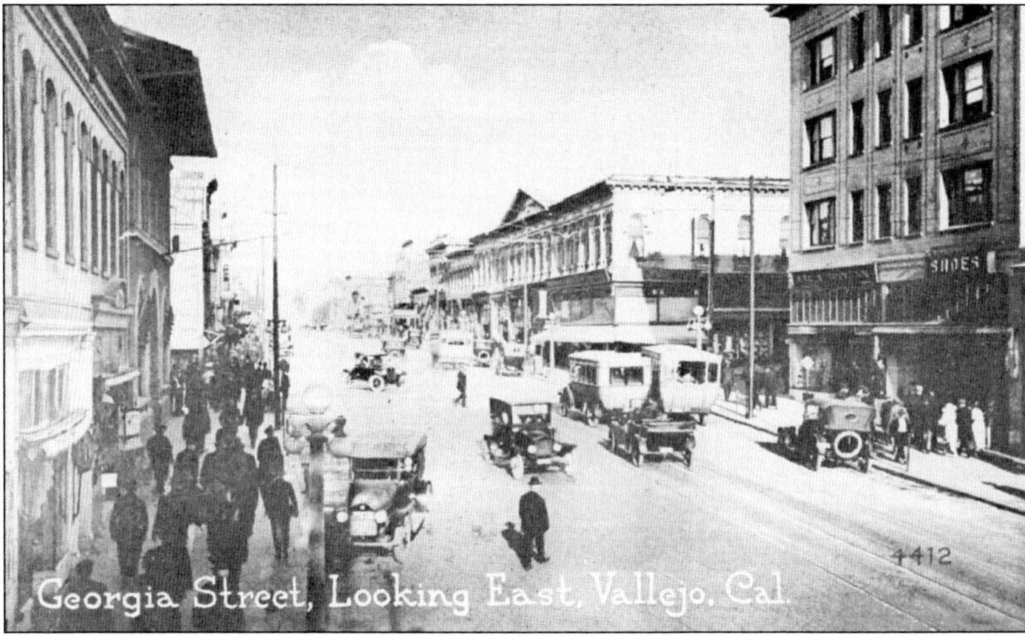

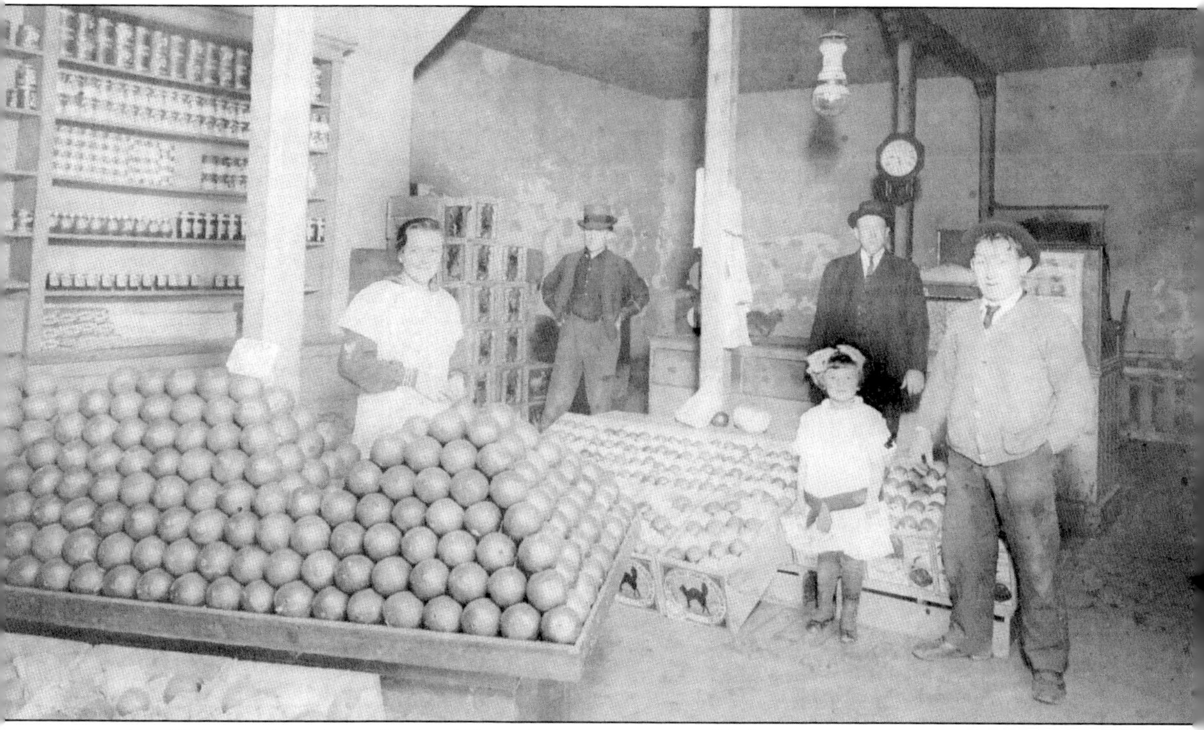

After the 1906 earthquake, Chaim (Heine) Bercu came to Vallejo, married a woman named Fanny, and opened the San Francisco Free Market on Marin Street where some recall that a Mr. Macheski was the butcher. Bercu is pictured here with his daughter Frieda, who later married Seymour Marcuse. Fred Sessler said of the past congregation president's store, "I don't know why it was called San Francisco Free Market, because it wasn't San Francisco and it wasn't free. This is how he made his living. People earned pennies in those days. And it's amazing how many little grocery stores there were—like the size of your living room—they were spread all over town." The Marcuses would later create Hadassah's 52/100 fundraiser. An optometrist, Seymour was famous for his sense of humor and encyclopedic mind until his death in 2013 at age 106. (VHM.)

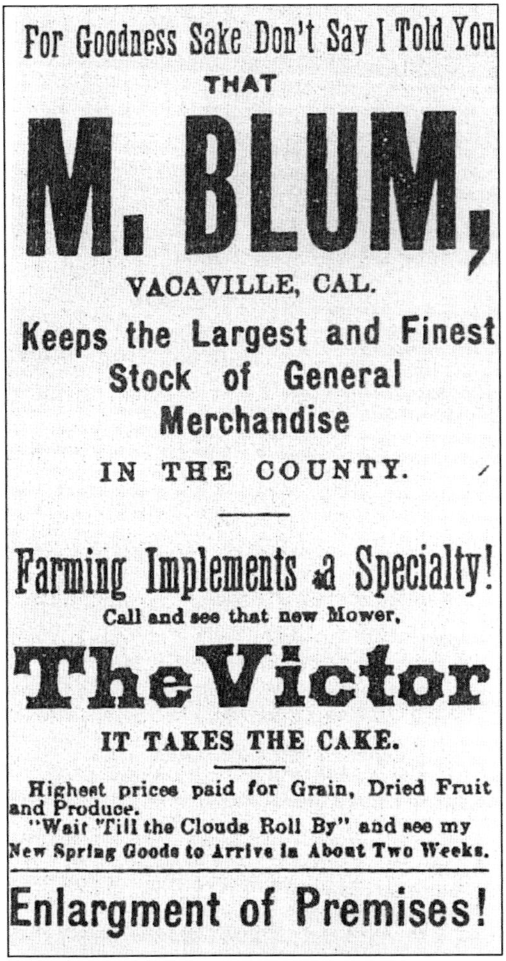

For Goodness Sake Don't Say I Told You

THAT

M. BLUM,

VACAVILLE, CAL.

Keeps the Largest and Finest Stock of General Merchandise

IN THE COUNTY.

Farming Implements a Specialty!

Call and see that new Mower,

The Victor

IT TAKES THE CAKE.

Highest prices paid for Grain, Dried Fruit and Produce.

"Wait 'Till the Clouds Roll By" and see my New Spring Goods to Arrive in About Two Weeks.

Enlargment of Premises!

"For goodness sake don't say I told you that M. Blum, Vacaville, Cal. keeps the largest and finest stock of general merchandise in the county." The left advertisement became a well-established feature in the *Vacaville Reporter* after Moses Blum and his two brothers opened a general store in a stone building on block 20 of downtown Vacaville. (VHC.)

After living in Gilroy, Maurice "Moe" Raphael and his wife, Bertha or "Bertie," moved their family to Vallejo at the end of the 1930s. He had been told of the opportunity to open a small shop downtown in an area that had a growing Jewish community. Moe opened Raphael's, which carried "gent's furnishings" at 527 Marin Street. His son-in-law Harry Gray worked in the store while building a career as a teacher. (CBI.)

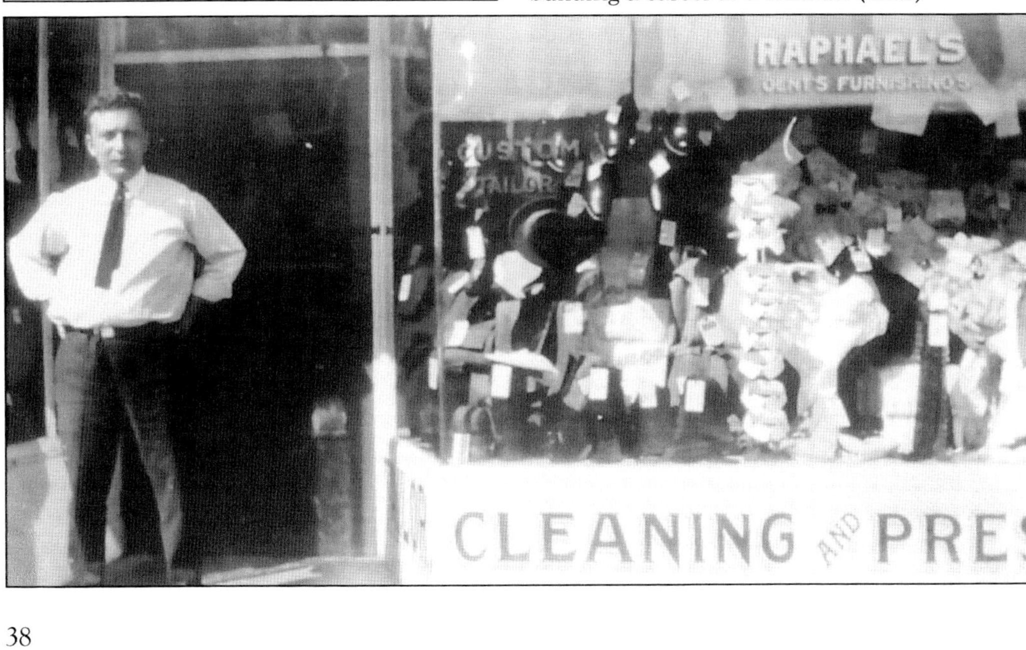

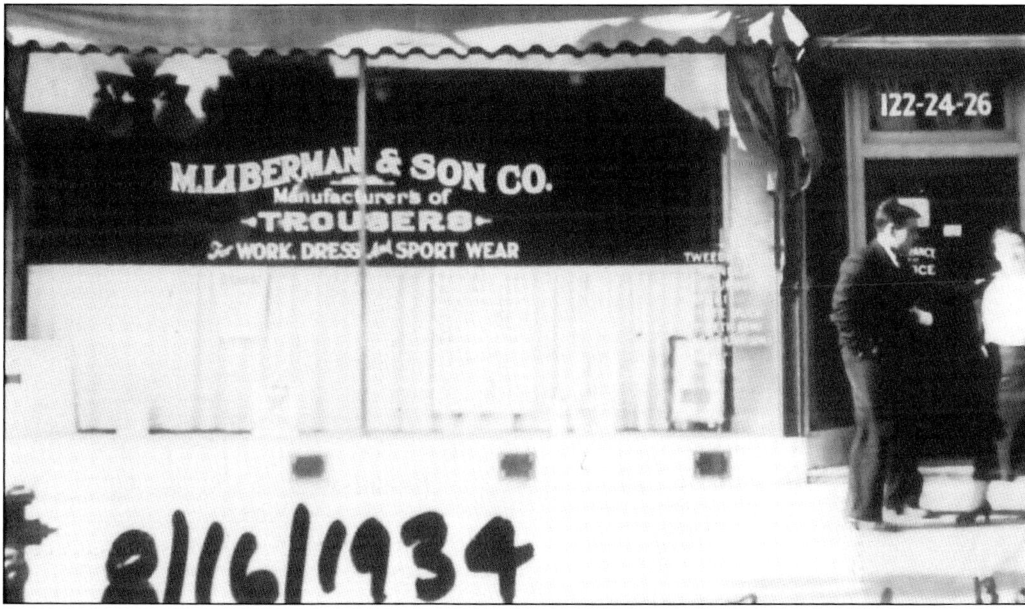

One of the founders of Vallejo's Jewish community, Meyer Liberman became an important manufacturer of work and mining pants after operating his own naval tailor shop on Georgia Street at a time when Vallejo's roads were still unpaved, with plank sidewalks and nearly impassable muddy streets in winter. The above photograph shows that the Liberman store stretched from 122 to 126 Georgia Street. Having come from Germany after the 1906 San Francisco earthquake to help with the rebuilding efforts, Liberman's unexpected death on the operating table in 1935 produced huge local headlines, illustrating his importance to the city of Vallejo. Some of his descendants remain in Vallejo and are active in the Jewish community in 2014. (Both, CBI.)

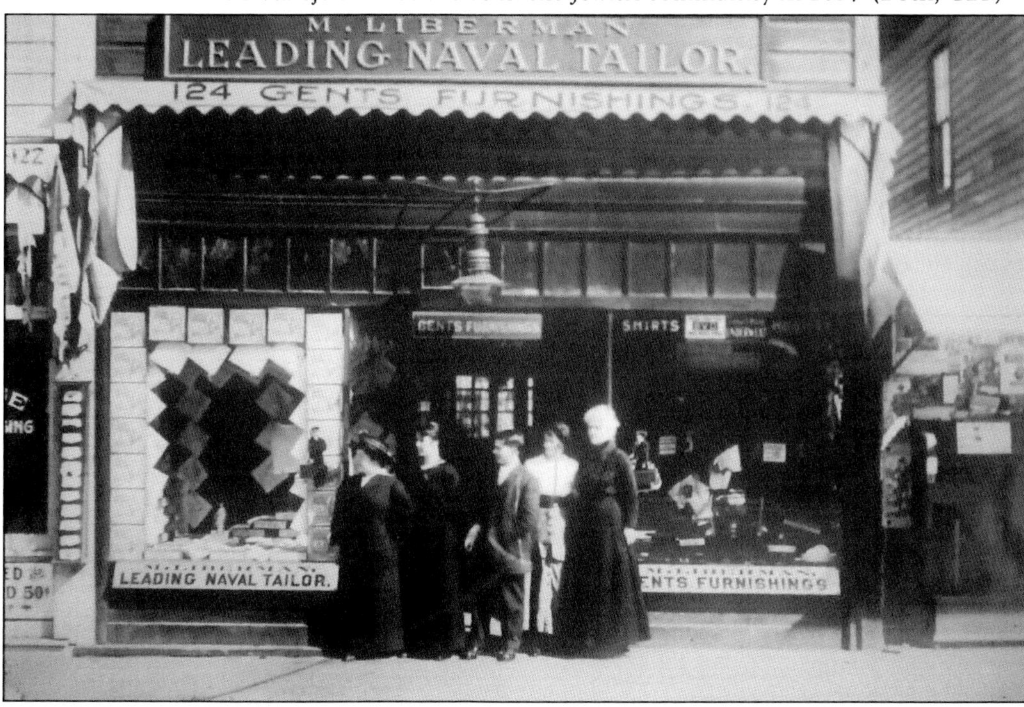

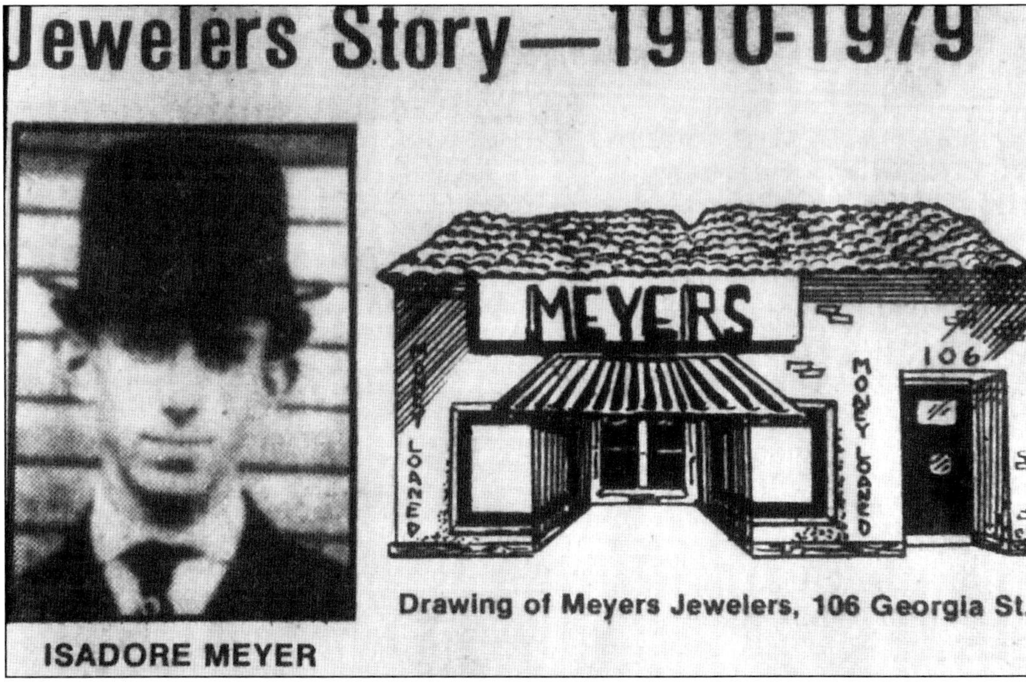

Cousins of Celia Harris Barsky, Isadore Meyer and his brother Wesley arrived in Vallejo in 1912 and founded a Georgia Street business that—before it became a jewelry store—was a pawnshop. A founding member and past CBI and B'nai Brith Lodge president, Isadore Meyer was named CBI's honorary lifetime president in 1950 at the Isadore Meyer Testimonial Dinner that was held in recognition of his 1947 trip to Washington, DC. Meyer's wife, Annie, served as Sisterhood president. (CBI.)

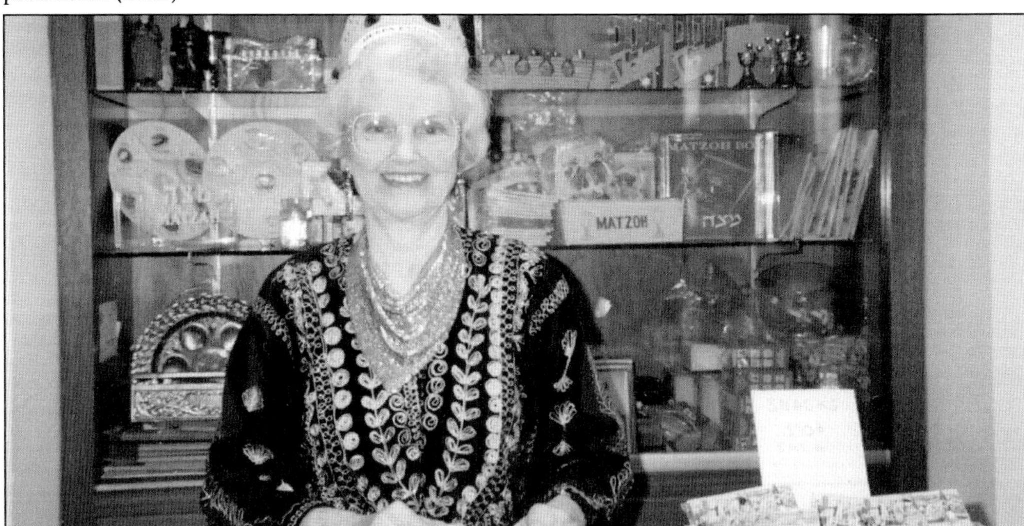

Beryl and Isaac Cohen opened Greens Liquors on Georgia Street, near Marin Street, in the 1950s. Around 1964, they moved their location to 318 Georgia Street, opening Pacific Gifts near the Alibi Clock. Beryl used her merchandising expertise for many years as she organized and ran the Sisterhood gift shop (pictured here) at Congregation B'nai Israel, where she and her husband were active members of the synagogue. (SDN.)

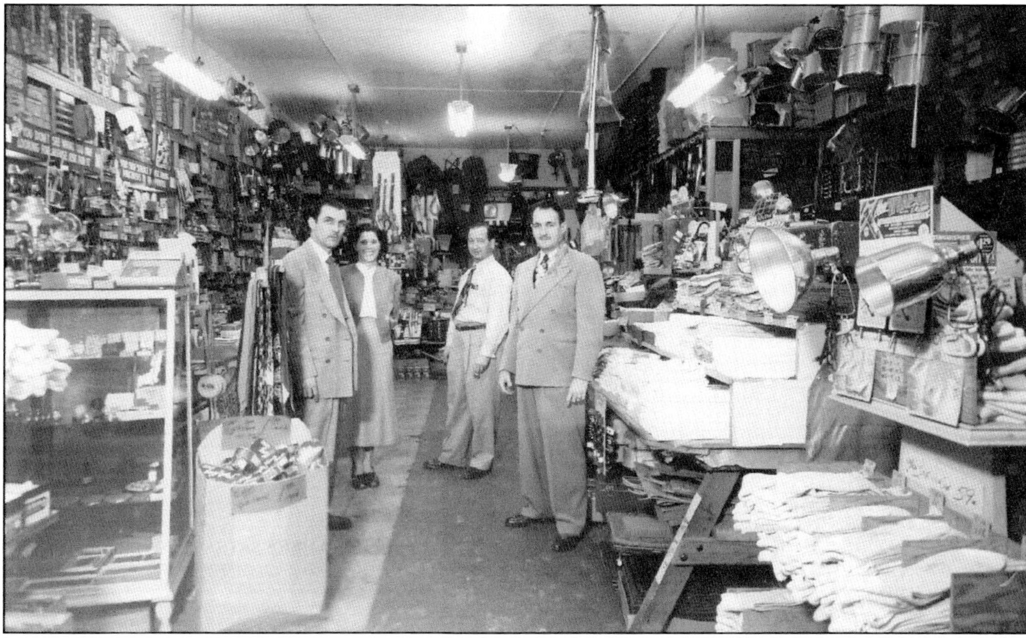

Al Ross's Victory Stores is among the earliest and longest-existing Jewish-owned enterprises in Vallejo. Founded in 1946 in a building on Georgia Street owned by Dr. Morris Zlot, it moved to its present site in 1960. Shown here in 1951, the store began as an Army/Navy surplus store and added work clothes and other items over the years. Al Ross's daughter Terry ran the business for many years before passing it on to her son, Raymond Prather. The Victory Stores has been a fixture in downtown Vallejo ever since, catering to a loyal working-class clientele from Vallejo and well beyond. (Both, courtesy of Ray Prather.)

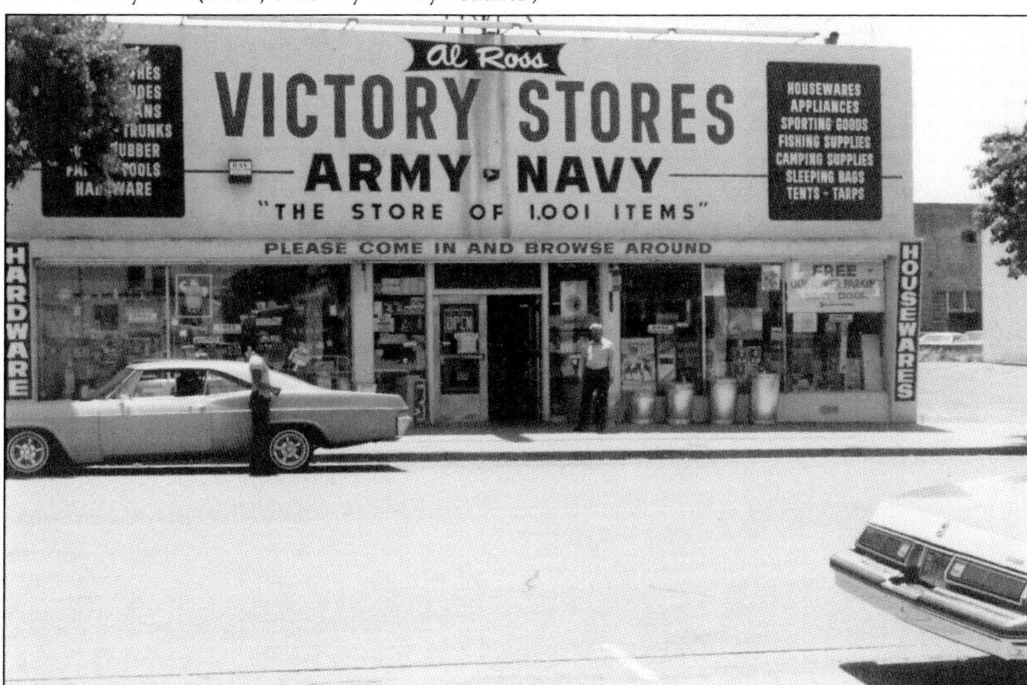

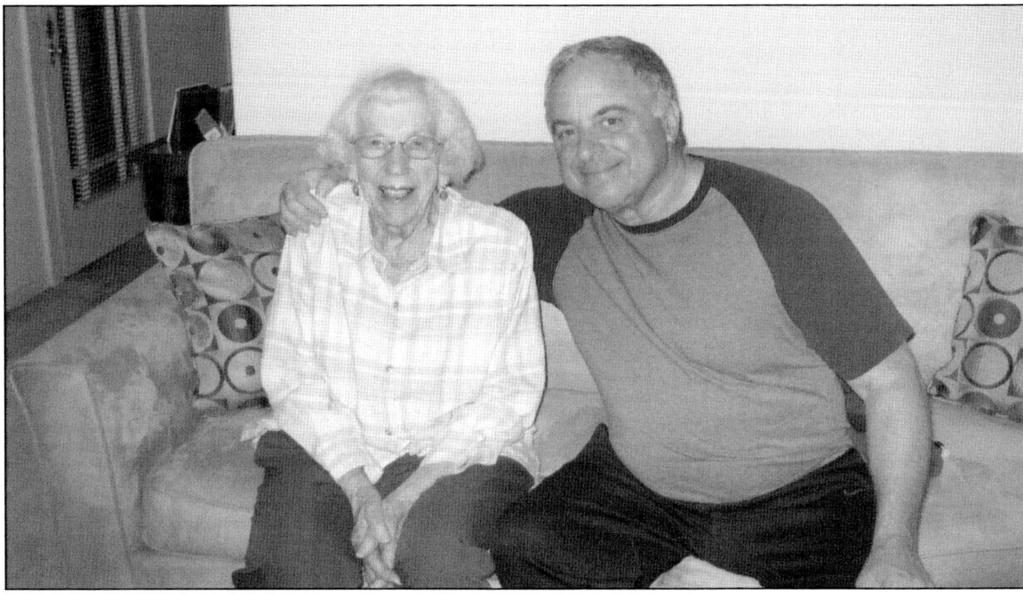

Coming to Vallejo in 1963, Mimi Farone, her son, David, and her brother Al Munter—who played trumpet—opened the Munter Music Company on the corner of Sonoma Boulevard and Georgia Street. There, they rented and sold musical instruments and gave music lessons. Mimi's husband, Louis—a singer and organist—was principal of Vallejo's Solano Middle School. A music major and violinist herself, Mimi started out as a schoolteacher but realized that she enjoyed a smaller class size. The entire family is full of musicians. Farone's sister, the stockbroker Bonnie Rogers, plays the cello, lives in Vallejo, and is an active member of Hadassah along with Mimi. David Farone played piano, and his son, Adam, plays guitar. (Both, SDN.)

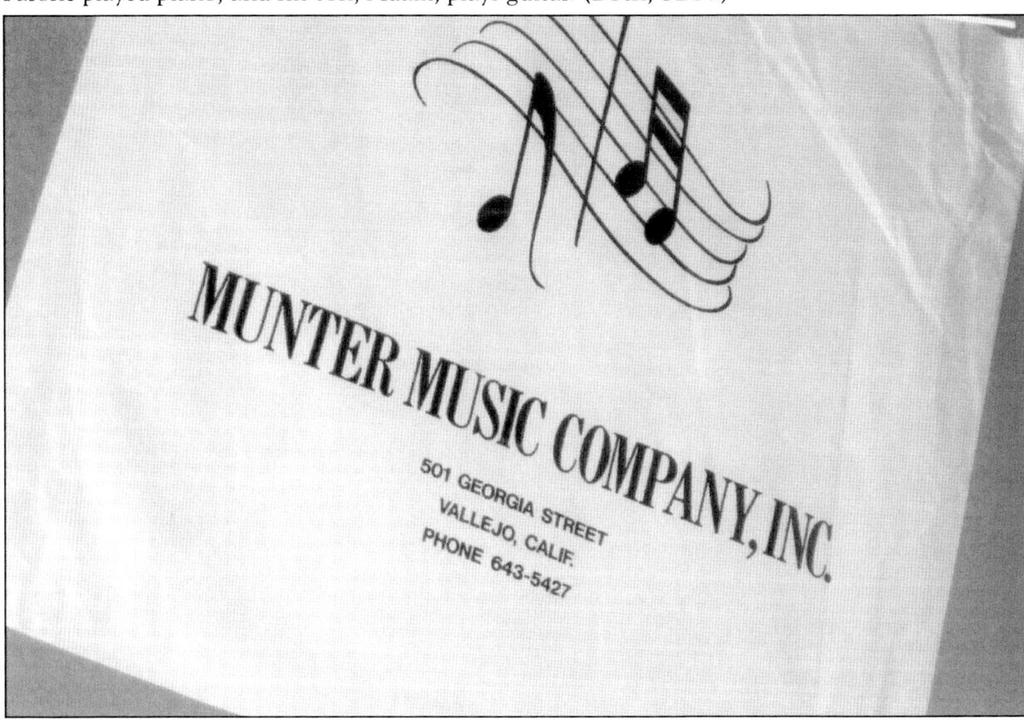

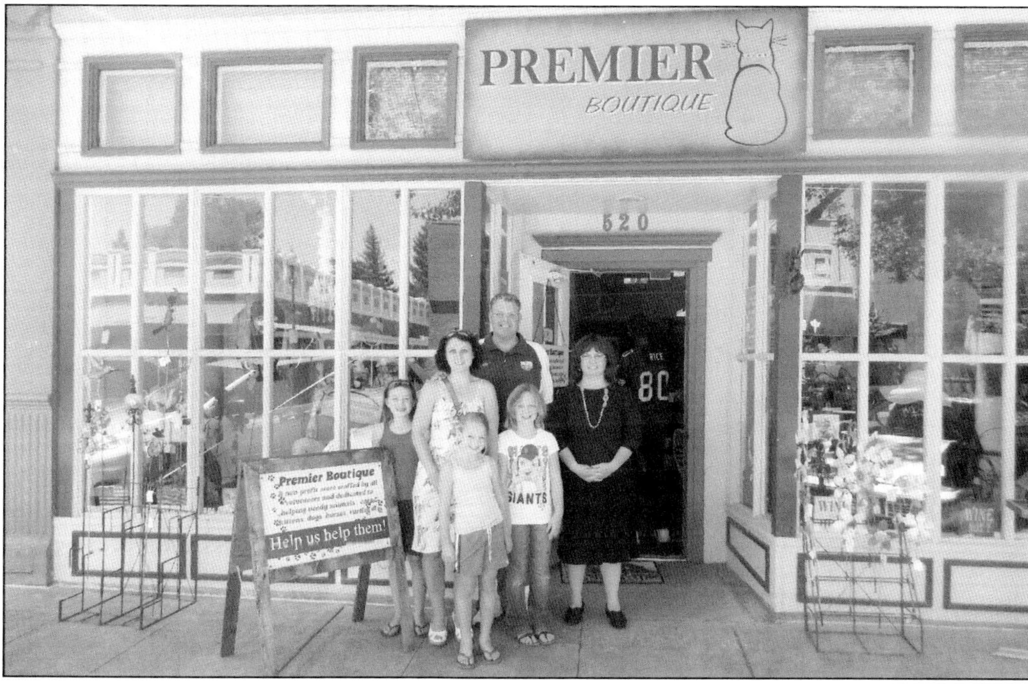

Finding a way to take a bite out of the high rate of animal euthanasia in Solano County was the idea that drove Kelly Fine—an active member of Solano's Chabad community—to found the Premier Animal Rescue Boutique in Vacaville, as seen here with Barbara Abeling and her daughters. They raise funds for animal rescue, spay/neuter services, and medical care. From left to right are (in front) Tessa Abeling; (second row) Brynna, Barbara, and Tiagan Abeling; (third row) Bill Abeling and Kelly Fine. (Courtesy of R. Lessem.)

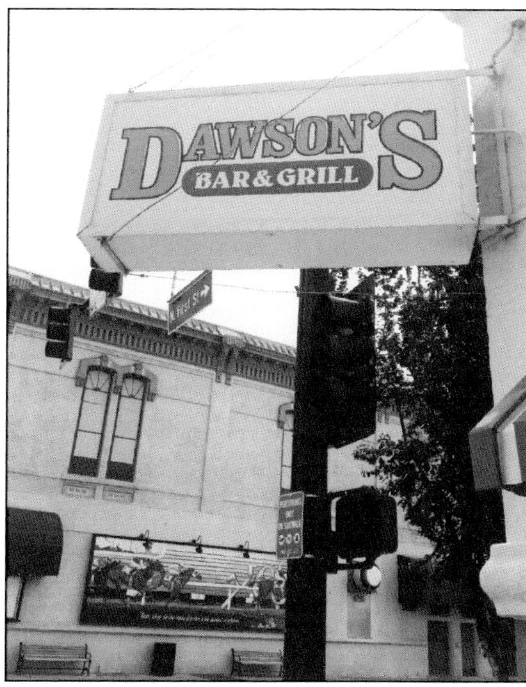

Harvey Kaplow realized a lifelong dream to own a restaurant when he and wife Lois opened Morgan's Coffee Shop in Vacaville in 1968. The family first came to Vallejo from San Francisco in the 1960s, and Harvey worked at Meyer's Jewelers. They later moved to Vacaville. While Lois pursued an education career, Harvey ran Morgan's and then bought Dawson's restaurant in Dixon in 1978, which they sold in 2002. (Courtesy of R. Lessem.)

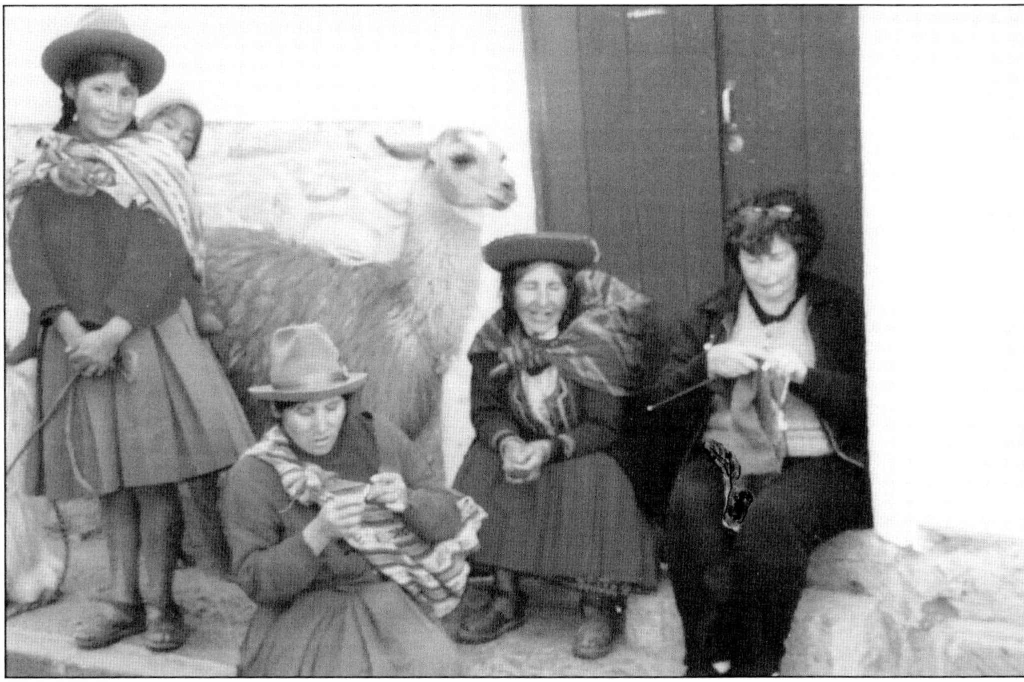

Employed by the Benicia Unified School District for 27 years, Ellen Blaufarb was a resource specialist, a counselor, a vice principal, and a principal. She says she worked hard to foster a vision of inclusiveness and equal access and opportunity. After retiring from education, Ellen—an avid traveler—opened a yarn shop where she taught knitting and sold yarn. She is also a columnist for the *Benicia Herald*. (Courtesy of Ellen Blaufarb.)

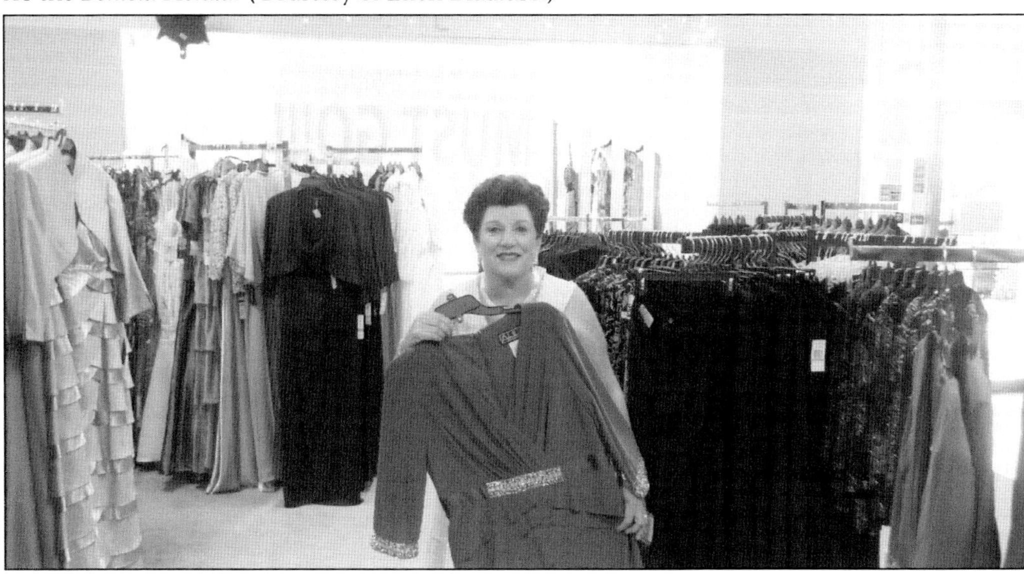

After starting out by selling clothes out of her car, Marjorie "Marge" Block has owned Napadashery, on Fairfield's Texas Street, for over 40 years. The secret of her success, she says, is "buying right" in New York and discounting everything. She is known for her "eye for fashion" and for knowing what looks good on a particular body type. Others believe that Block's success is due to her honest, caring, and genuine nature. (Courtesy of R. Lessem.)

Four

Big Shots

נכבדים (Nichbadim)

מאכרז (Machers)

. . . Making names for themselves

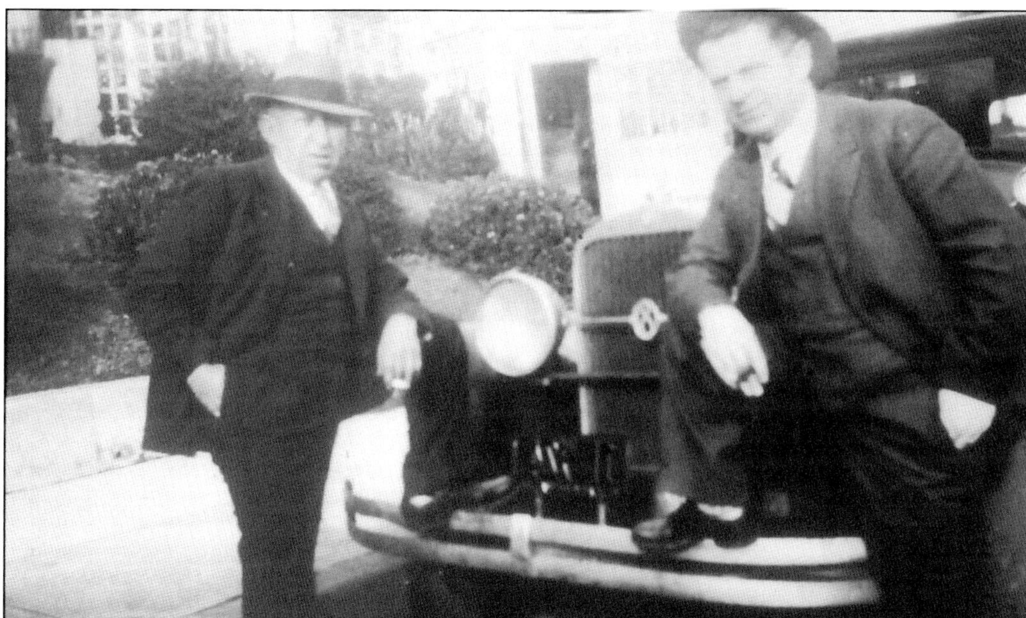

Isadore Meyer (left) and Meyer Liberman, big shots in both the Jewish and larger community, pose here with an older-model car in the 1930s. These men are simply two Jewish community members who were, or are, machers in some other arena of life. Since the beginning, there have been Jewish religious leaders, civic leaders, business leaders, and professionals who have left their mark on Solano County. (CBI.)

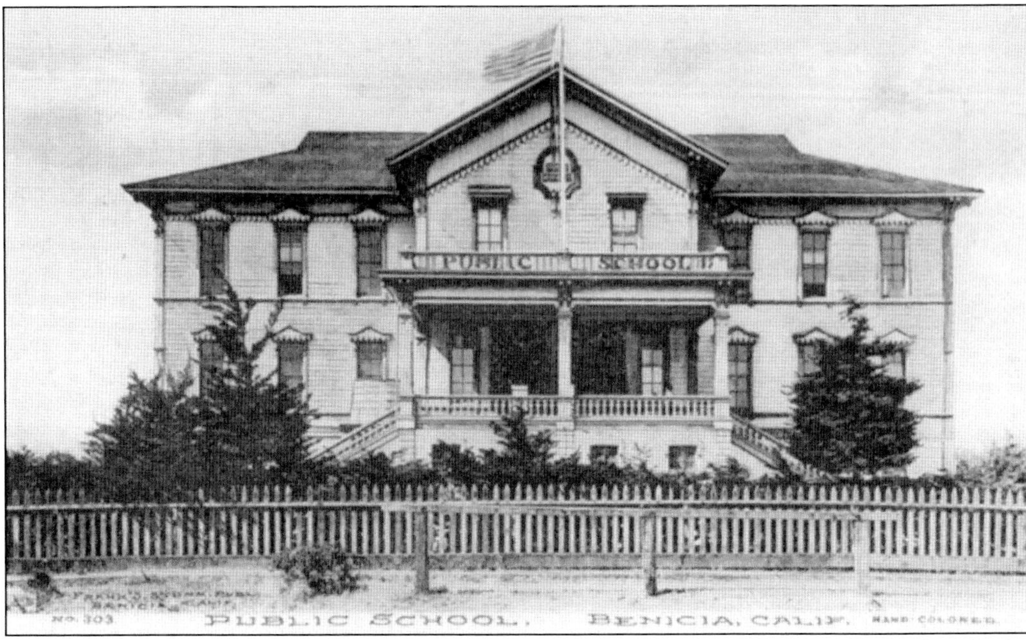

Before dying in 1898, at age 35, Samuel Weyler—a German Jew born in Russia—was raised Orthodox but converted to Christianity after arriving in America, although he steadfastly refused before leaving Russia, where he was under pressure and persecution of the Russian Orthodox Church. His knowledge of Talmud and Hebrew served him well after he became an ordained Methodist minister and was hired to pastor at Benicia's Congregational church. His unique perspective as a "Christian Hebrew" made him a popular lecturer at conferences and meetings. In 1896, he founded a classical academy that is believed to have later become Benicia High School. At about the same time, in Suisun City and Vacaville—at the other end of Solano County—Jewish children were attending the Pena School in the school district named for Austrian Jewish immigrant Morris Milzner. (Above, BHM; below, VHC.)

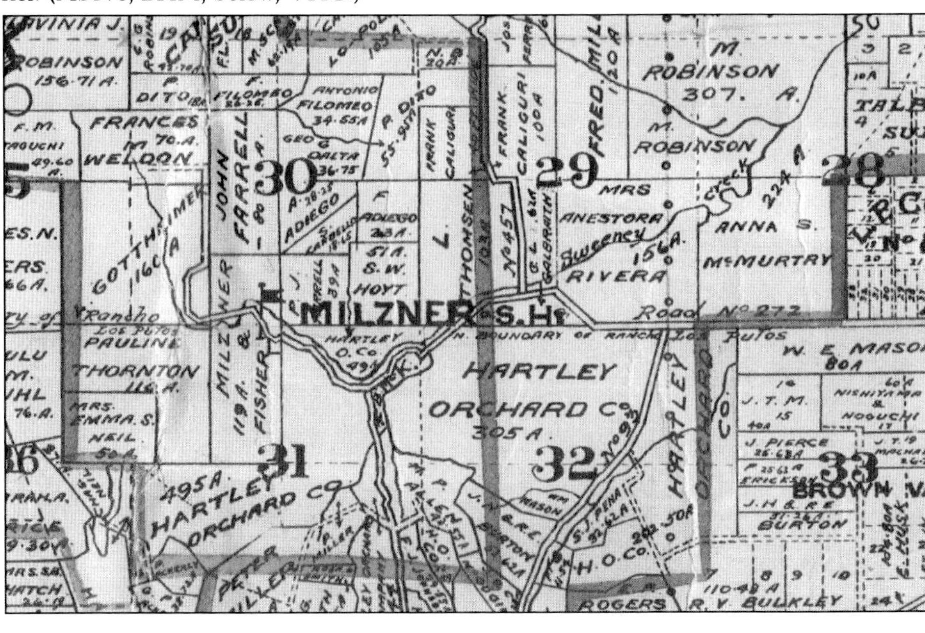

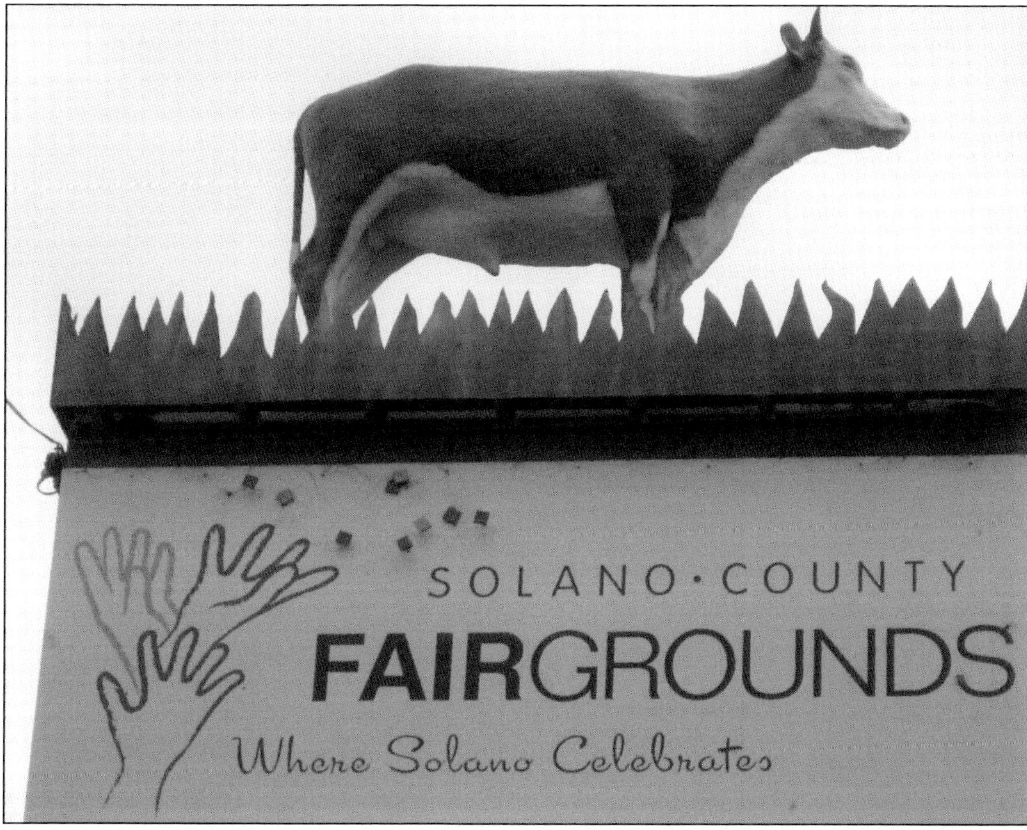

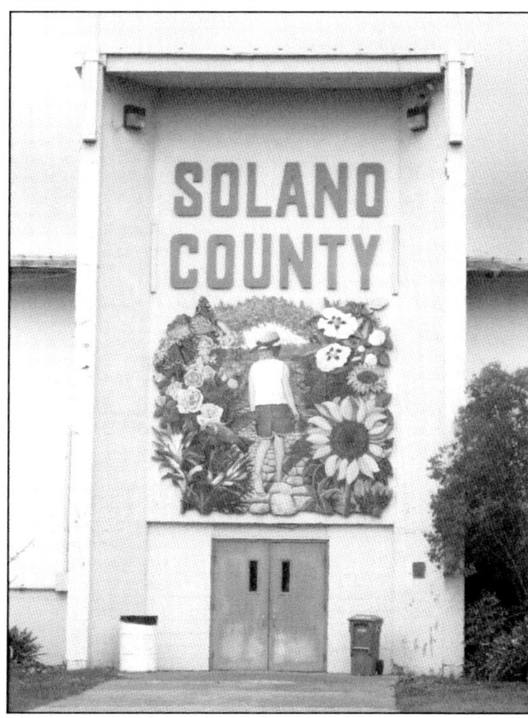

Arriving in the United States with his older brother in 1902, Harry Handlery—then 14—began a rags-to-riches story that, as a newspaper story once said, "became more impressive with each new venture." Toiling first in a New England wool factory, he arrived in San Francisco two weeks before the 1906 earthquake. Jobless and homeless in its aftermath, Handlery slept outside for three days before moving to Vallejo, where he found work and later opened a Georgia Street clothing store. In 1911, he married fellow earthquake refugee Rose Braun and started buying properties. The couple had two sons, belonged to a slew of local organizations, and always maintained strong ties to Vallejo—donating 100-plus Vallejo acres for the Solano County Fairgrounds. Handlery is also credited with "dreaming up" the glass elevator. He died in 1965, at age 77, and Rose died in 1970. (Both, SDN.)

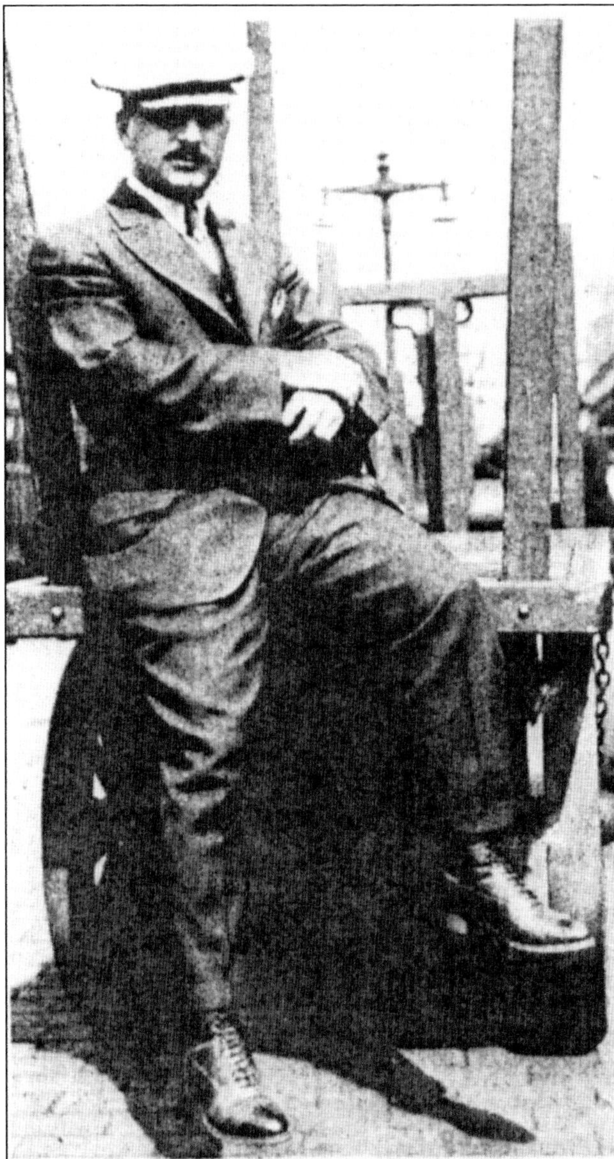

DOCTOR ERVIN J. CASPER
. . . waiting for the new ferry to San Francisco

In 1913, San Quentin Prison's attending physician, Dr. Ervin Casper, earned $75 a month. In 1933, he won acclaim for developing a prostate surgical technique that an Irish surgeon claimed as his own 15 years later, though he eventually backed down. A plaque commemorates Ervin and his Vallejo High School track star brother, Albert's donation of the field's lights before PG&E bought the family's power company (the track is named after Albert). In 1940, while acting as commodore of the Vallejo Yacht Club, Ervin hosted movie stars Clark Gable and Carole Lombard on his boat before the pair took "a casual stroll up Georgia Street," according to the *Times-Herald*. Albert Casper later helped fight what the *Times-Herald* referred to as "an unholy alliance" that tried "to steal Mare Island from Vallejo," traveling to Washington, DC, and staying for two weeks "until they had beat back the aggressors." (VTH.)

In the congregation's 100-plus years—first as the Sons and Daughters of Israel and then as Congregation B'nai Israel—it has been served by a string of rabbis and other spiritual leaders, including Jacob Waldman (right), Abrom Gray, Leo Abrami, Harold Friedman, Sol Horowitz, Dan Dorfman, David Kopstein, Bella Bogart, Sam Broude, Yitzhak Kaufman, Elchonon Tenenbaum, and David White. Northern Solano County has also had a number of spiritual leaders over the years, including several at Travis Air Force Base and Stephen Vale and Chaim Zaklos. Rabbi Gray's son, Harry Gray, was a Solano Community College history professor and the author of several regional history books. They contain photographs of California's Jewish personalities, cemeteries, and institutions; general Judaica; and the 1967 Arab-Israeli War. Pictured below, Harry (second from right) also wrote, produced, and performed in several CBI productions, like *Shikker*. (Both, CBI.)

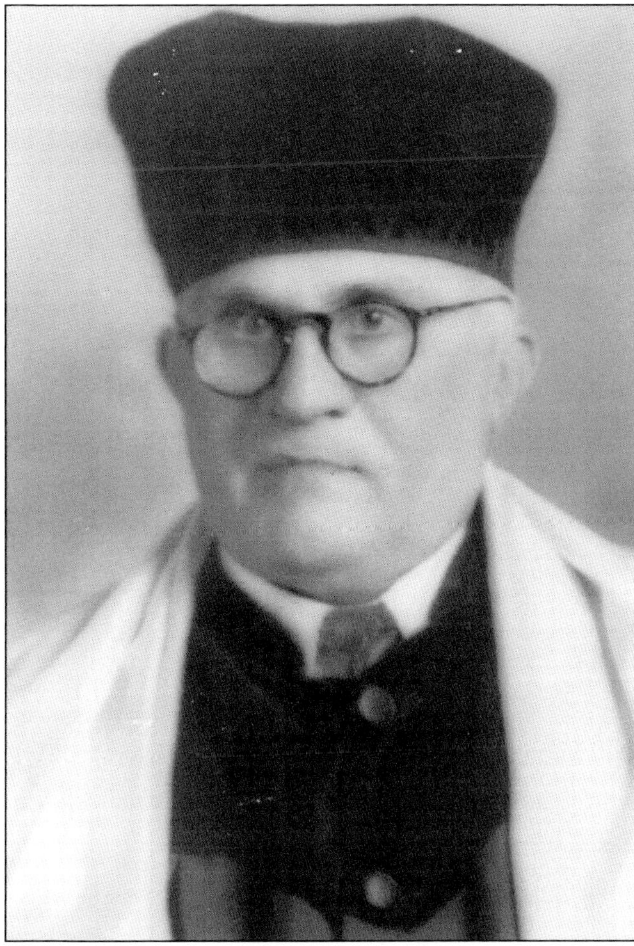

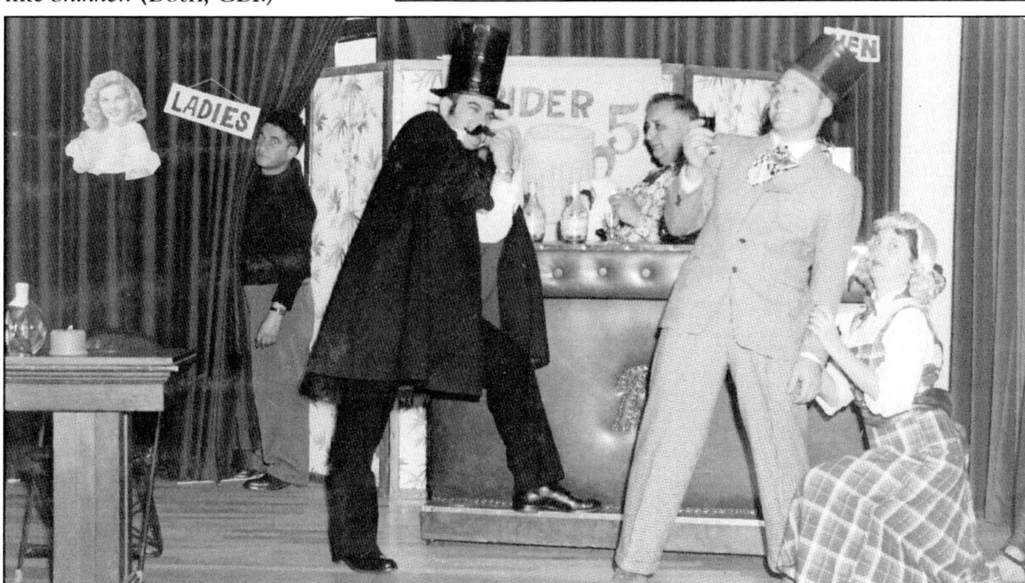

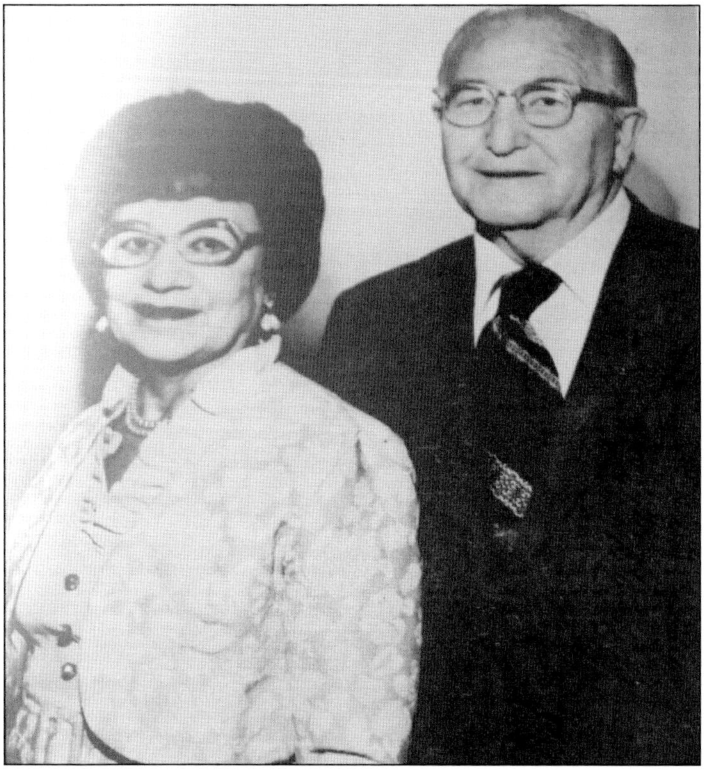

In 1948, Congregation B'nai Israel hired Rabbi Sol Horowitz to serve as its spiritual leader—a post that he held for 35 years. He and Rebbetzin Jennie Horowitz made public speaking engagements, led the establishment of the religious school, and, together, came to be recognized as among the finest religious leaders in the region. Their deaths in 1983 left a wound that took the congregation years to recover from. (CBI.)

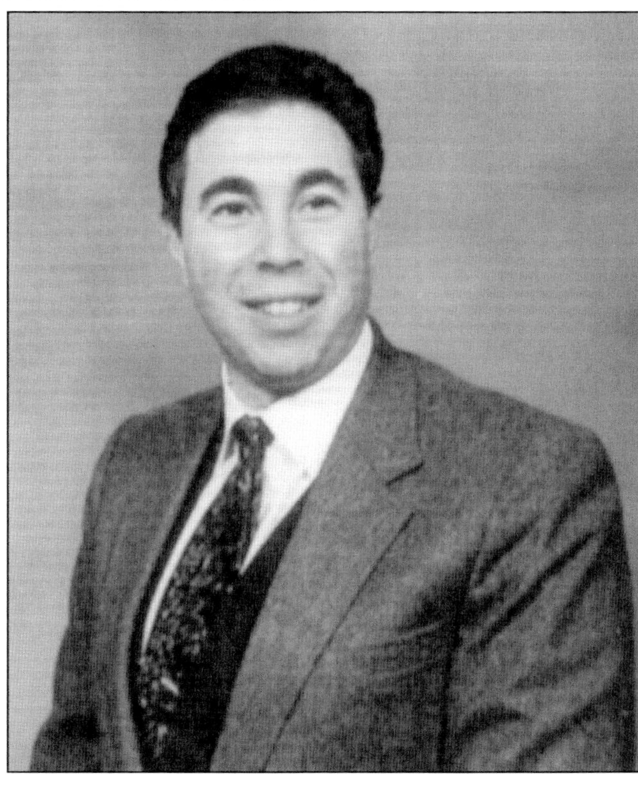

For many years, Jim Heilborn—the CBI confirmation instructor and cantor—touched many people with his soulful and powerful singing voice. The highlight of the High Holidays in Solano County was the opportunity to hear Jim sing both the "Kol Nidre" and the "Hineni" prayers at Yom Kippur. Having eschewed a career as a secular vocalist, Heilborn chose to use his considerable talents for religious purposes. (CBI.)

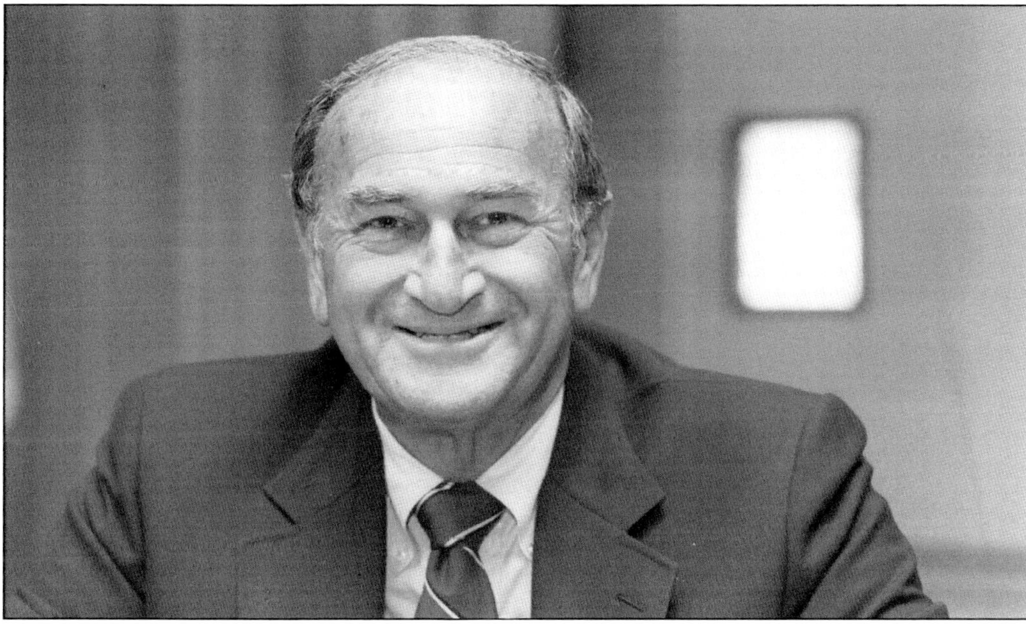

A Vallejo native, Fred Sessler was elected president of the Vallejo Junior Chamber of Commerce in 1956. He went on to head the Vallejo Municipal Center Corp., the Downtown Association, the Vallejo Chamber of Commerce board, and the Board of Realtors. He was also elected to head the Vallejo General Hospital board in 1970, succeeding attorney Kenneth Casper. A planning commissioner through the 1980s, at 86, Fred still brokers some of Vallejo's biggest commercial real estate deals. (VHM.)

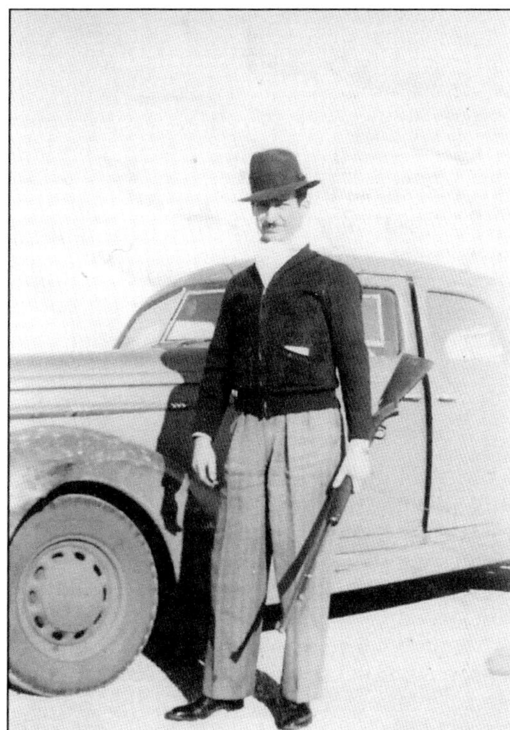

In 1945, Russian native Abbe Rosenblatt left Canada with his bother Sam, changed his name to Al Ross, and opened an Army/Navy surplus store in Vallejo. Terry Ross said that her parents, Al and Sylvia "Babe" Brown Ross, met at CBI and operated the store believing that "the main thing is to always be as fair as you can." In 1960, the store moved from Georgia Street to its present Virginia Street location. (Courtesy of Ray Prather.)

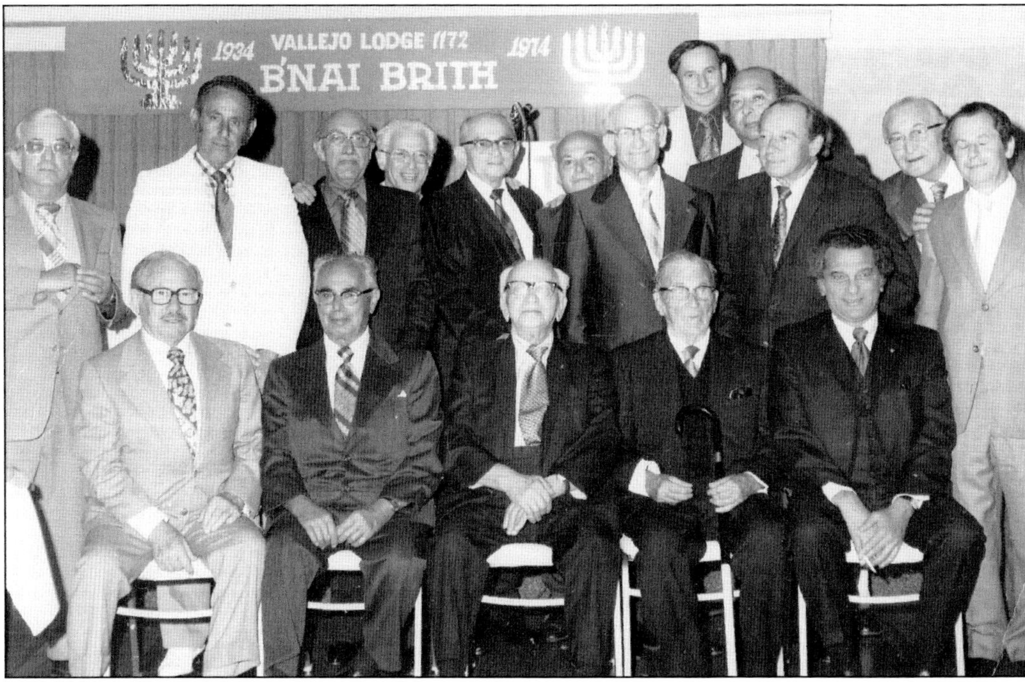

Optometrist Morris Zlot, a pioneering CBI member and a B'nai B'rith chapter founder and also a Vallejo city councilman, is pictured below. He was also vice-mayor from 1955 to 1959 and onetime head of the local Red Cross. With his wife, Isabel, he donated the stained glass windows in CBI's vestibule, and, even into his 90s, Zlot read from the Book of Jonah at Yom Kippur. As a child, Zlot visited Ukraine and was trapped there for more than a decade by the Russian Revolution. The family eventually escaped with help from the American embassy in Turkey. "When he came back to California, he couldn't speak English anymore," his son later recalled. Pictured above are, from left to right, (first row) Dr. Zlot, Sam Abouaf, Mr. Heller, Asher Plutchok, and Isadore "George" Pizante; (second row) Leo Liberman, Harry Policar, Dr. Michael Wallin, Seymour Marcuse, Mr. Baylinson, Albert Pizante, Sam Leavitt, Marty Rothman, Walter Bogner, unidentified, Rabbi Horowitz, and Alan Rothman. (Both, CBI.)

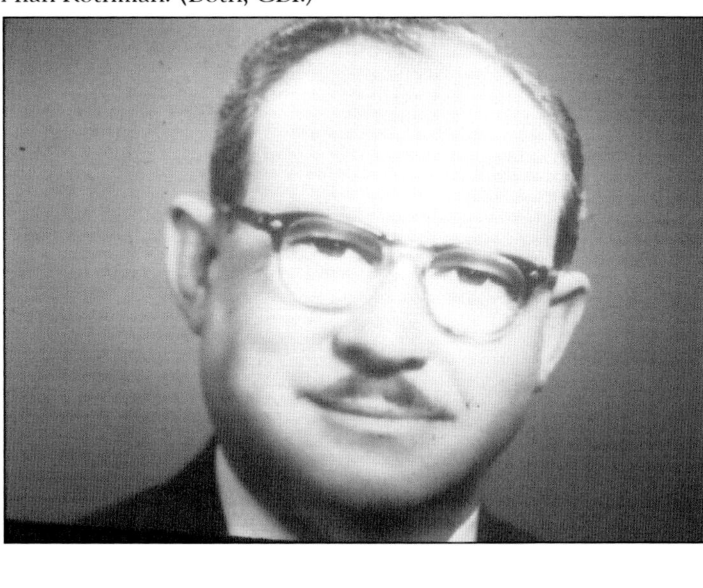

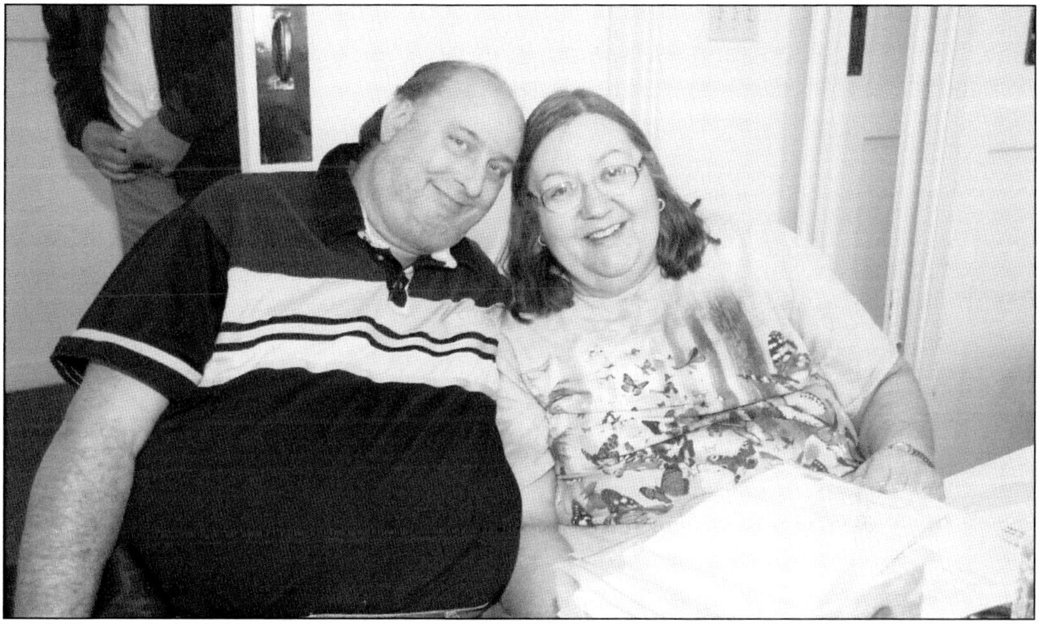

Alan and Mary Schwartz came to Congregation B'nai Israel in 1988, and, by 1990, Mary had organized the religious school and was its principal. She has also served several terms as president and treasurer of the local Hadassah chapter and has retired as the Vallejo City Unified School District financial manager. Alan, a former Levi Strauss executive, has also served as CBI president. Their children and grandchildren remain actively involved in the CBI family. (SDN.)

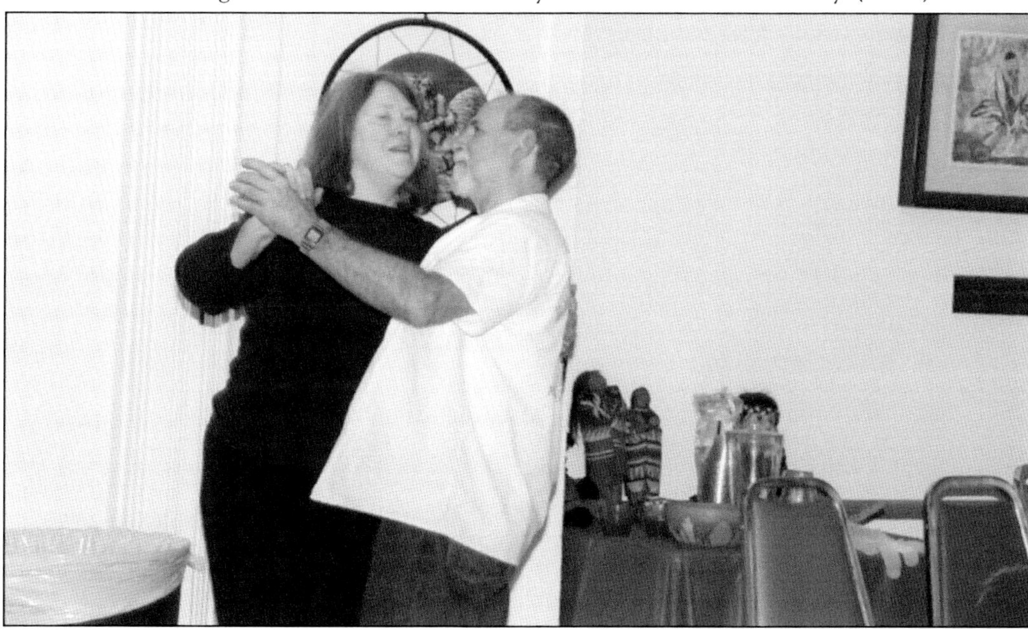

Napa residents Roy and Sue Barush are active in both the Napa and Vallejo synagogues, having followed Rabbi White to CBI. A bluegrass musician, Roy is an important force in public safety and communications at both temples and can often be found setting up speakers, computers, and other technology. He has also served on both temples' boards. Sue is CBI's administrator and a member of the Bay Area Temple Administrators. (SDN.)

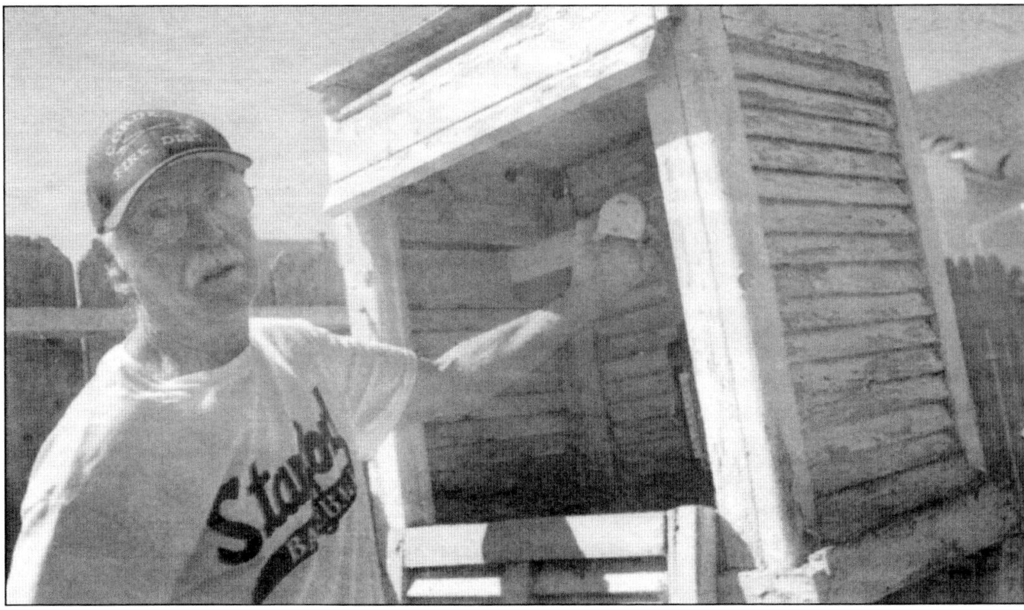

Mike "The Weatherman" Pechner has been the Golden West Meteorologists' consultant since 1967. A Solano County resident since 1988, Mike has been part of numerous Jewish communities and once served as a board member of Rabbi Vale's Ha-Makom in Fairfield/Vacaville. Pechner volunteers at a Bay Area midrasha, has worked at Jewish kids' camps, has been an ambassador at Fairfield's Rockville Park since 1989, and is a volunteer with the fire department in Cordelia. (CBI.)

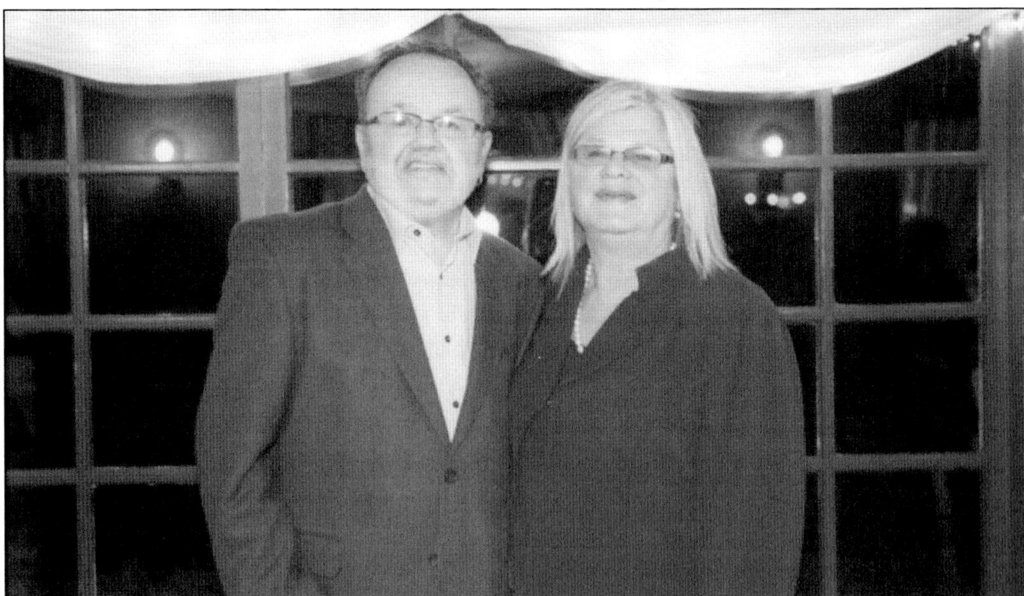

Before founding Event Solvers, Robin Gross—seen here with her husband, Ken Mullen—was Touro University's food service director, helped launch two of its programs, served on the CBI and Hadassah boards, and helped produce several fundraisers. She currently volunteers with Planned Parenthood and Rebuilding Together and is the board president of Youth and Family Services. She has also helped with Unity Day and Vallejo's Mad Hatter Holiday Festival and mentors Vallejo High School Hospitality Academy students. (Courtesy of R. Gross.)

Nationally regarded phobia expert Dr. Howard Liebgold—also known as "Dr. Fear"—freed people from their phobias in Kaiser Vallejo's PhobEase classes. As a psychiatrist who suffered from claustrophobia for 31 years, Liebgold spent most of his time at the hospital—feeling safe only there and at home—before overcoming his disorder. Enthusiastically embracing life, he used his personal experience to craft freedom-from-fear classes in 1986. He believed that phobias are cured not by information but through experiences. (Courtesy of PhobEase.)

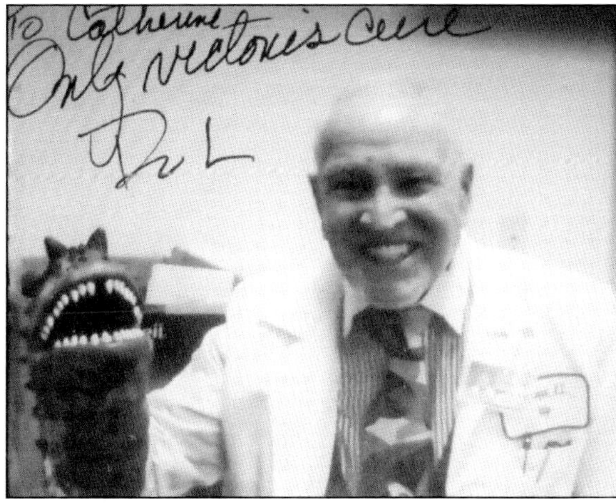

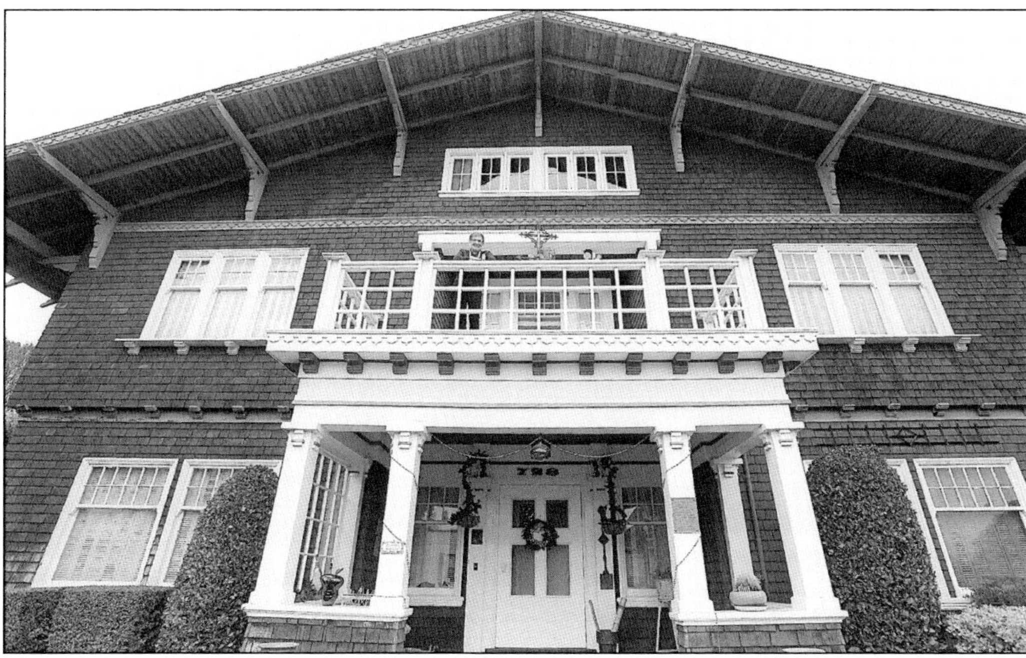

Judith Hilburg moved to Vallejo in the 1970s, bought and restored the city's only Julia Morgan–designed house (seen here), and helped stop the California Department of Transportation from extending I-780 through the center of Vallejo. She also spearheaded the creation of Vallejo's Architectural Heritage District—then the largest such district west of the Mississippi—sat on several boards and commissions, and was a fierce advocate for the JFK Library's McCune Room collection of rare books and manuscripts. (VTH.)

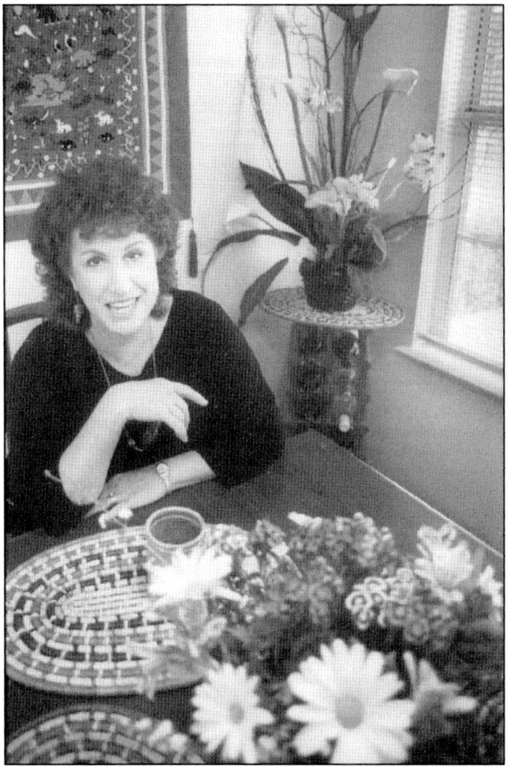

Marilyn Citron O'Rourke (left) moved to Benicia from Sacramento in 1978, beginning her political career. After serving as a school board trustee, she was the third woman elected to the Benicia City Council and the first elected mayor. Serving as mayor from 1984 to 1992, she was instrumental in establishing a safe water supply through the North Bay Aqueduct, created an art task force, cleaned up the toxic IT Corporation Panoche Facility Class One landfill, and oversaw the building of a new library that opened in 1991 and houses an art gallery bearing her name. Lisa Hirsh, Sheli Ryan, and Rhea Zaks (below) also served on the Benicia Unified School District Board as trustees. Jews have also been influential in educational matters in Northern Solano County. At the time of writing, Michael Kitzes is the vice president of the Vacaville Unified School District Board. (Left, VHM; below, courtesy of Rhea Zaks.)

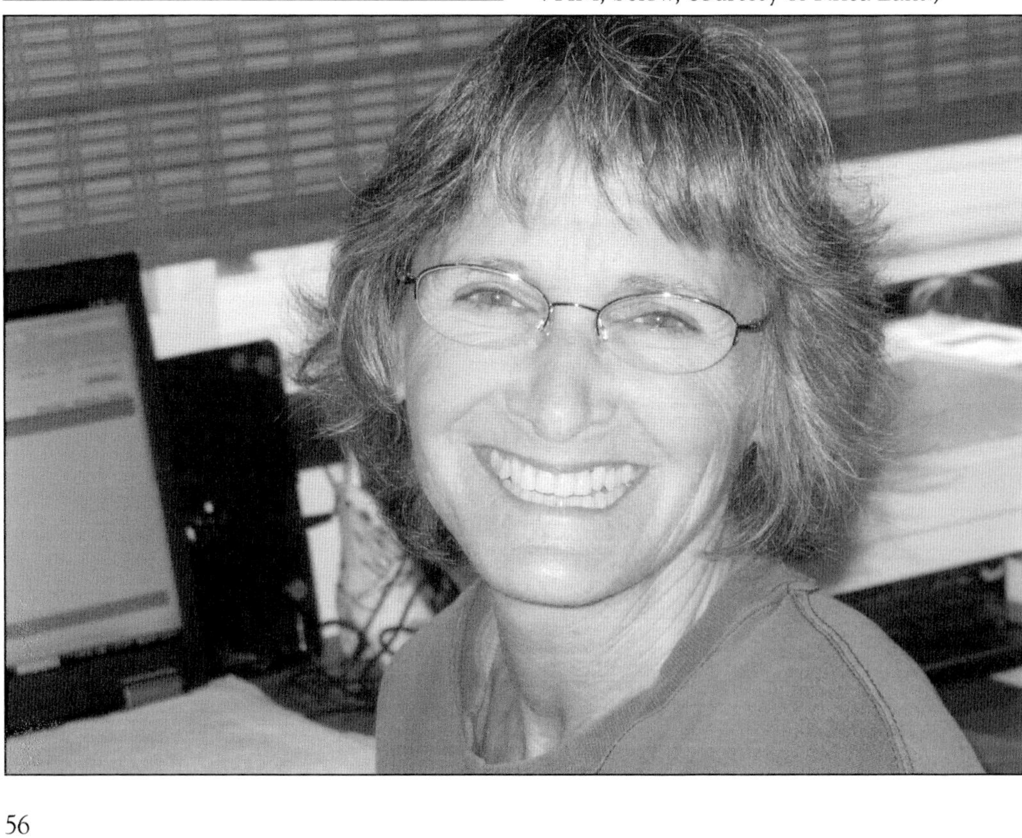

As of 2014, state senator Lois Krepliak Wolk had attained the highest public service position of any local Jew. A former schoolteacher, she was elected to the state senate in 2008, representing all or part of Solano, Napa, Yolo, Sonoma, Contra Costa, and Sacramento Counties. Through three terms in the state assembly, time on the Davis City Council—including two years as mayor—and as a Yolo County supervisor, Wolk earned a reputation as a problem solver. (Courtesy of Lois Wolk.)

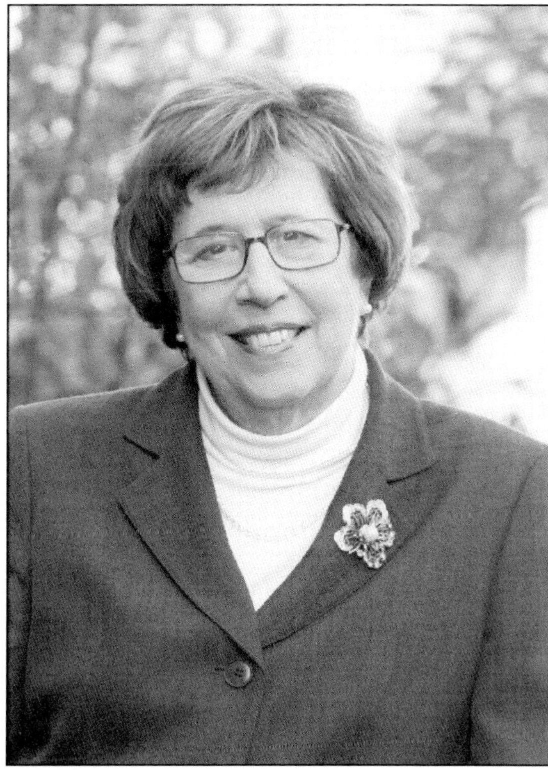

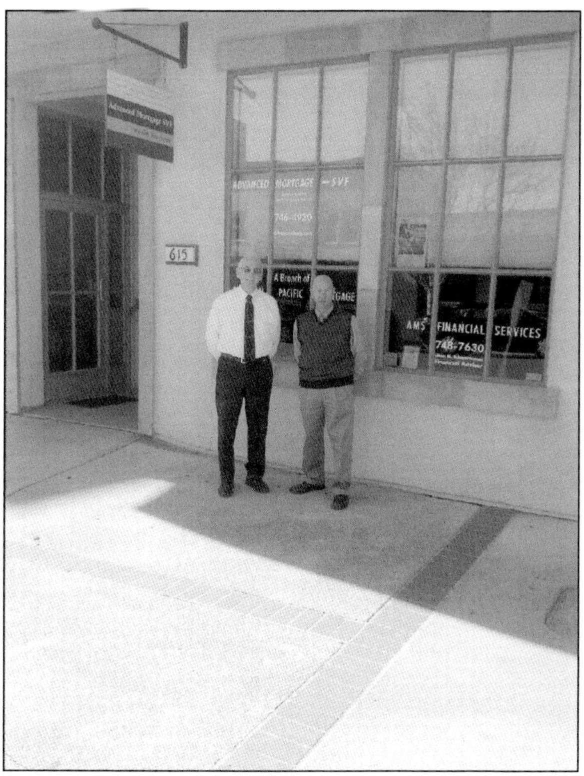

Business partners Mitchell Chernock (left) and Alan Schwartzman (right) are a financial mortgage and real estate powerhouse in Benicia. Schwartzman is also a two-term city councilman, and Chernock is a professional speaker and author who was appointed by the Contra Costa Board of Supervisors as the special rehabilitation lender for its low- and moderate-income home buyers program. (Courtesy of Mitch Chernock.)

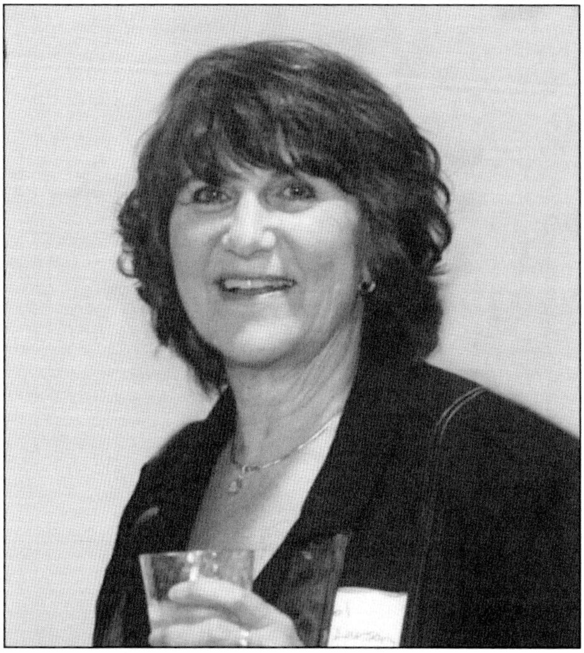

The granddaughter of 1906 Russian immigrant Samuel Raskin, Vallejo businesswoman Carol Raskin Larson has won numerous civic awards, served on many boards of directors—some as president—and coproduced the Vallejo Jazz, Art & Wine Festival for about a decade. Winner of the 2012 Humane Society of the North Bay Humanitarian of the Year award and the 2012 & 2013 Mayor's Community Recognition Award, Larson came to Solano County in 1975. (Courtesy of the Vallejo Chamber of Commerce.)

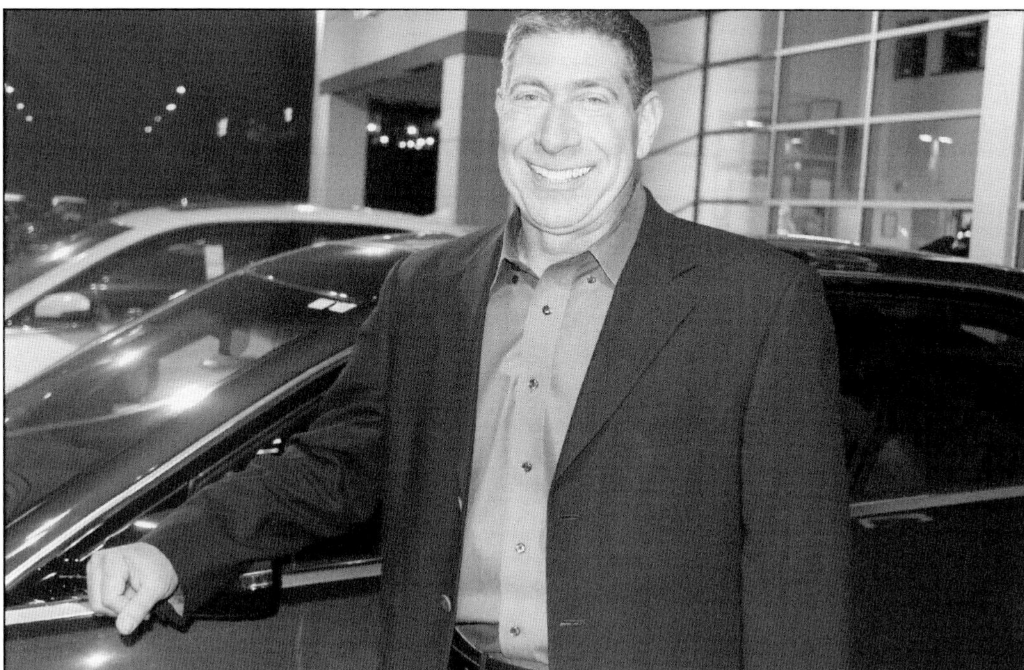

Counting the Vallejo Chamber of Commerce's 2013 Humanitarian of the Year award among numerous accolades, Vallejo businessman and philanthropist Ken Ross is the self-described "black sheep" of his family. The son of Vallejo native Bernice Bregman Ross, Ken's grandfather worked on Mare Island, and his grandmother owned a candy store. Over the years, he sold cars, raced for NASCAR, and advanced corporately. Helping to create Vallejo's Auto Mall, Ken grew Team Superstores to the point where he donates some $200,000 to local causes annually. (Courtesy of the Vallejo Chamber of Commerce.)

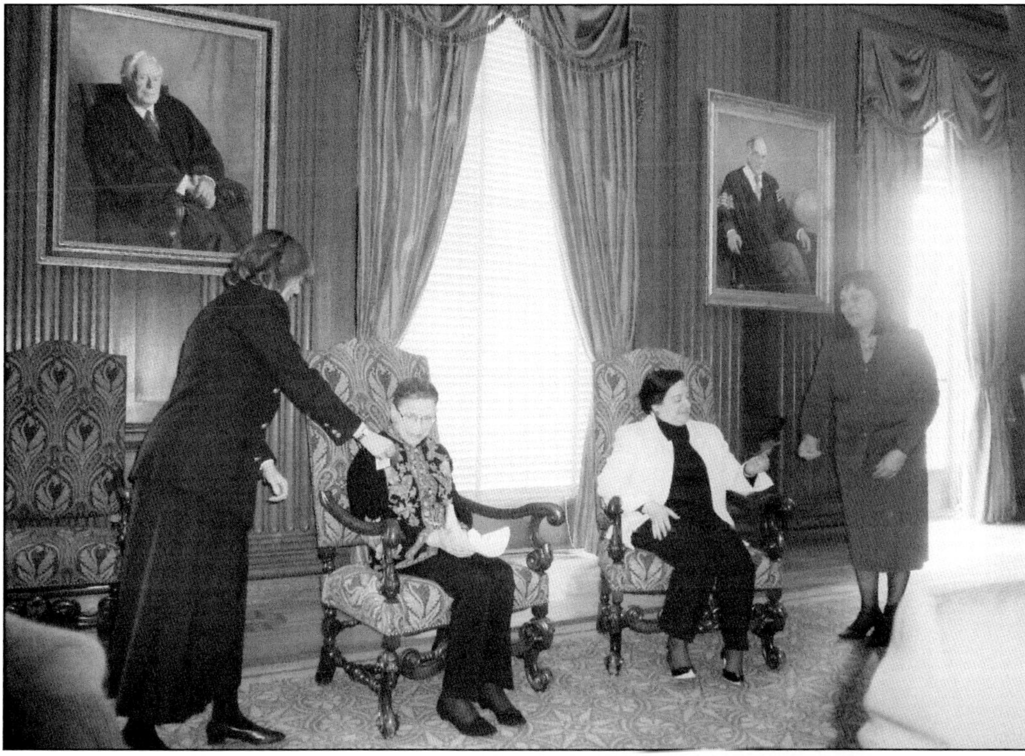

Benicia resident Geri Kahn is seen above (at far left) with Jewish Supreme Court justices Ruth Bader Ginsberg (seated left) and Elena Kagan (seated right) on behalf of Hadassah on the occasion of her swearing in as an attorney. She is one of many professionals that the Solano County Jewish community has produced. These have included other lawyers like Jeffrey Nurik, Robert Bernstein, and Shana Farber and teachers like Lois Pierce, Eileen Marks, and Teri Rosenmann (pictured at right). Other professionals include business tradesmen Raphael Zrihen, Danny Jacob, and Shlomo Ovaide; area realtors Eileen Stern, Malcolm and Mary Tipp, and Bonnie Falk; law enforcement official Steve Harris; and investigators Harvey Shapiro and David Salter. Other big shots have included Woodstock's producer Karin Moss, who was briefly Vallejo's economic development specialist. (Above, courtesy of Geri Kahn; right, SDN.)

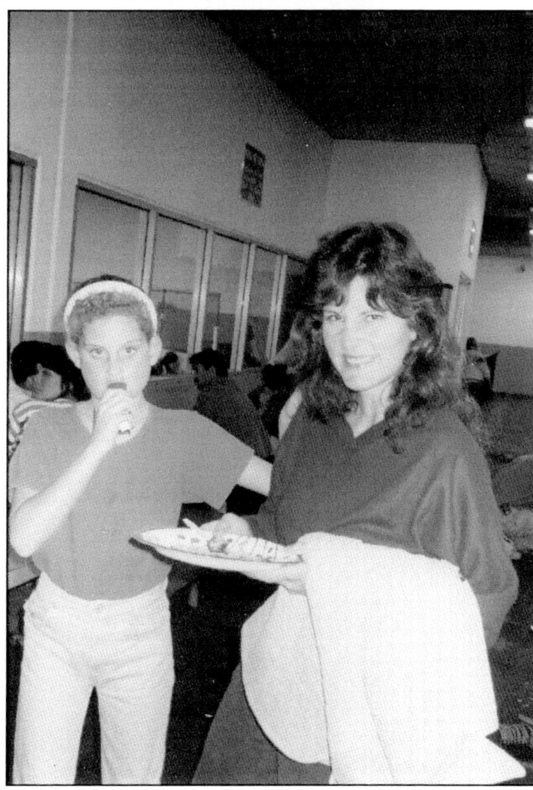

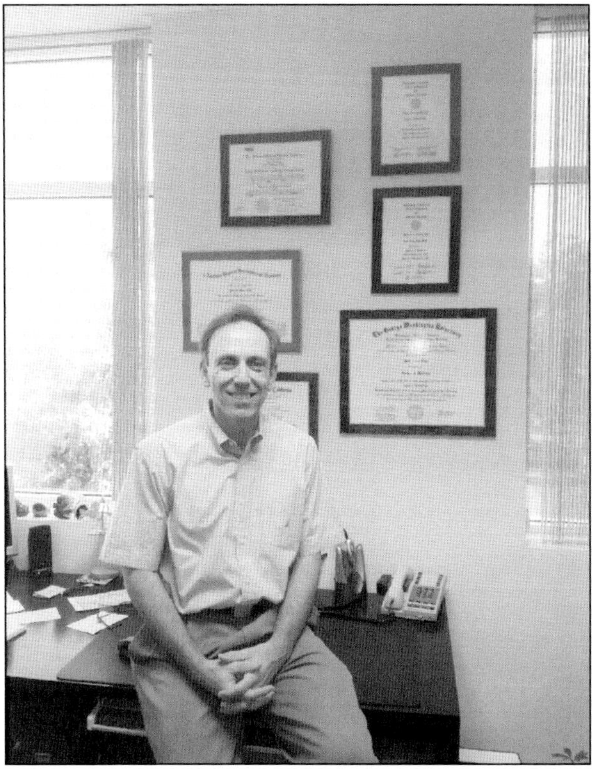

Psychiatrist and author Joel Fine moved to Solano County in 1990 and connected with local Jewish groups. Six congregations and 23 years later, the Fines helped bring Chabad to Solano County. Not having begun life as an observant Jew, Fine wrote the book *Arc of the Covenant: A Psychiatrist Tracks His Path in Judaism* to chronicle his journey from secularism to orthodoxy. (Courtesy of J. Fine.)

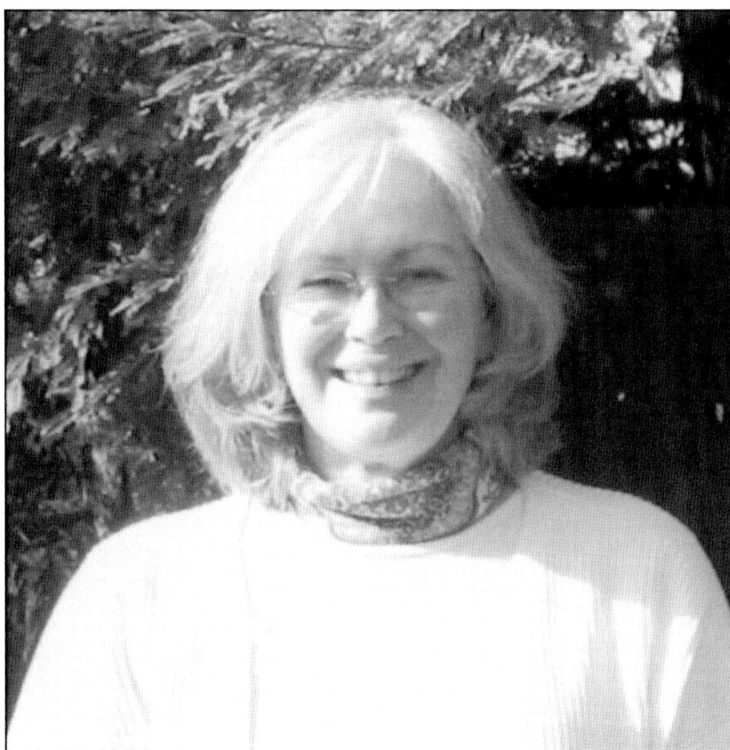

German immigrant Sabine Goerke-Shrode came to Travis in 1987 with her husband, Mark, after studying classical archeology in Heidelberg and Jerusalem. She is an author and historian who wrote the book Images of America: *Fairfield* and founded the Solano History Exploration Center. A Vacaville Museum curator, freelance historical writer, independent business owner, knitter, and opera enthusiast, Sabine believes in actively volunteering and serving her community. (Courtesy of S. Goerke-Shrode.)

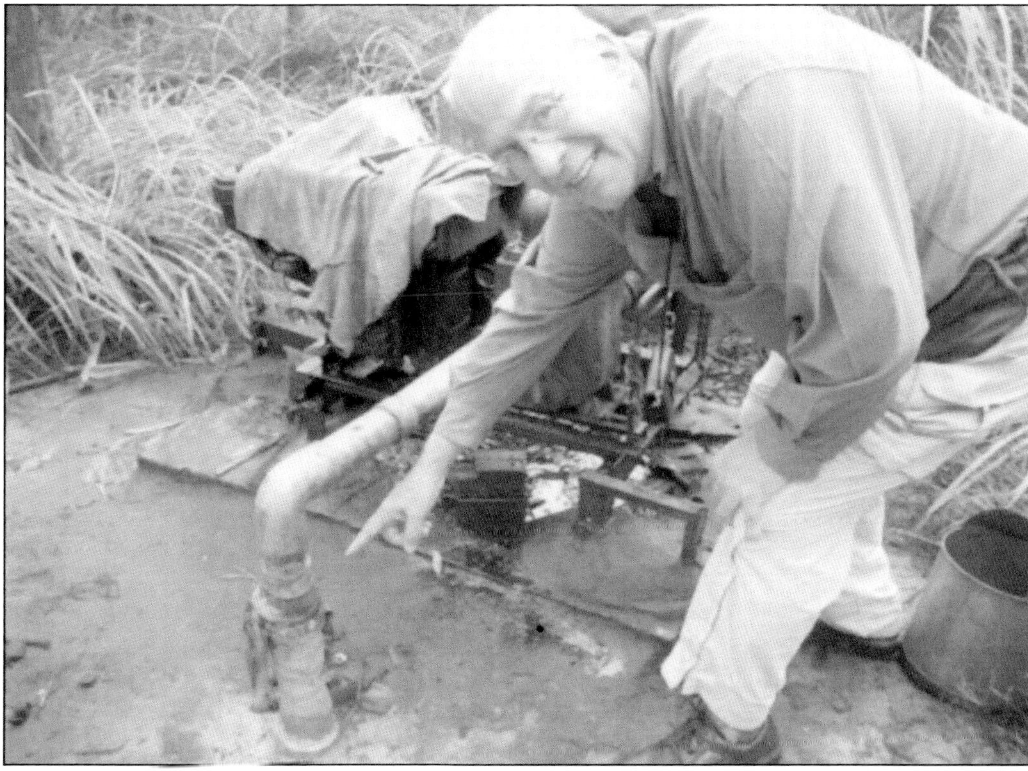

Working both privately and with USAID, Barney Popkin is a sought-after water, waste, soils, geological, and environmental expert who made Vallejo his home base for several years in the 2000s. Mostly, he was overseas, helping those in developing countries—including many Arab nations—with their water issues. (Courtesy of Barney Popkin.)

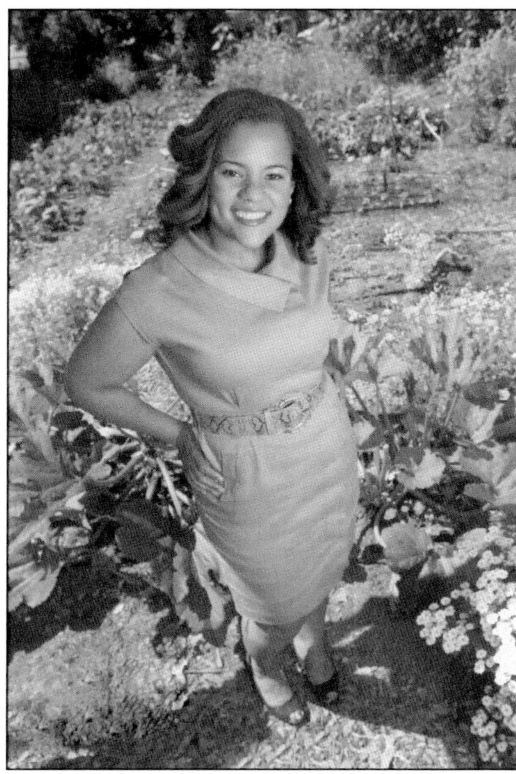

The "Robin Hood of Silicon Valley," and named among *San Jose Magazine*'s 100 Most Powerful People, Phaedra Ellis-Lamkins has helped to shepherd local, state, and federal policy changes. Phaedra was raised in Solano County by her single mother, onetime CBI president Gail Lamkins. As the chief executive officer of Green for All, Phaedra advocated for green jobs as pathways out of poverty. She has also been recognized by many major media outlets. (Courtesy of Phaedra Ellis-Lamkins.)

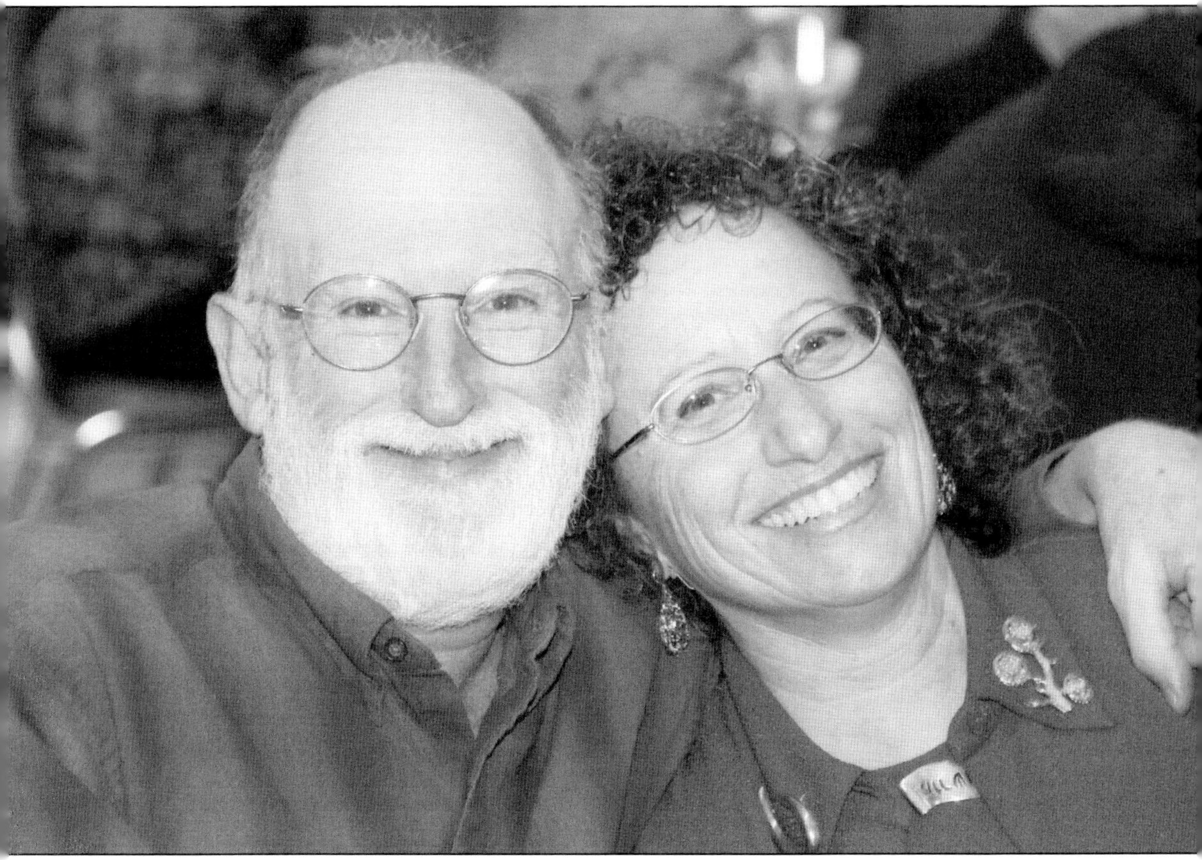

A Benicia power couple, Larry Grossman and Susan Cohen-Grossman have a long list of accomplishments between them. An entomologist and public administrator in Solano County since 1989, Susan was the first woman hired by the USDA Forest Service to survey for specific dangerous bugs in Idaho and, later, in Monterey. She was the California Department of Food and Agriculture's Dutch elm disease expert, was named to the Agricultural Commissioner's Office for Monterey and Solano, and was appointed Solano County's agricultural commissioner/sealer of weights and measures in 1989—spending 16 years in that position. Since then, she has been UC Davis's Integrated Pest Management Program's pesticide safety writer, a Contra Costa County Public Works manager, a Benicia planning commissioner, and chapter president of the Solano-Napa Hadassah. Meanwhile, Larry chaired Benicia's Finance Committee in 2014, established Grossman Financial Management in 1998, launched an online Jewish streaming audio webcasting site in 2004, has been active in the American Israel Public Affairs Committee for decades, and served on the Jewish Federation of the East Bay and CBI's board of directors. (Courtesy of the Grossmans.)

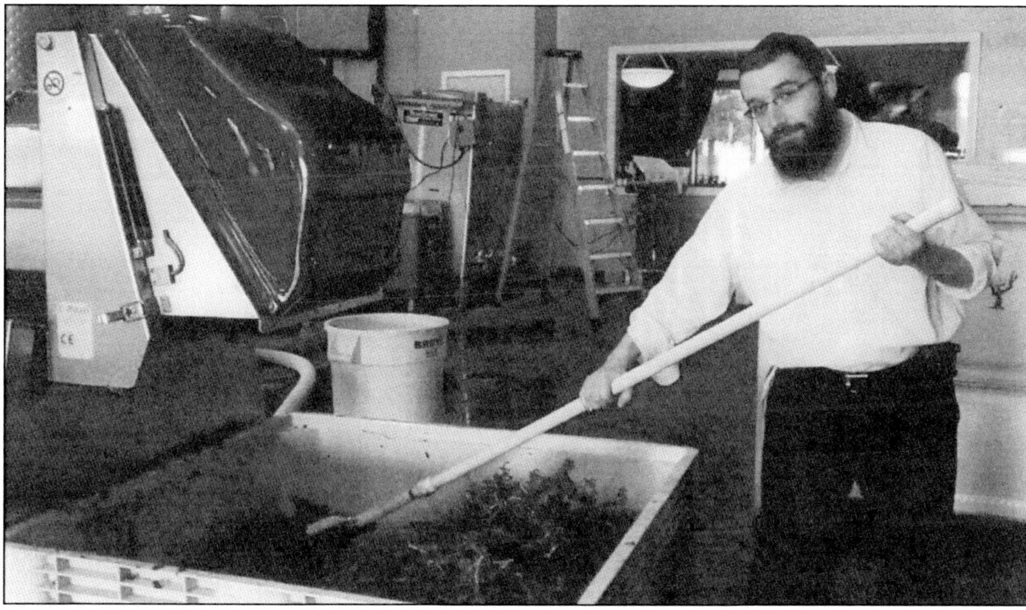

One way that Touro University works to maintain its Jewish nature is by making sure that there is a rabbi serving its students and faculty. Those rabbis, who have included Yitzhak Kaufman and Elchonon Tenenbaum (above), always make an effort to include the wider Jewish community at events. University officials also ensure that the kitchen is kosher by appointing overseers (*mashkiachs*) like Joseph Plotkin and Yehuda Welton. On campus, there is a kosher café and catering company as well. Since coming to Mare Island, Touro officials have hired several Jewish faculty members, including Bruce Silverman, pictured below, who is a biology and cadaver instructor. (Both, courtesy of Touro University.)

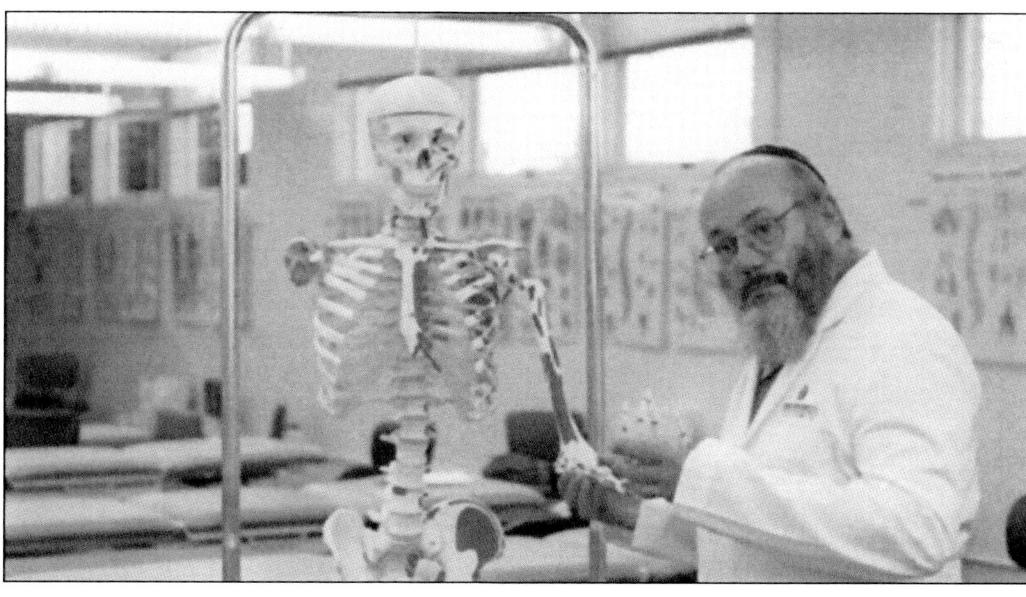

Several attempts were made to create a cohesive Jewish community outside of Travis Air Force Base in northern Solano County before Chabad's Rabbi Chaim and Aidel Zaklos (pictured at left) succeeded. These attempts, including the short-lived B'nai Avraham in the 1970s, were made by well-meaning Jewish leaders like Rabbi Stephen Vale, who led Congregation Ha-Makom (The Place), and allowed some, like Mike Povitsky, Steve and Jack Harris, and the Kaplow, Bousley, and Block families to find spiritual nourishment for a time. (Courtesy of Chabad.)

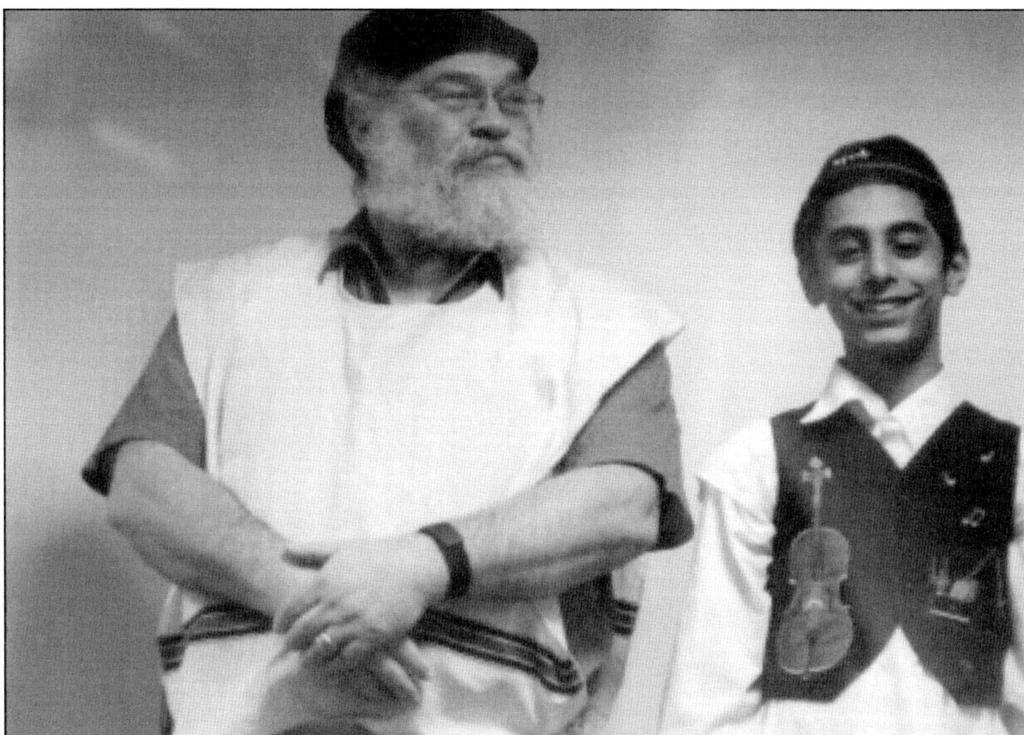

Dr. Martin "Marty" Markovits (left) of Vacaville is a retired Kaiser Vallejo pediatrician—seen here in Purim costume with Lidoor Levy (right)—and one of many medical professionals in Solano County. Other local, Jewish pediatricians include Alan Sher, Gary Winston, and Sandy and Larry Corman, while the list of other physicians includes Ed Levin, Mark Susskind, and Walt Zaks. Jan Leventhal, Susan Stern, Debbie Williges, Barbara Abeling, and Abby and Tobi Lessem are also medical professionals. (Courtesy of Chabad.)

Five

Artists and Athletes

אמנים וספורטאים (Amaneem v'Sportayeem)

קינסטלער און אַטליץ (Keinsteller und Atleetz)

. . . On a playing field, in a studio, or on a barge in the bay

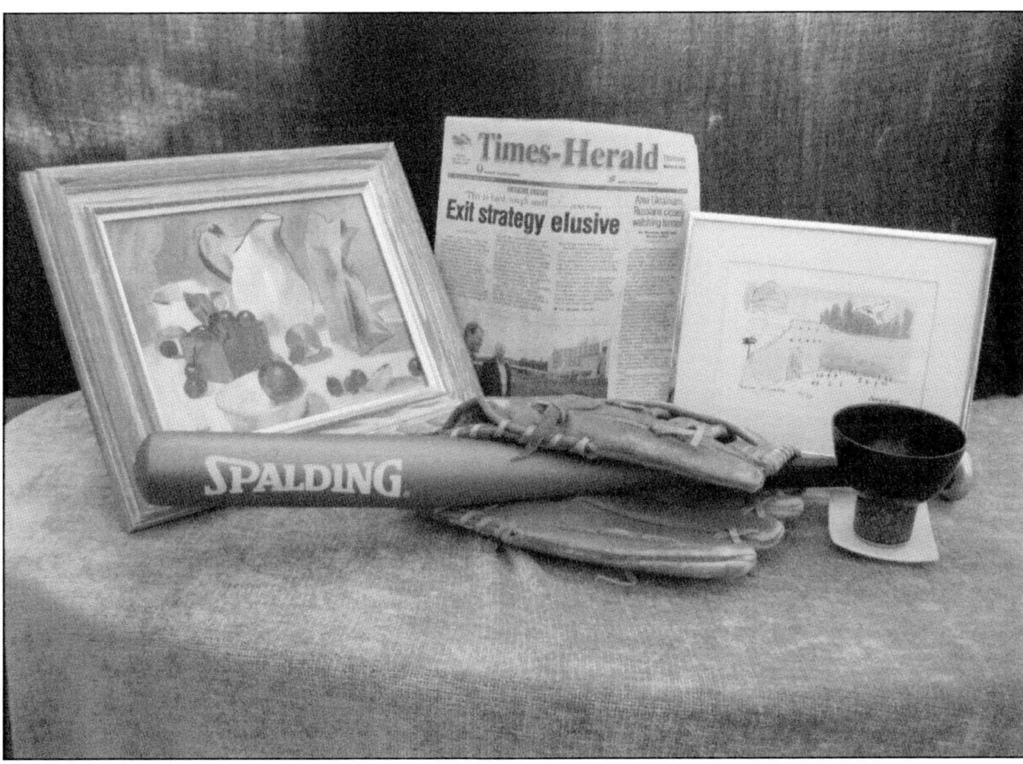

Sometimes art is more of an avocation than a vocation, but throughout history—from David and his harp to Miriam and her timbrel—there have been Jews with a need to express themselves artistically. For others, the camaraderie and competition of sports fulfills that passion. Seen here are pieces by Alma Friedman, whose husband Irv was CBI's caretaker for years; the Mazers; and Kathy Ertemann. (SDN.)

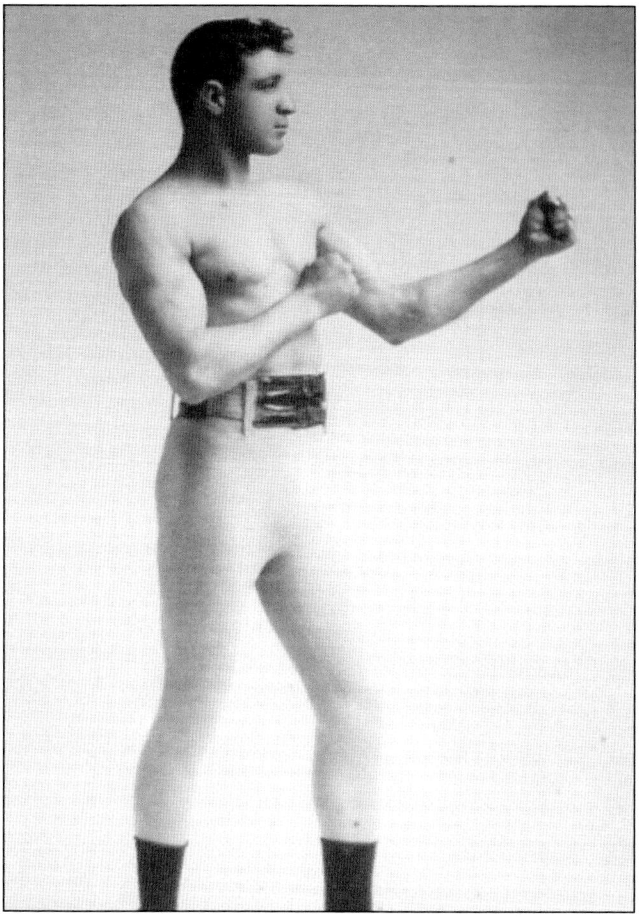

Joseph Bartlett "Joe" Choynski, also known as "Chrysanthemum Joe" and "The Fighting Jew," fought professionally as a heavyweight but never had the opportunity to fight for the title. A highlight of his career was a bout—fought on a wheat barge off the coast of Benicia—against "Gentleman Jim" Corbett on June 5, 1889. While Corbett wore two-ounce boxing gloves, Choynski had been hoping for a bare-knuckle fight and ended up wearing kid gloves used for driving carriages. It proved to be a bloody battle lasting 28 rounds. Choynski went on to fight and have success against such heavyweights as Jack Johnson, Jim Jeffries, and John L. Sullivan, winning 52 out of 79 fights. In 1991, he was inducted into the International Jewish Sports Hall of Fame, and in 1998, he was inducted into the International Boxing Hall of Fame. (Left, BHM; below, courtesy of Boxing.com.)

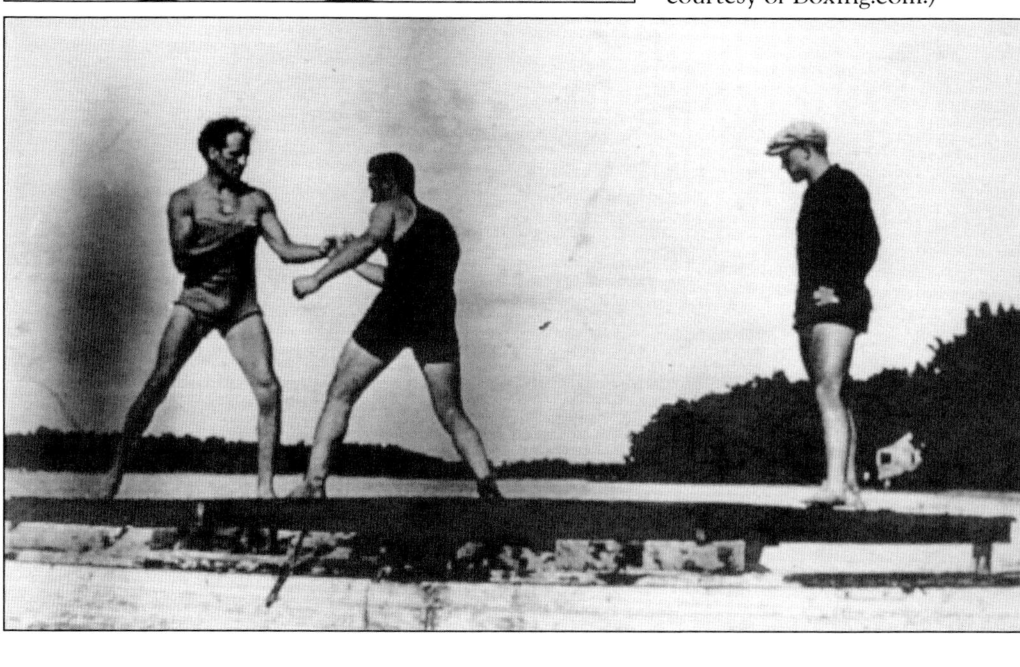

Benicia and Vallejo are home to painters, sculptors, photographers, illustrators, metal smiths, ceramicists, jewelry designers, and other artists, with studios scattered throughout the city but primarily concentrated in Benicia's Arsenal arts district. Known Jewish artists date back to Helen Salz, an artist (work pictured at right) and art collector, and, later, Judy Cohen Chicago, who designed her Birth Project in a studio in the arsenal. Ceramicist Kathy Ertemann had a studio in the old Yuba Mfg. Co. and was a founding member of Arts Benicia. Nikki Basch Davis is a plein air artist and participates in a gallery in downtown Benicia. Cheryl and Jack Mazer are painters and graphic designers, and Cheryl also makes jewelry. Shoshana and Alexandra Nurik (work pictured below) have studied at Arts Benicia. Finally, Isaac Nurik (Judaica pictured below), the studio manager and designer at Phase Design, designs Judaica "for the current Jewish identity." (Both, SDN.)

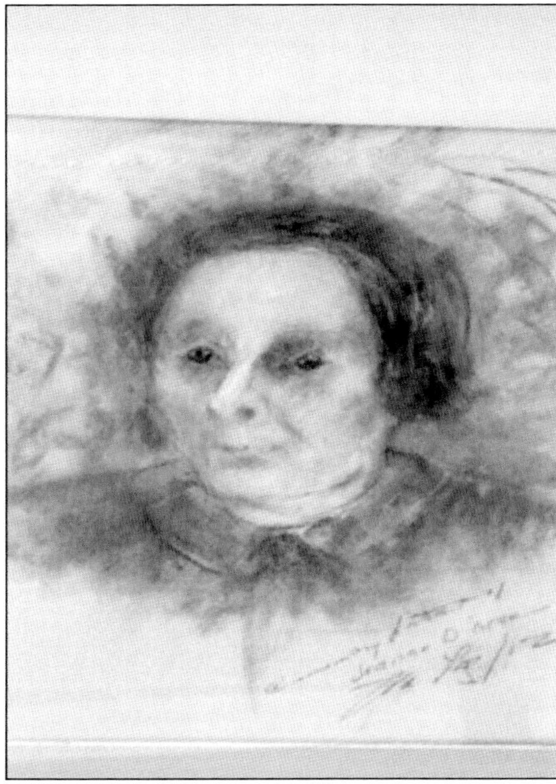

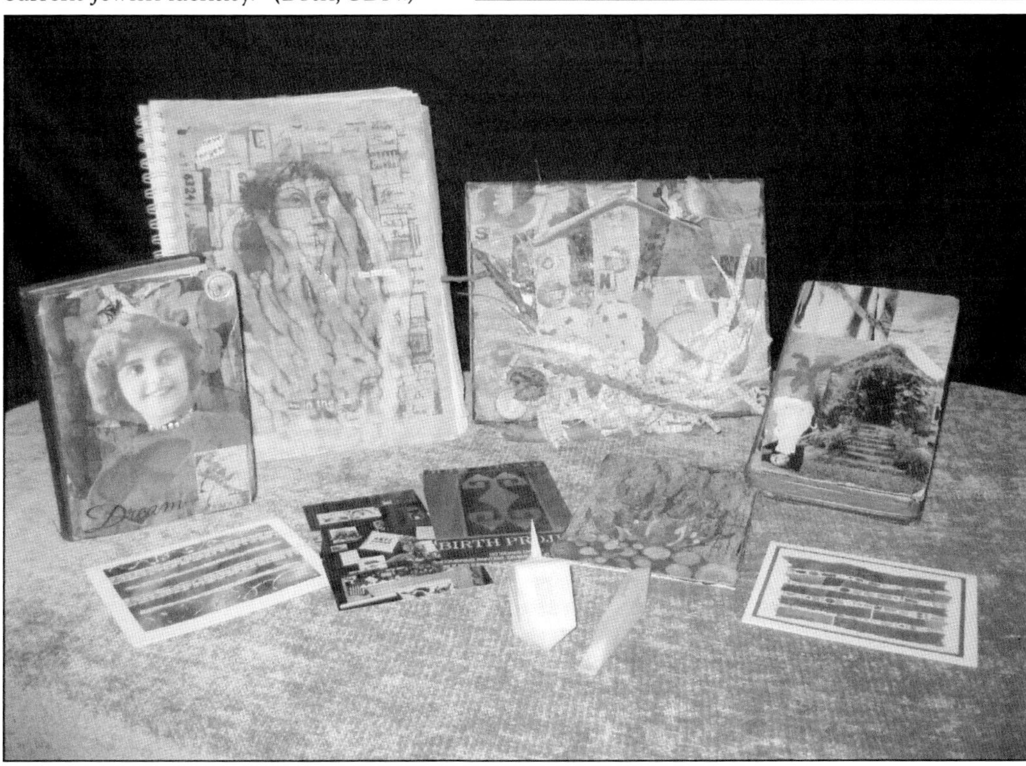

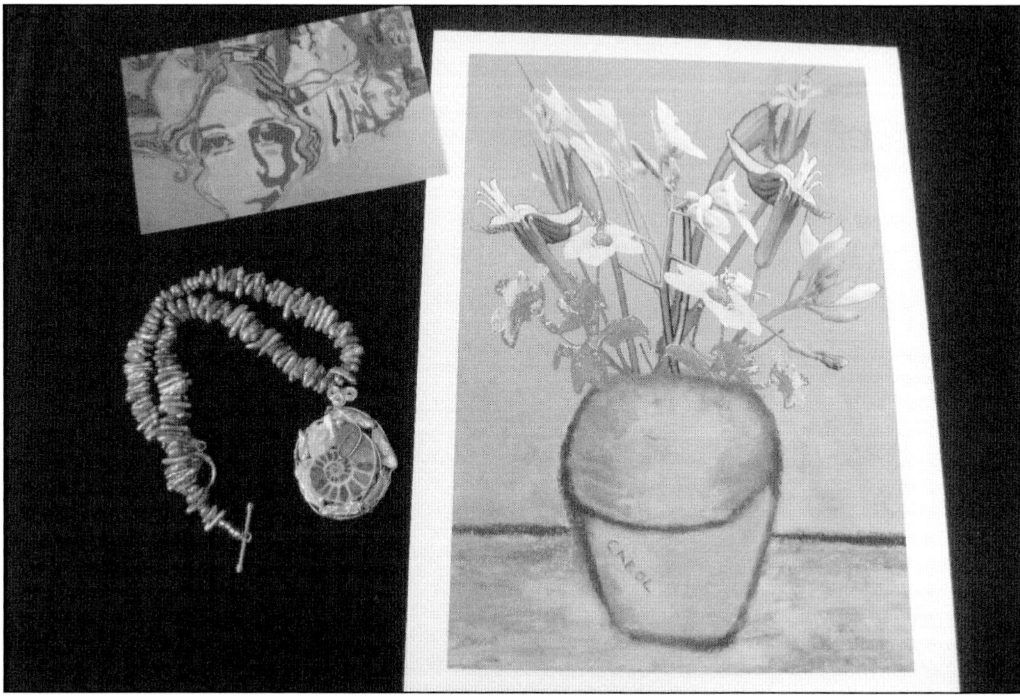

Vallejo and Benicia are not the only Solano County art areas; the northern part of the county also produces its share. Fran Bond, whose husband was a Silicon Valley CEO, is an artist and former dancer with the New York City Ballet. Spending her golden years in Fairfield, Fran was instrumental in bringing a Trader Joe's store to town. She also started the first ORT chapter in Huntington, Long Island, decades ago. ORT is derived from the original Russian term *Obschestvo Remeslenovo i. Zemledelcheskovo Trouda*, which literally means Society for Trades and Agricultural Labor. Through the years, the term "ORT" has become synonymous with quality high-tech education that gives people necessary training to obtain meaningful employment in their local economy. An artist and designer, Fran's work has been exhibited in various art shows and can be viewed around the county. Other north county artists include visual artist and photographer Carol Levin; Laura Susskind, who designs wearable art; and others. (Both, SDN.)

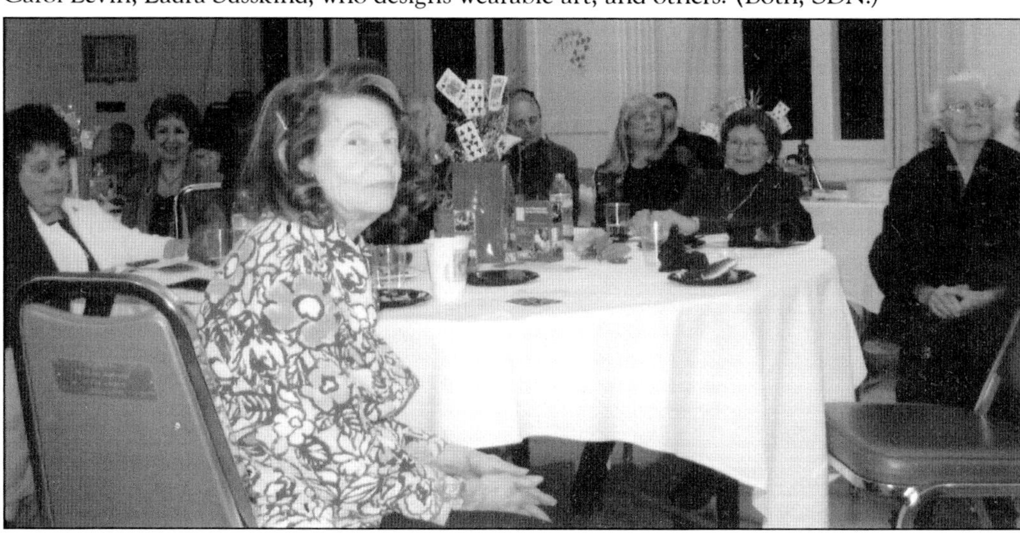

A contributing member of one of America's pioneering rap groups—the all-Jewish Beastie Boys—disc jockey Mike "Mix Master Mike" Schwartz of Vallejo also made a name for himself as a solo artist. Schwartz was also a member of San Francisco's Invisibl Skratch Piklz Crew, a respected battle DJ, and a pioneer in "turntablism," an art form using the turntable as a musical instrument. (Courtesy of R. Zrihen.)

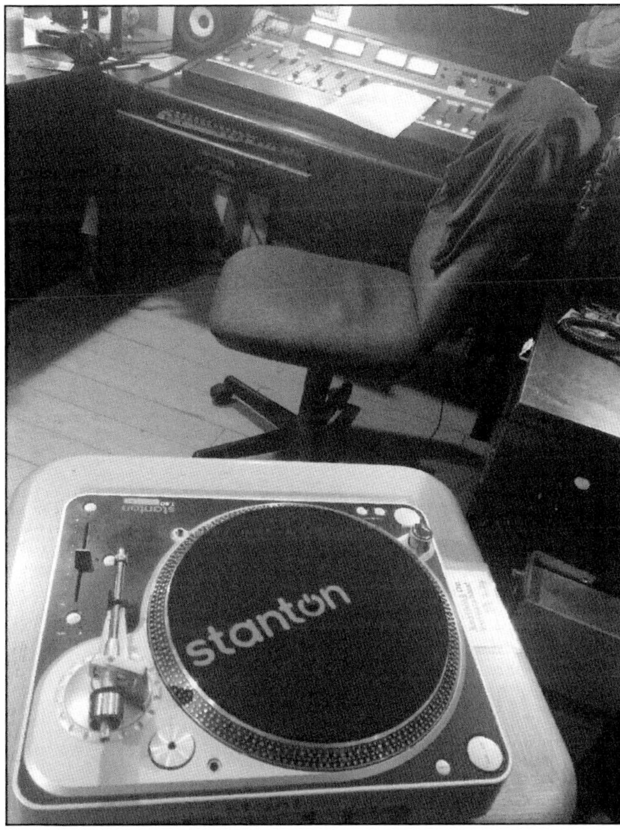

Francesca Biller of Benicia is a writer, humorist, author, speaker, singer, dancer, artist, and mom who grew up a Japanese Jew in Santa Monica and Hawaii. Both of her parents and all of her siblings are also in the arts. An award-winning former investigative journalist, Biller is writing three books, is regularly published in various magazines and websites, and occasionally appears on radio and television. (VTH.)

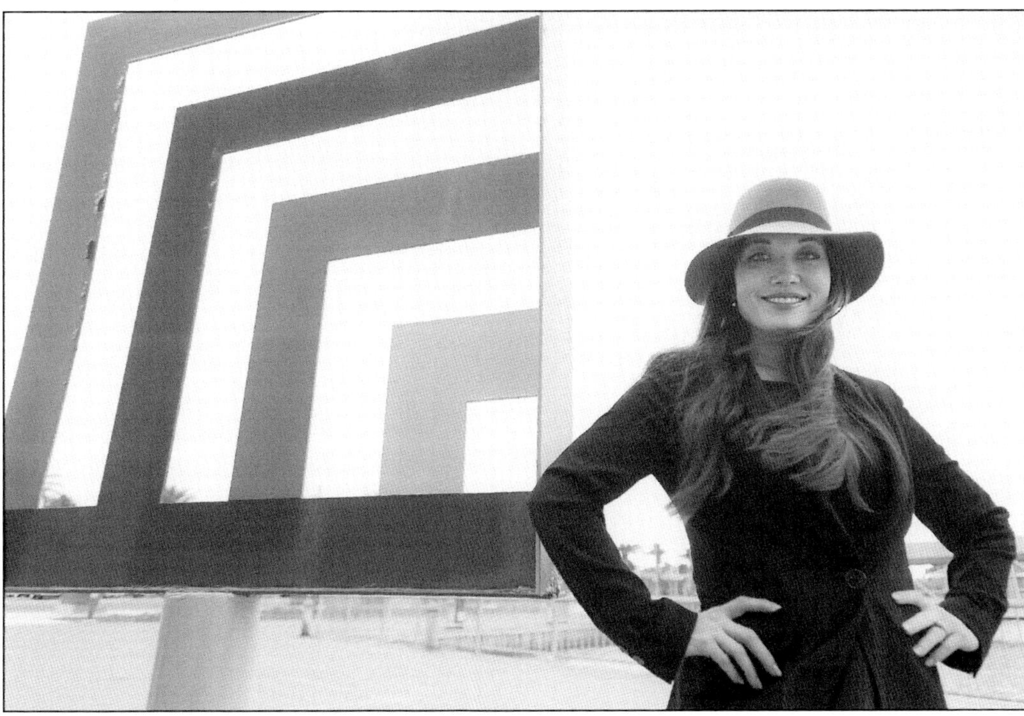

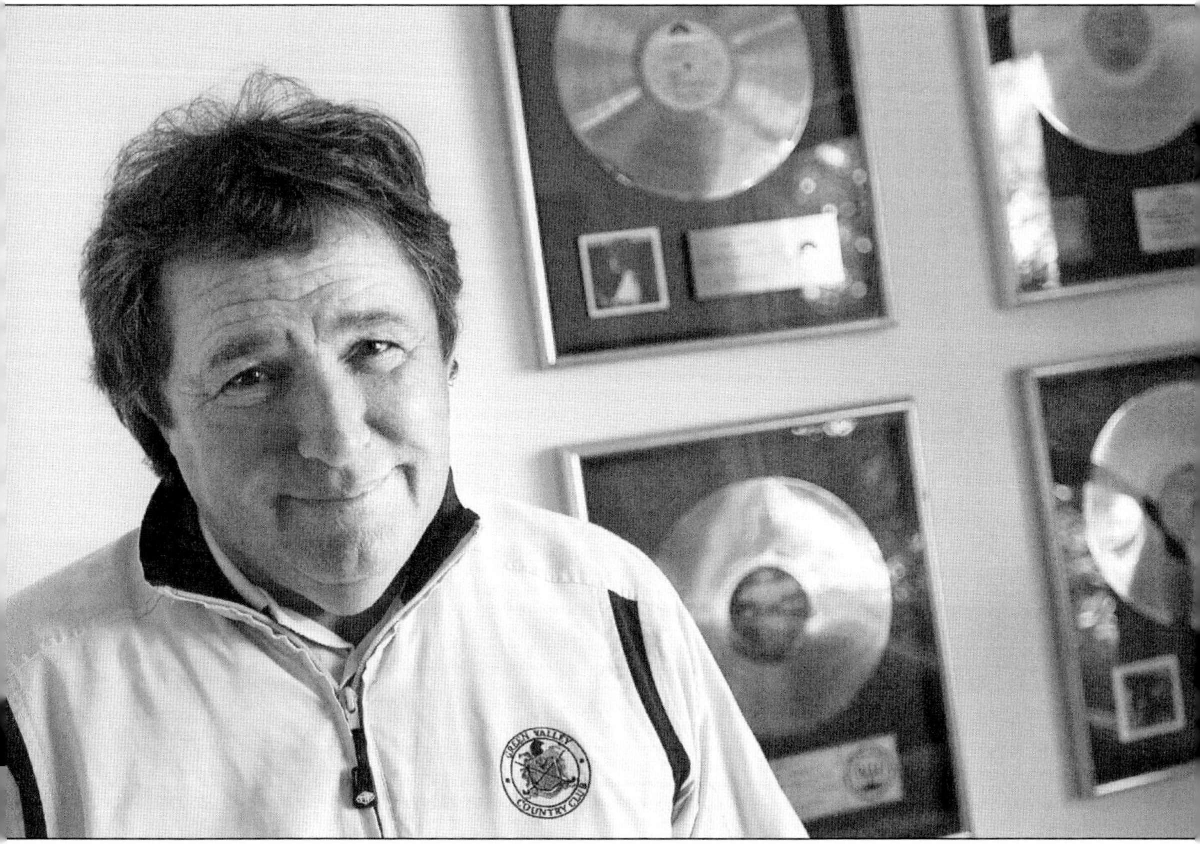

A San Francisco native who has lived in Solano since 2000, Jeff Trager is a 40-year veteran record promoter and has worked with the likes of Gene Simmons, the Moody Blues, Tom Jones, and Joni Mitchell. The son of a former Vallejo elementary school teacher and principal, the Blues Hall of Fame inductee's anecdotes about iconic American entertainers include getting the Bee Gees to sing Christmas carols at a children's hospital and floating down the Mississippi River on a paddlewheel with singer Al Green. He has helped jump-start the careers of stars like Tina Turner and Carlos Santana, but Trager is now best known for promoting fundraisers for local causes. (Courtesy of J. Trager.)

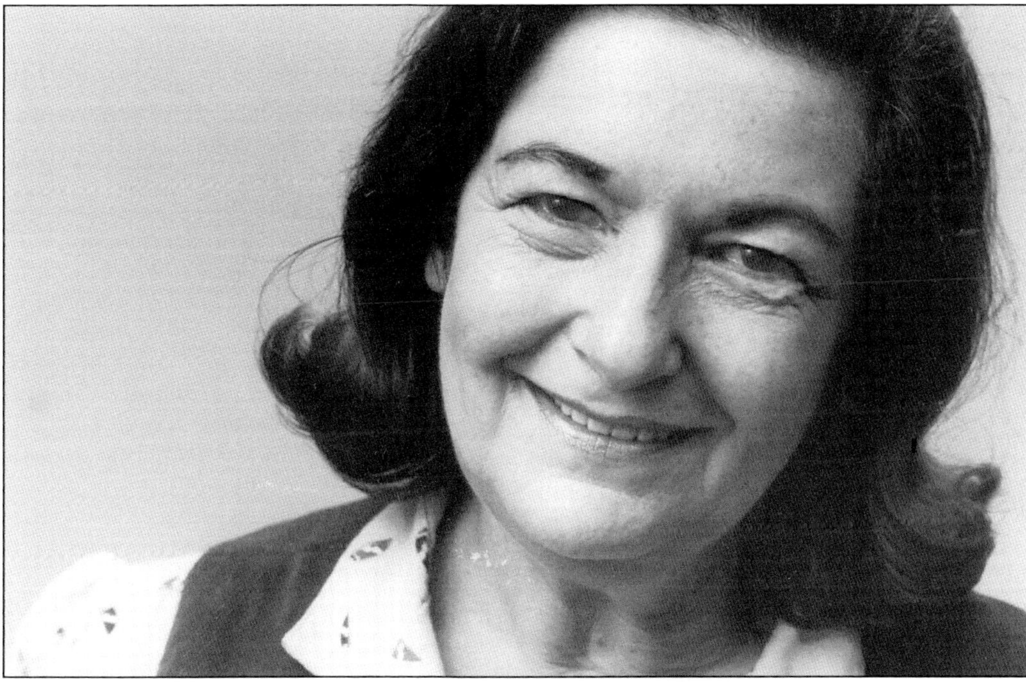

Editor of the *Davis Enterprise*'s Living section in the 1970s and author of the cooking column "Eating In," Gene Silverman was with the *Times-Herald* and active in Vallejo from 1981 until her death in 2003 at 77. For years, she appeared each summer at a special Solano County Fair gourmet-cooking event, where she was honored for her years of participation at her last public appearance just before her death. (VTH.)

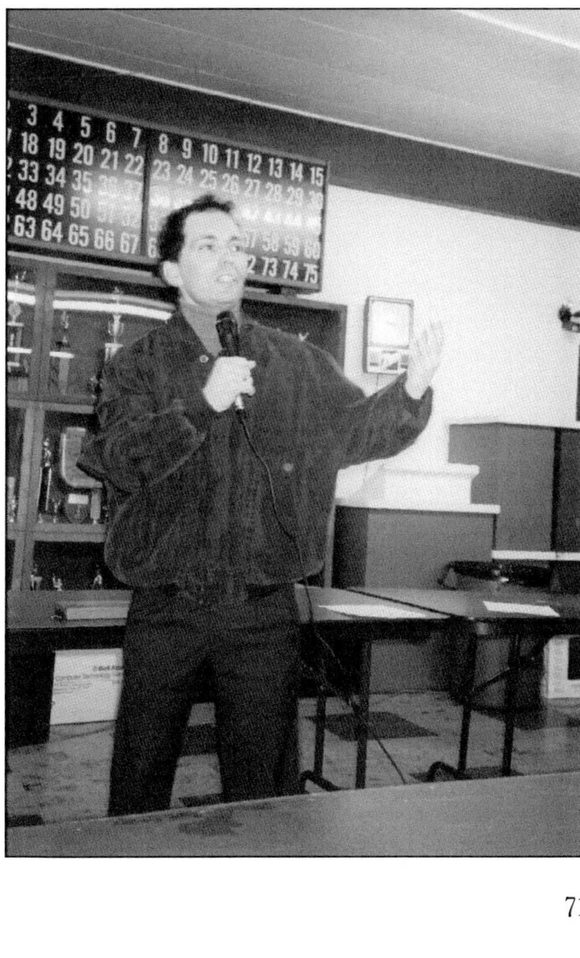

In June 1989, while living in Benicia, Jim Weiss developed his storytelling hobby into a business. Along with his wife, Randy, a teacher at Benicia Middle School, he formed Greathall Productions. Producing 48 storytelling productions, from classical literature to the Bible, the couple has won more than 100 national awards. Jim has shared his interactive storytelling with the children of Benicia and instilled in them a love of literature. (SDN.)

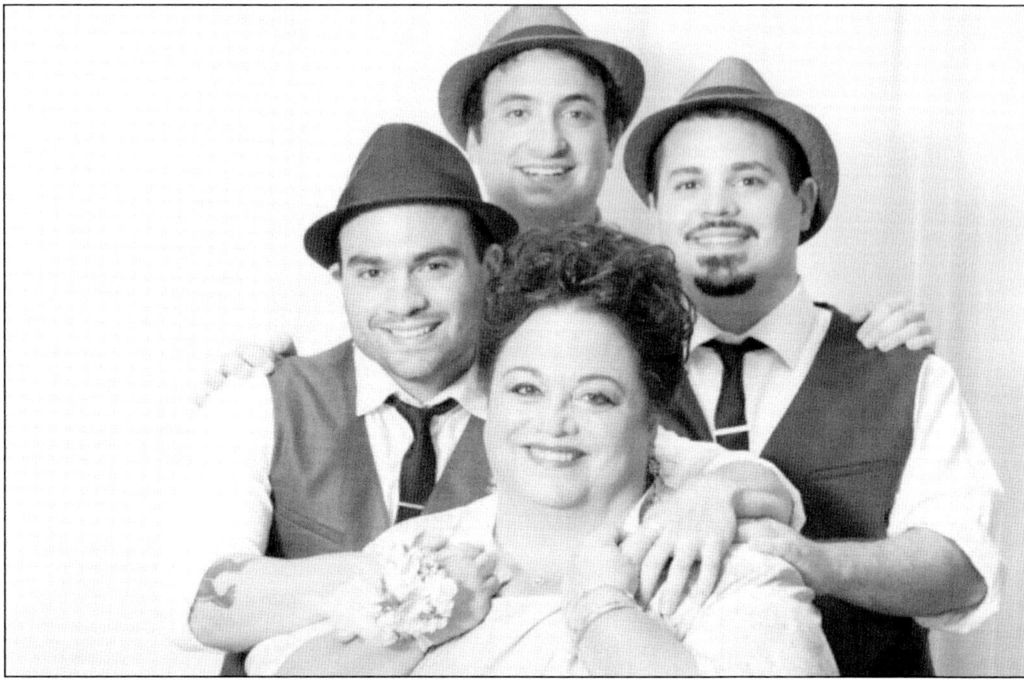

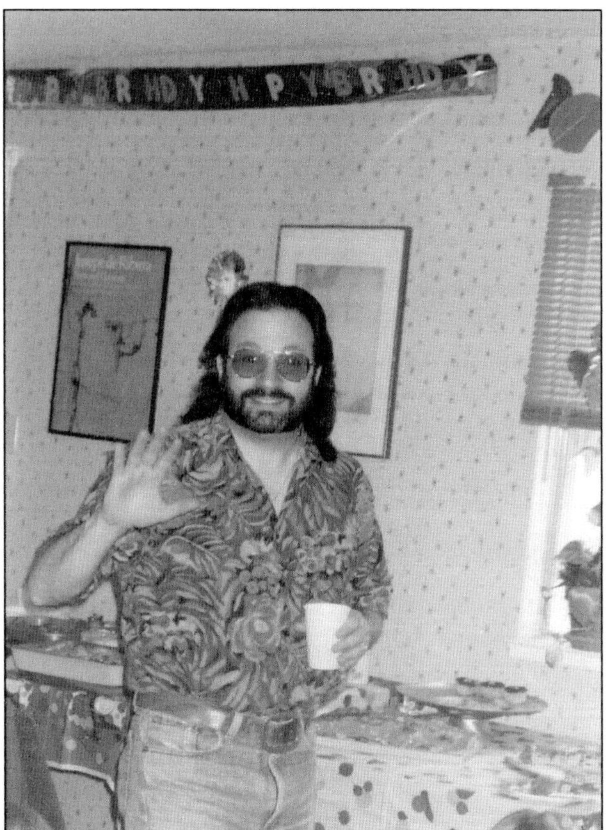

Her love of theater and talented sons set Serena Kreamer on a path that not only led her to organize and direct one of CBI's best productions—1997's *Fiddler on the Roof*—but also paved the way for her to open a school that teaches acting, singing, dance, and theater to Solano County's young people. With her sons—from left to right, Adam, Jeremy, and Josh—helping to teach, direct, and otherwise keep things running, Kreamer's S&J Performing Arts Center (named for Serena and her late husband, Joel, pictured at left) continues to help dozens of Solano County's children and teens find their hidden talents and the self confidence to use them. (Both, courtesy of Serena Kreamer.)

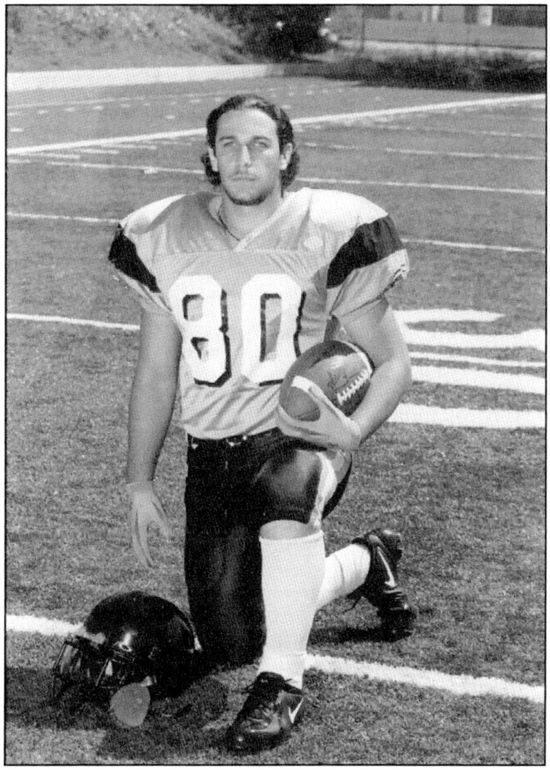

The Zrihen brothers of Vallejo were both student athletes. In 2014, Danny (right) is a successful businessman, and Jonathan (below) is studying for a career in law enforcement. Both were on the varsity football and the varsity wrestling teams at Vallejo High School in the early to mid-2000s. Proof that they were not the school's only Jewish athletes can be found in the 1980s plaque honoring Vallejo High School track star Albert Casper—for whom part of the school's athletic field, Casper Oval, is named. Caleb Natov was a Vallejo High School baseball star. Another young local athlete, Nicole Oettinger, swam with the Benicia Blue Dolphins swim team. (Both, courtesy of the Zrihen family.)

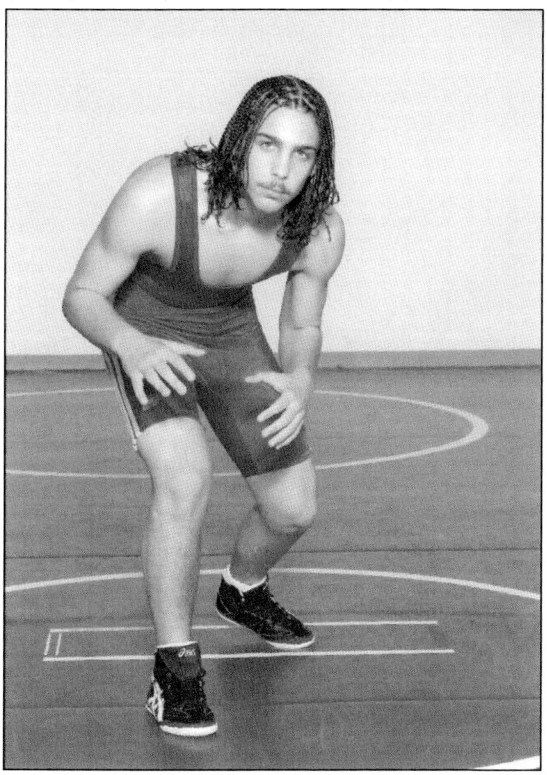

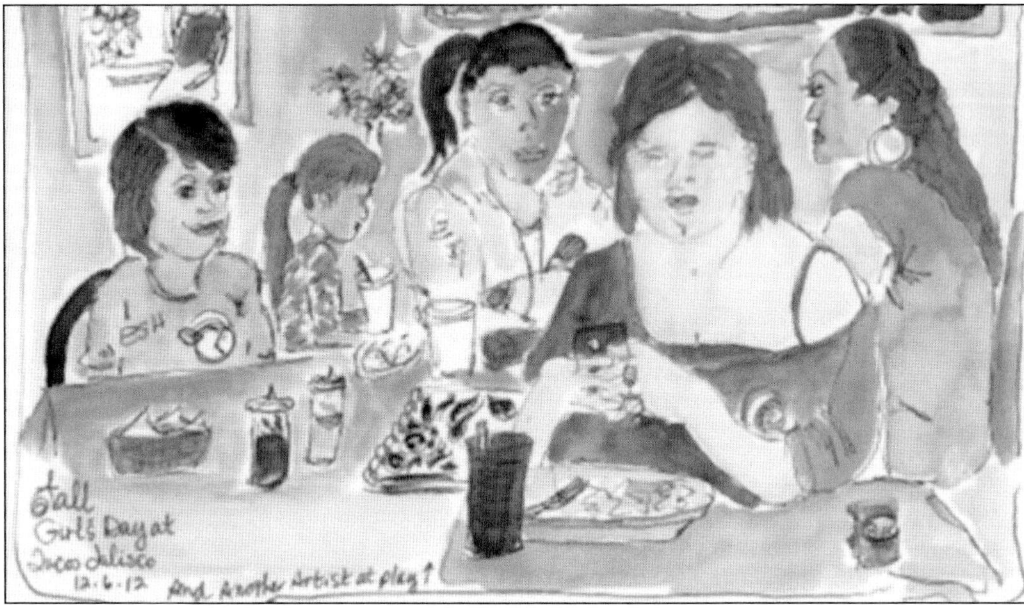

A marriage and family therapist, Lynn Cohen of Vacaville also paints, quilts, writes, and illustrates in her spare time. She published a book of sketches called *One Fish Taco and Half an Order of Guacamole: A Year of Drawing Over Lunch at Tacos Jalisco*, and her blog, *Somewhere to Sketch*, is a place where artists can discuss their work. (Courtesy of Lynn Cohen.)

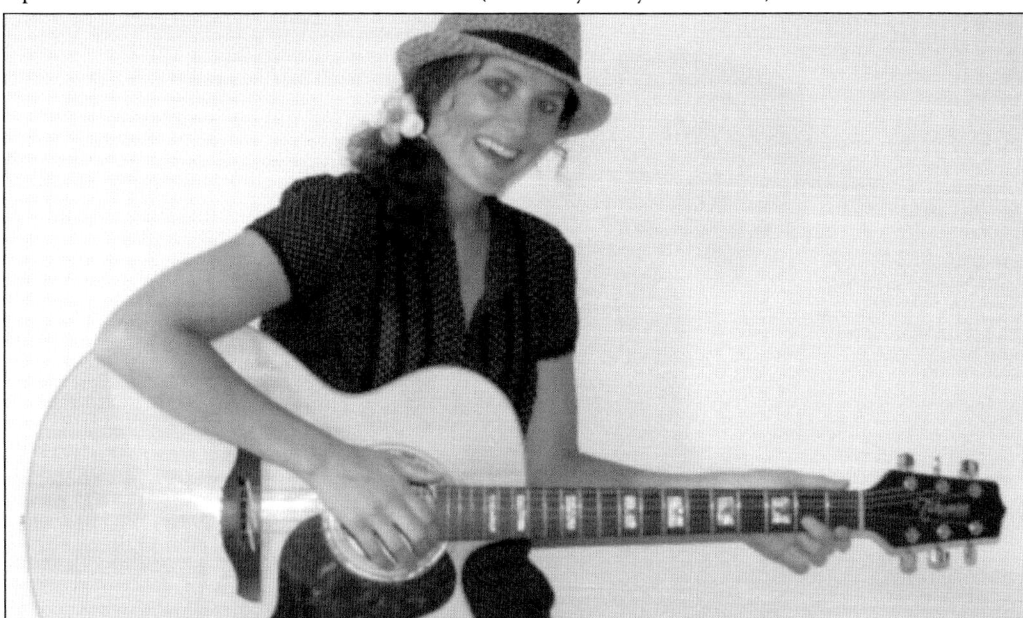

Some of Katie Goudie Fry's first musical experience was with CBI's choir. She has since mastered several instruments, including the flute, piano, guitar, and drums, and toured both with a band and as a soloist, performing original music as "Katie Jane." She is also a musical director at Rocklin Youth Theatre Company, teaches music at a Jewish preschool, and is a volunteer songwriter and producer for Songs of Love, a foundation that provides personalized music for seriously ill children. (Courtesy of Katie Fry.)

Richard Freedman of Vallejo, seen here with his wife, Megan (a singer), has been a columnist, reporter, and editor at the *Vallejo Times-Herald* since 1994. He has also produced or hosted dozens of fundraisers for various nonprofits and earned dozens of awards and honors. He has produced benefits on behalf of a slew of worthy causes, including the Special Olympics, the Make-A-Wish Foundation, the local Humane Society, the Vallejo Police Activities League, Toys for Tots, and the local food bank. (CBI.)

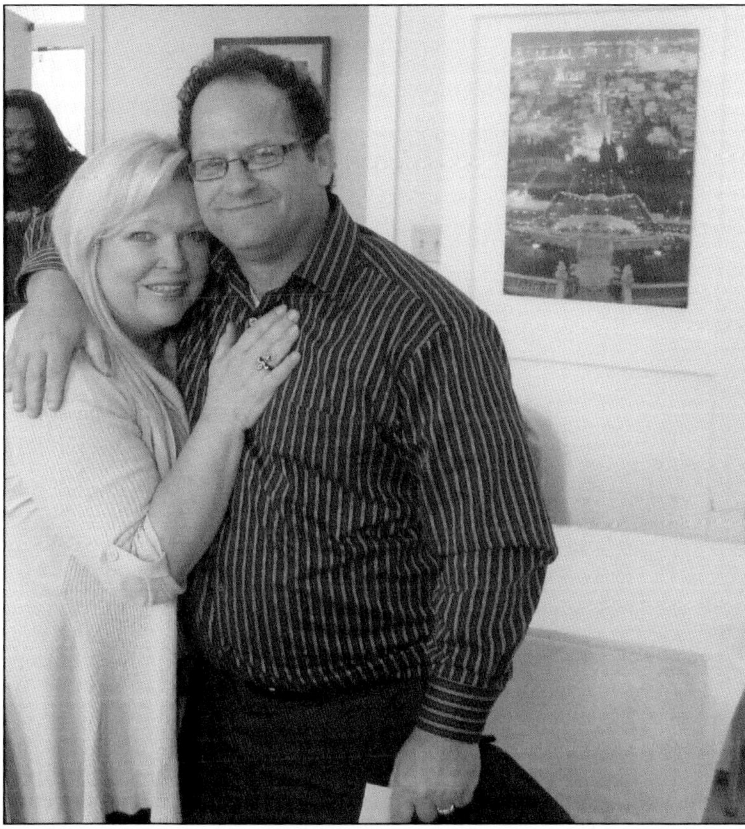

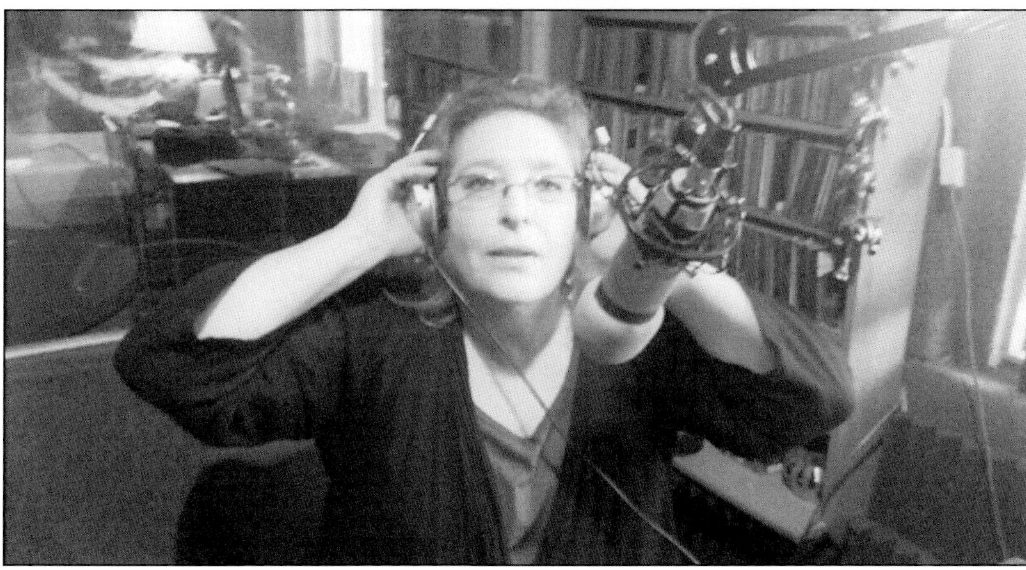

A columnist and *Vallejo Times-Herald* reporter since 1999, Rachel Raskin-Zrihen married her Moroccan-born, Israeli-American husband, Raphael, in 1982, and the couple raised two sons. She created the *Ha!* humor magazine and was honored with the Soroptimist Club's Marion Devlin Journalism Award in 2010 for a series chronicling her battle with breast cancer. She is pictured here as a volunteer DJ on the local Jewish radio show she helped found. (Courtesy of Geri Kahn.)

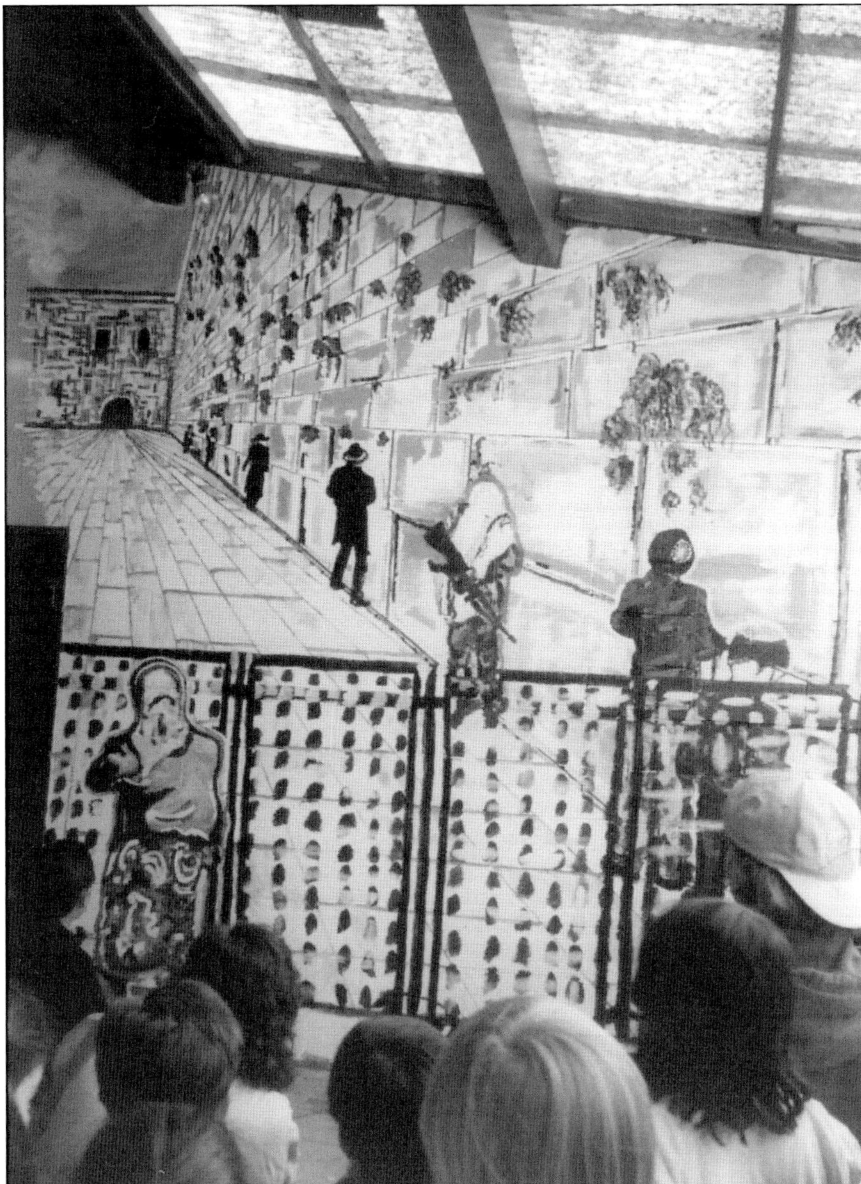

In May 1995, during the Jewish year 5755, B'nai Israel congregant and artist Steve Biering symbolically brought Jerusalem's Western Wall to Vallejo by painting a Kotel scene on the walls surrounding B'nai Israel's courtyard. Biering told the local newspaper that it took him 65 hours to complete the work of recreating the image of Judaism's holiest site. "I painted it from the perspective of looking at the men's side [of the Kotel] from the women's side," he said, calling it a unique view for many. The mural was dedicated in a ceremony commemorating Israel Independence Day. During the ceremony, Rabbi David Kopstein paraphrased Yossi Gamzu's take on the so-called "Wailing Wall," saying, "There are people with hearts of stone and stones with human hearts." Gamzu reportedly wrote those words just hours after the liberation of Jerusalem's Old City, while standing with a group of military reporters. Biering also painted the backdrop of the village of Anatevka for the congregation's 1997 production of *Fiddler on the Roof*. (SDN.)

Six

COMMUNITY

קהילה (KEHILAH)

קעהילע (KAHILAH)

. . . Embracing and celebrating our uniqueness

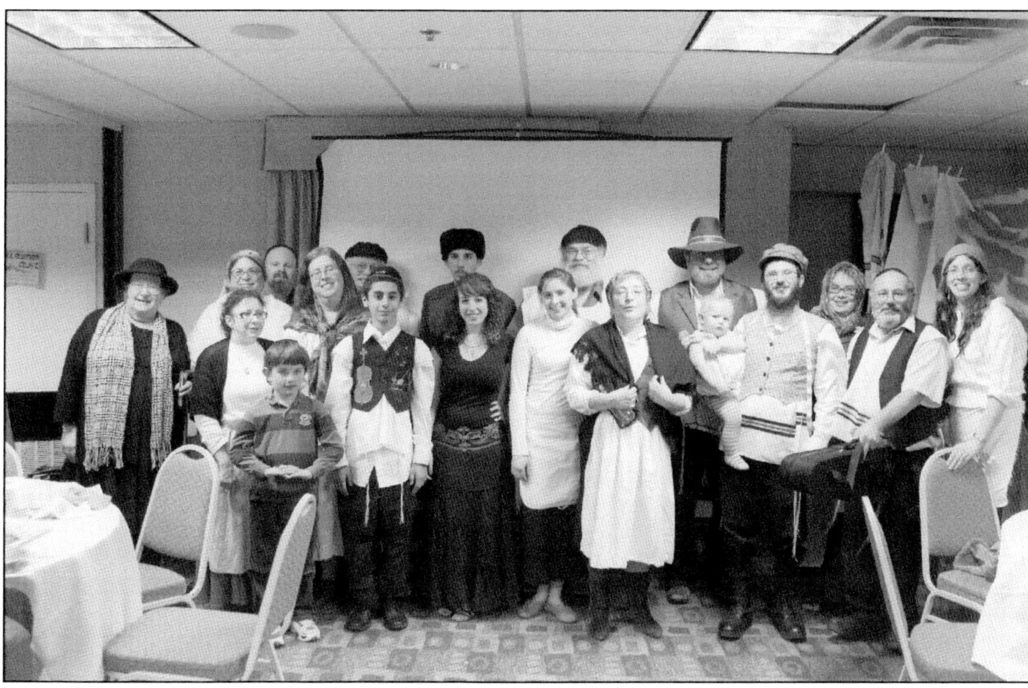

This *Fiddler on the Roof*–themed Purim party from 2011 is among the many public events sponsored by Chabad of Solano County. At this gathering, participants performed a humorous "where-are-they-now" skit, updating the *Fiddler* characters' lives. Solano County's Jews have often reached out to the greater population and have been involved, in various ways and times, with important local occasions. (Chabad.)

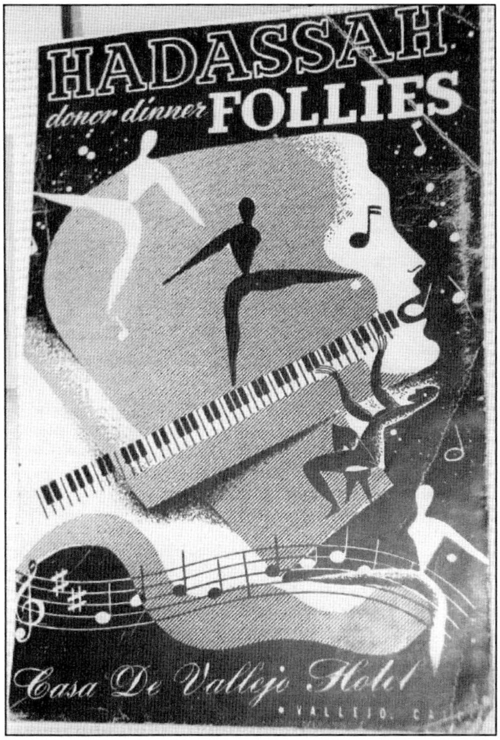

From the beginning, Solano County's Jewish community has produced shows of various kinds. The Center Players Guild, formed in 1948, presented several productions to entertain and raise funds. These included *The Redeemers*, *The Shikker*, and *The Hanukapades*. This 1949 poster advertises the Hadassah Follies donor dinner, which included performances by Isabel Zlot, Kate Monetta, Mrs. Stern, Mrs. Hal Liberman, and Sylvia Weinberg. (Courtesy of Bernard Monetta.)

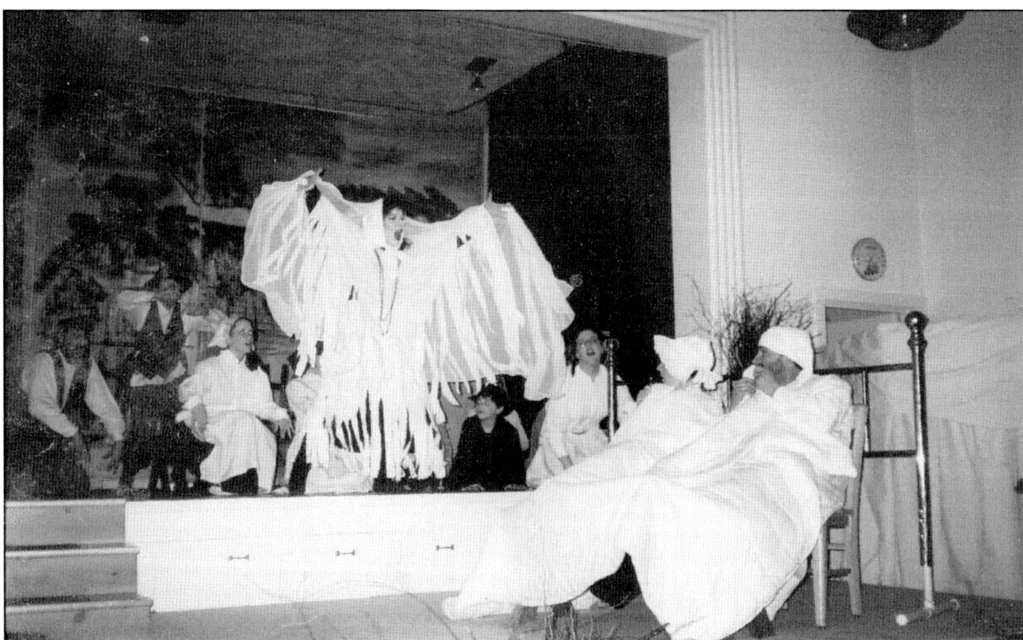

In 1997, CBI members performed a production of *Fiddler on the Roof*, which was directed by Serena Kreamer, featured music by Francie Gross, and was open to the general public. Pictured is the dream scene, with Rachel Raskin-Zrihen as Fruma Sarah's ghost and Steve Harris and Melissa Edwards seen in the bed as Tevya and Golda. Also on stage are, from left to right, Gary Levy, Sarah Rozett, Katie Goudie, Josh Kreamer, and Meghan Campbell. (Courtesy of the Zrihen family.)

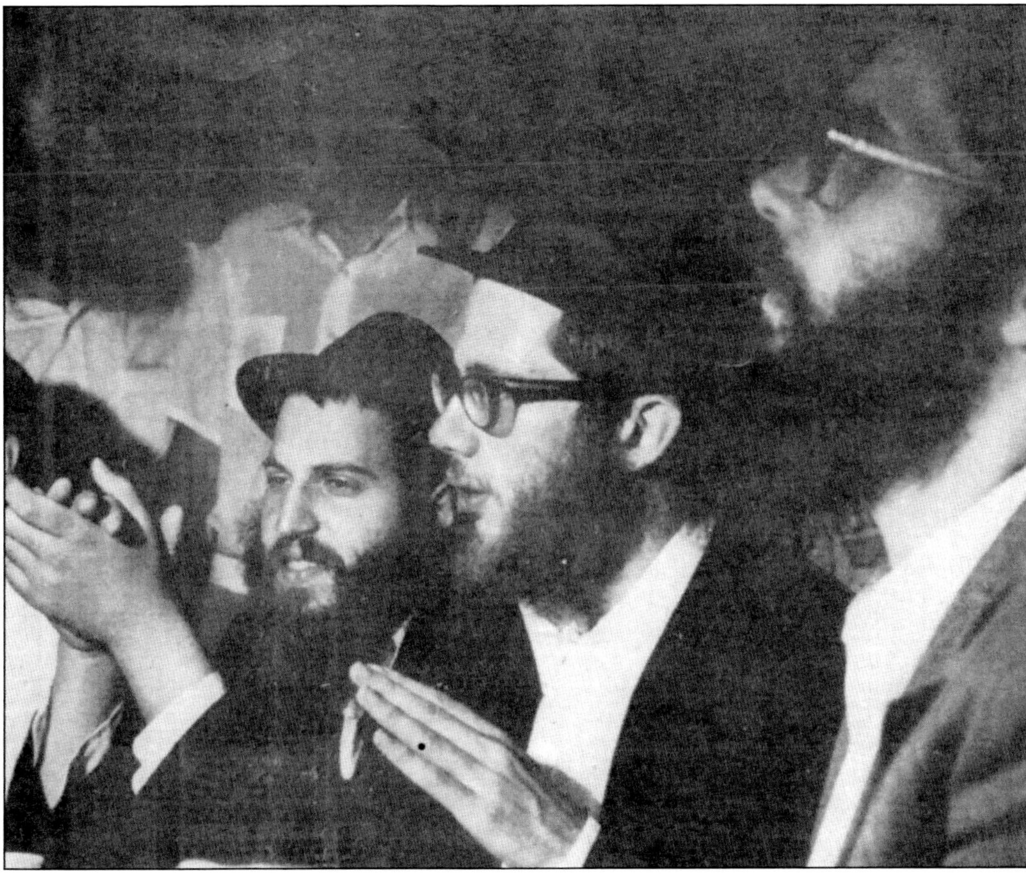

Dr. Lawrence Wanetick came to Fairfield in 1968, working for the California Department of Corrections medical facility in Vacaville. Wanting his children to receive a Jewish education, Wanetick contacted a Bay Area rabbi, Joseph Langer, who sent a teacher. This worked so well that Wanetick met with other Jewish parents and started B'nai Avraham, which operated a Sunday school that hosted rabbis from around the region. Wanetick was congregation president, Intercommunity Hospital's chief of staff, Solano Medical Society president, and a professor of surgery at the UC Davis Medical School. Vacaville's first Chassidic *fabrengen*, or gathering, was held at Wanetick's home in 1977. It started at 9:00 p.m. and at 3:00 a.m. was still going strong, with stories, songs, and philosophies that brought Judaism's deepest traditions to those needing spiritual restoration. Wanetick invited these rabbis to show his children Judaism's many traditions. A Travis Air Force Base chaplain, Rabbi Israel Haber, was also there. (Both, Chabad.)

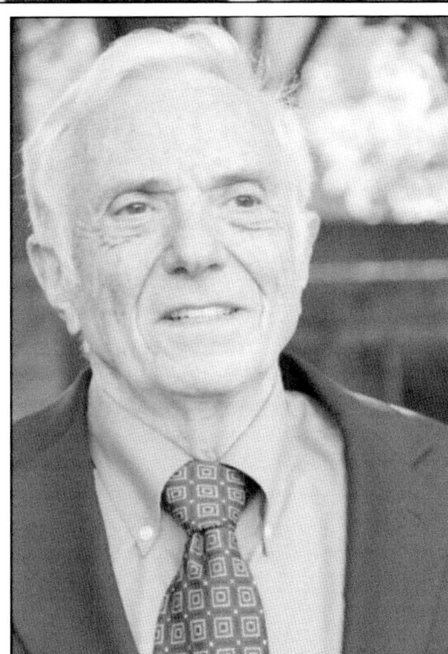

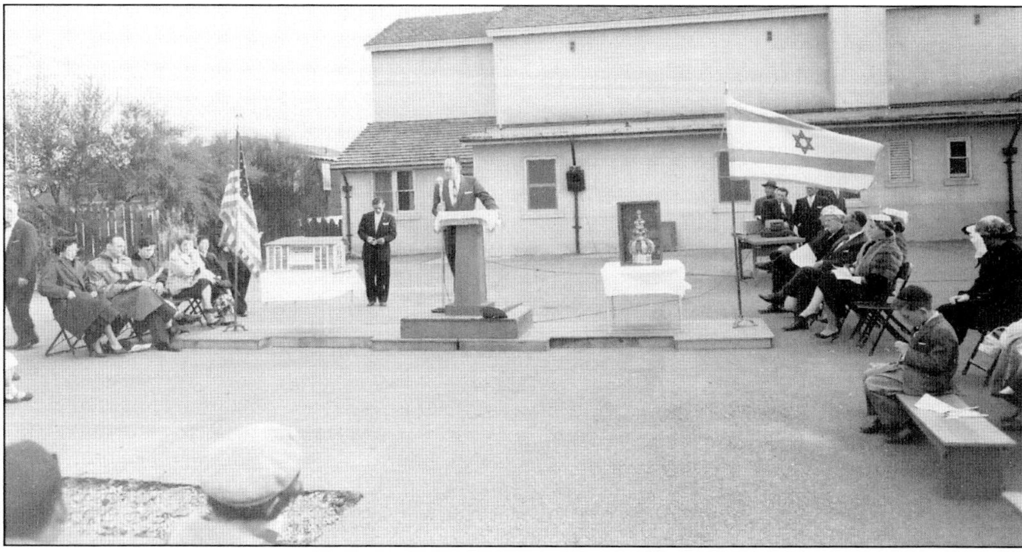

In 1956, in honor of National Brotherhood Week and as part of a citywide pulpit exchange, Rabbi Sol Horowitz and Rev. Kenneth Tuttle of the First Congregational Church traded platforms. Continuing the tradition years later, members of CBI and Benicia's St. Paul's Episcopal Church partnered in producing an Interfaith Thanksgiving Service, in which members of a growing number of different faith communities have begun participating. Rev. Jeanne Forte and Rabbi David White are seen below at the church, with the rabbi reading the Litany of Thanksgiving and the pastor giving the sermon. The next year the location and roles are reversed. The 2012 and 2013 events saw a marked increase in the number and variety of churches attending as a result of CBI's involvement with Common Ground. (Above, CBI; below, VTH.)

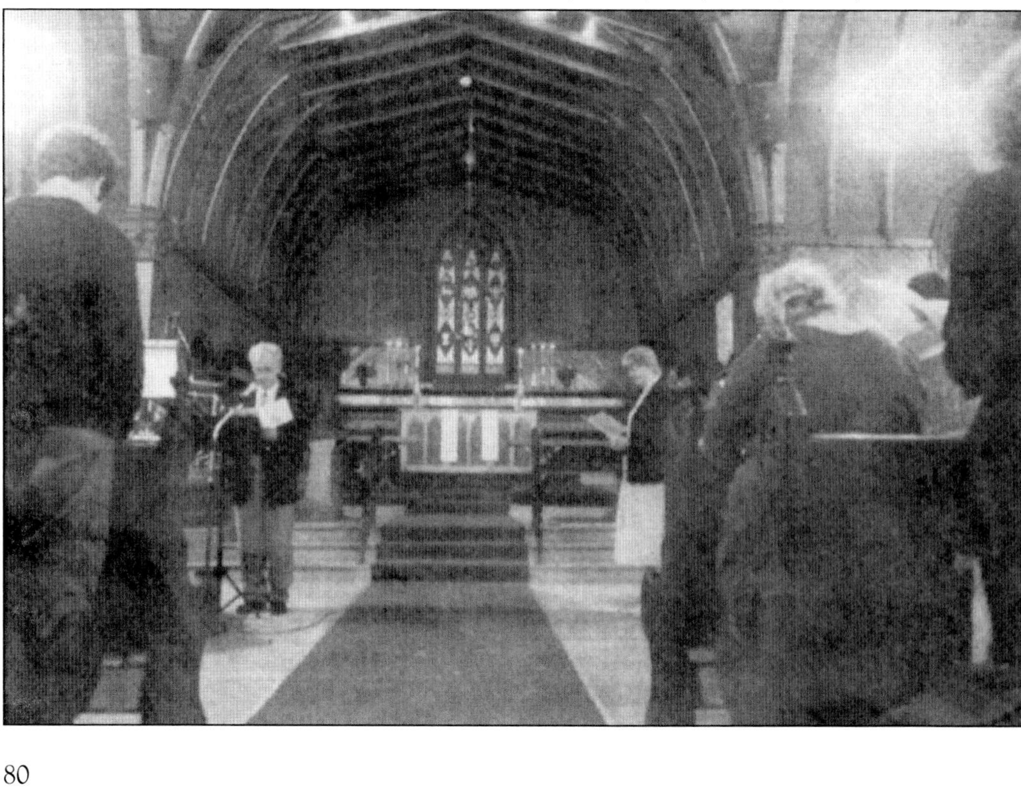

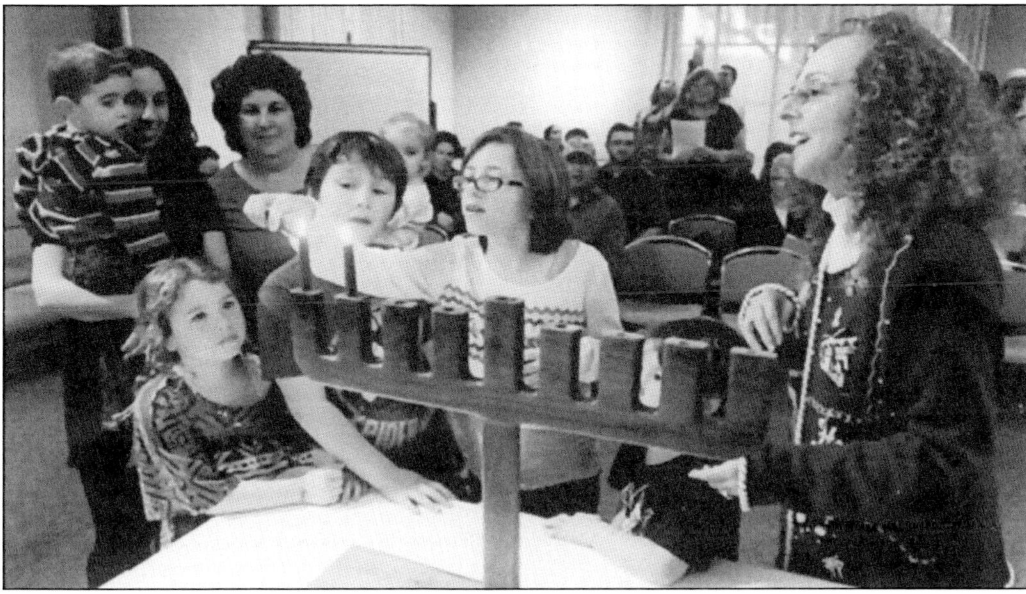

In 1989, the Benicia-Solano Jewish Women's Network launched an annual menorah lighting in downtown Benicia and invited the community to attend. At the event, the Chanukah story is told, songs are sung, and dreidels are distributed. Organized by Shoshana Deutscher-Nurik, Alisa Danyeur, and Heather Campbell (pictured at right), the event was renamed the Meghan Campbell Memorial Menorah Lighting in 2010 in honor of Heather's daughter, who lost her life at age 26. John Campbell designed the menorah. (SDN.)

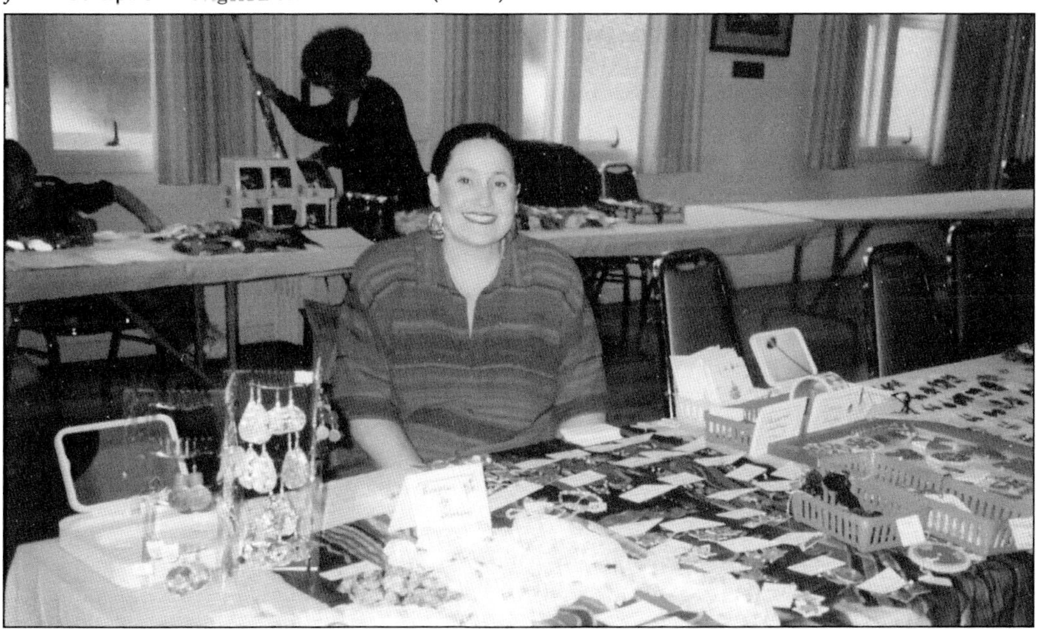

The Chanukah Boutique is an annual mainstay at Congregation B'nai Israel. Vendors occupy tables and sell everything from homemade crafts to jewelry to Judaica. Potato latkes and bagels and lox are sold in the synagogue café. Shoshana Deutscher-Nurik is pictured here selling homemade head covers and jewelry. She also instituted the annual Pixie Boutique, where young children can buy gifts for their families on their own. (SDN.)

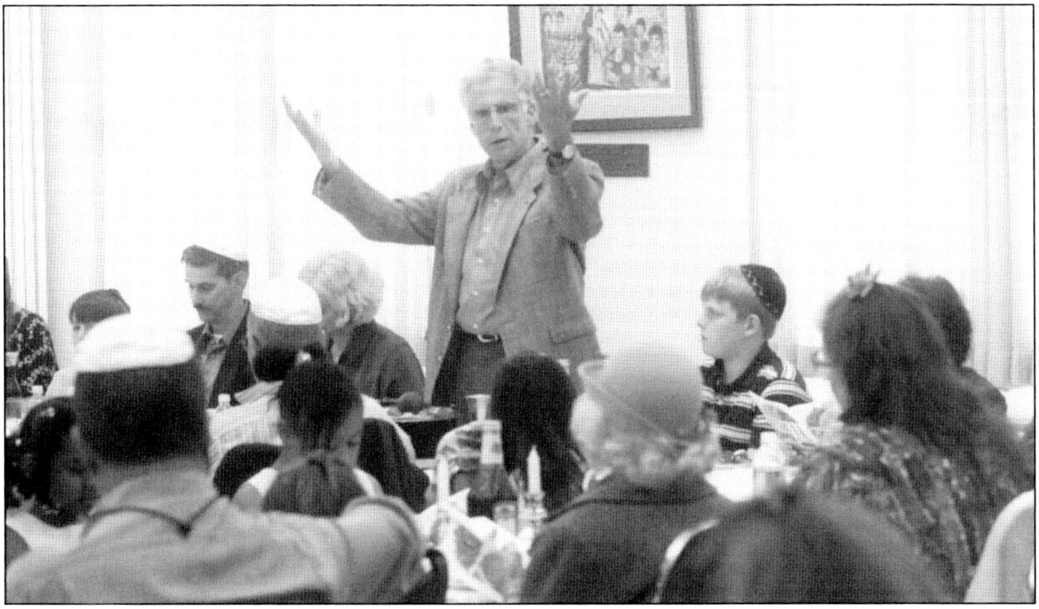

Since the congregation's earliest days, Passover Seders have been open to the community, because we are commanded to open our doors to all who hunger. Usually, this means that Jewish travelers can find a friendly Seder in an unfamiliar city. In this photograph, Rabbi David White addresses a highlight of the Hagaddah, containing the Passover story. Rabbi White is the son of the late Rabbi Saul White, of San Francisco's Congregation Beth Shalom. (VTH.)

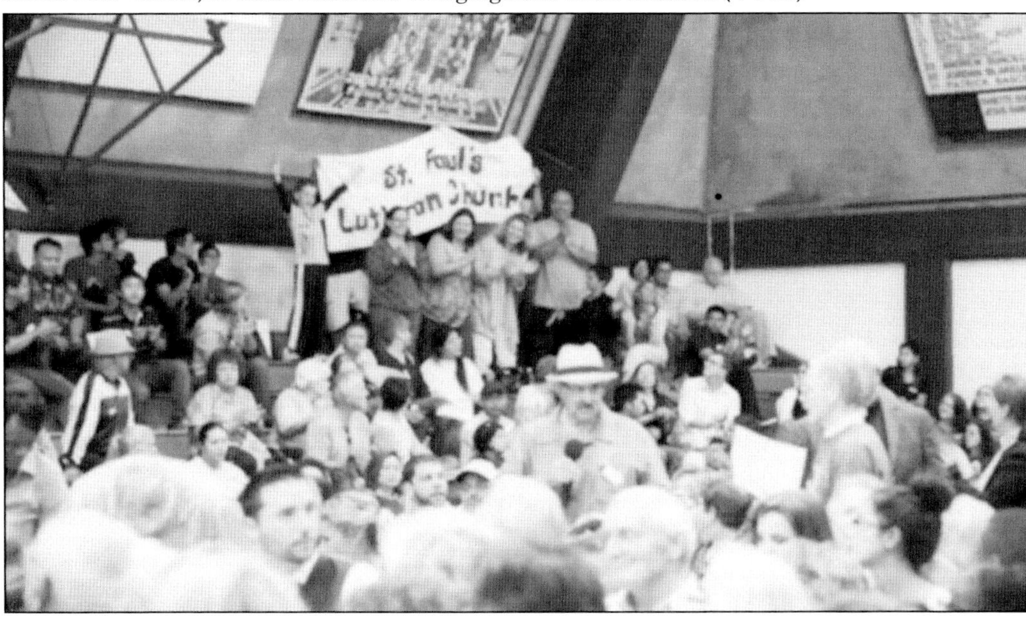

In 2013, CBI leadership helped found the local branch of Common Ground, a 14-year-old civic organization formed to address community issues. Common Ground consists of some 15 nonprofit and faith-based organizations from Napa and Solano Counties that meet regularly to discuss local issues like violence, drugs, immigration, and homelessness in an effort to determine root causes and consider ways to address them. The group is part of the 70 nationwide chapters of the Industrial Areas Foundation. (CBI.)

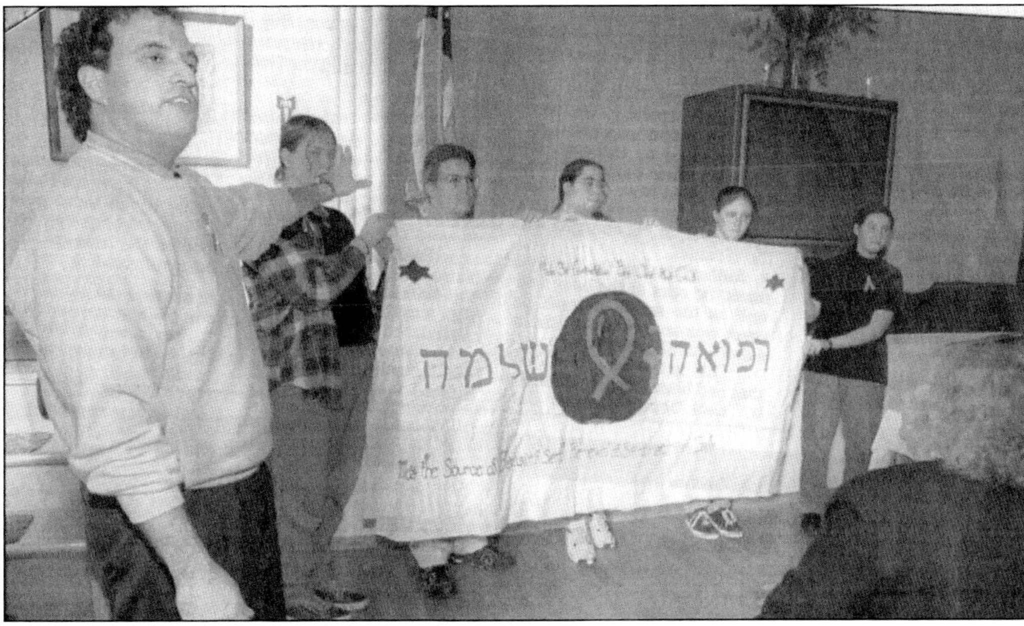

After the AIDS-related death of her beloved son Joseph, Leah Schmall became involved in observing National AIDS Day on December 1. Working with the Young Judea youth group, she encouraged the creation of a quilt panel for display in Solano County and then as part of the National AIDS Quilt. She sewed the quilt—designed by Alexandra Nurik—with Meghan Campbell, Jennifer and Becky Schwartz, and Tanya Tackaberry. (VTH.)

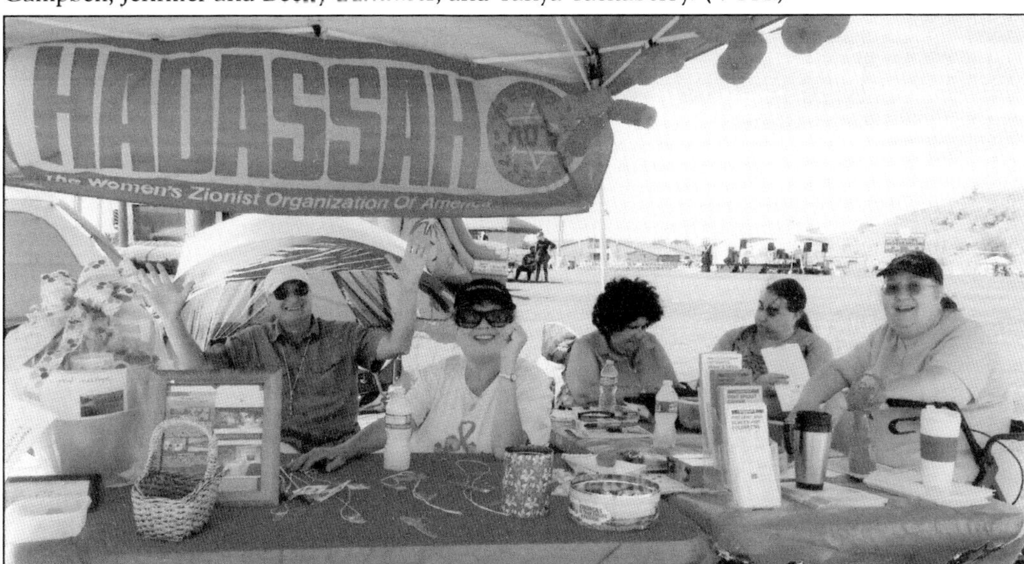

Relay for Life is a fundraiser for the American Cancer Society. Congregants from B'nai Israel in Vallejo and the Solano-Napa Chapter of Hadassah join forces for it annually and raised over $2,500 in 2013. Pictured here at the CBI-Hadassah Friends and Family booth are, from left to right, Frank Candido, Rachel Lessem, Sharon Petrellese, Becky Stevenson, and Mary Schwartz. Not pictured are the booth chairpersons: Shoshana Deutscher-Nurik, Geri Kahn, and Heather Campbell. (SDN.)

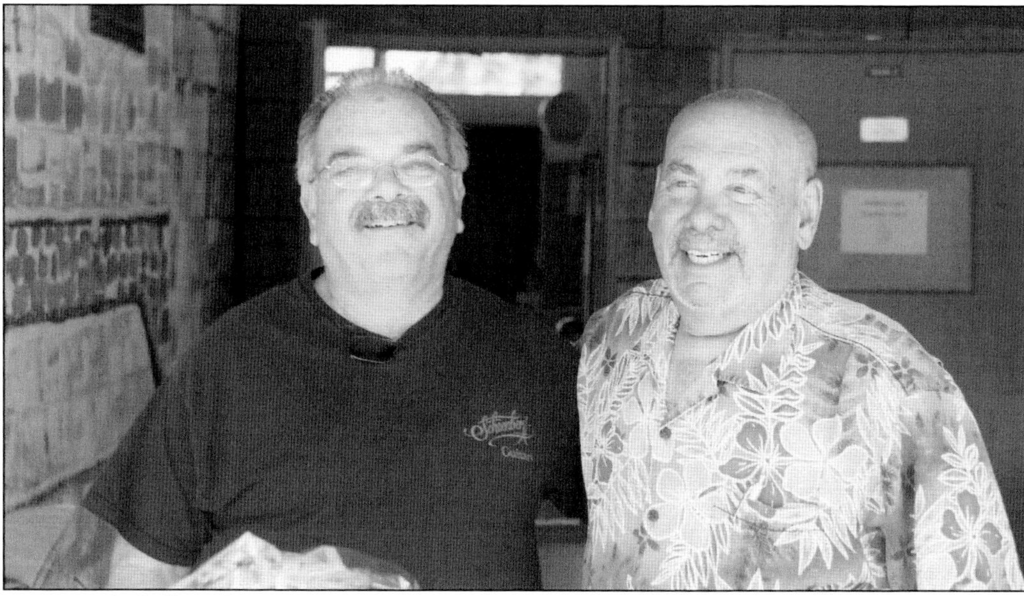

Dan Joseph (left) and Alan Pluchok (right) were CBI's auctioneers for many years. They are seen here at the large annual fundraising event—consisting of a dinner and an auction—that was first initiated by Joyce Georgetti. Many have chaired the event, including Helene Falk, Donna Plantz, Sheryl and Dennis Meade, the Petrelleses, the Zolas, Syd Nazarenko, and current chairperson Robin Gross. Items sold often include artwork, antiques, sports tickets, and cabin getaways. (Courtesy of Donna Plantz.)

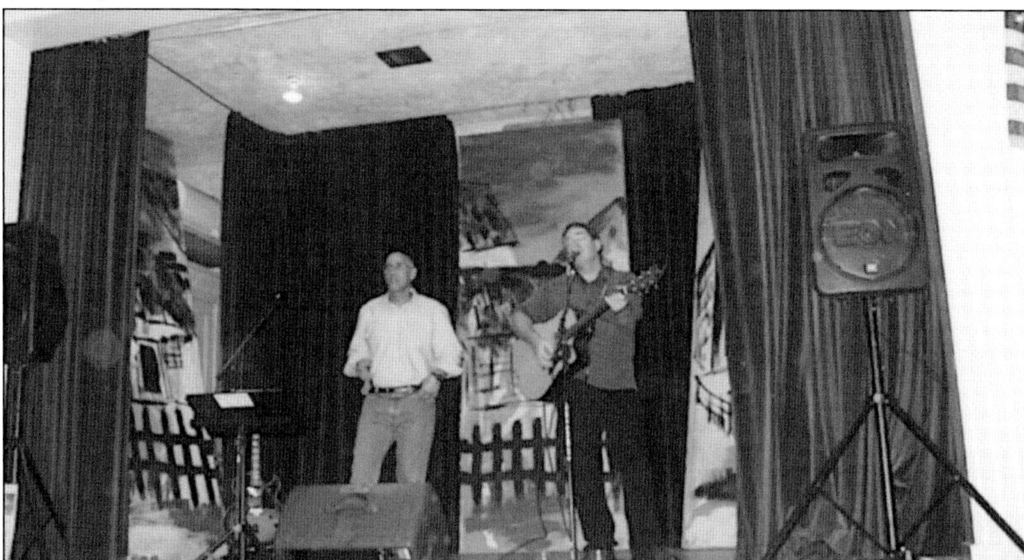

In 2008, psychologist and Benicia resident Doug Cort (seen at left) organized a fundraising concert to help CBI members who were struggling with medical expenses. The now-annual TLC concert features Cort on guitar and vocals, "Jewish Blues" guitarist and songwriter Saul Kaye, keyboardist Dan Zimmelman, and vocalist Steve Sicotios, and the audience has grown each year. Thousands of dollars have been raised, helping hundreds to worry less about skyrocketing medical bills. (Courtesy of the Cort family.)

In 1999, Eric Strong Bear, seen with here his Native American drums, and other Vallejo Intertribal Council members joined CBI in the synagogue's sukkah for the Jewish harvest holiday. In 2005, several Jews—including Rabbi Yitzchak and Devorah Kaufman, Bruce Silverman, and George and Jan Farber—signed an official letter supporting the Vallejo Intertribal Council's efforts to block the development of a park near the ancient Shell Mound burial site at Vallejo's Glen Cove waterfront. (VTH.)

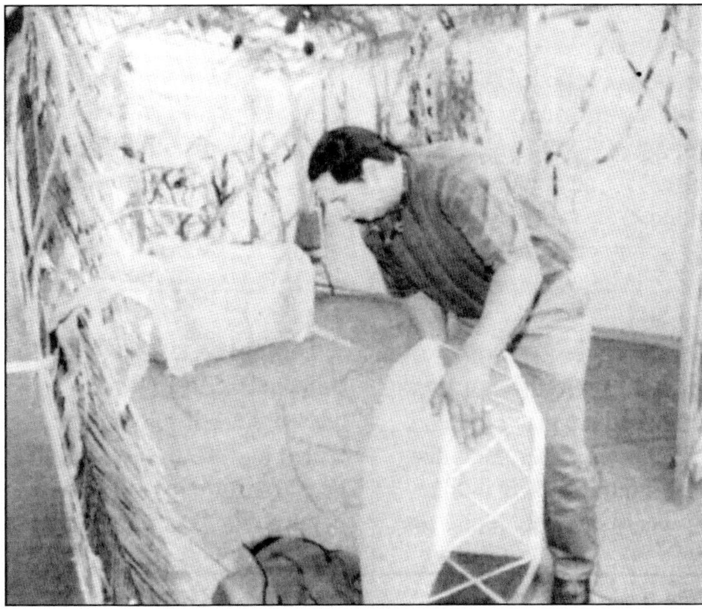

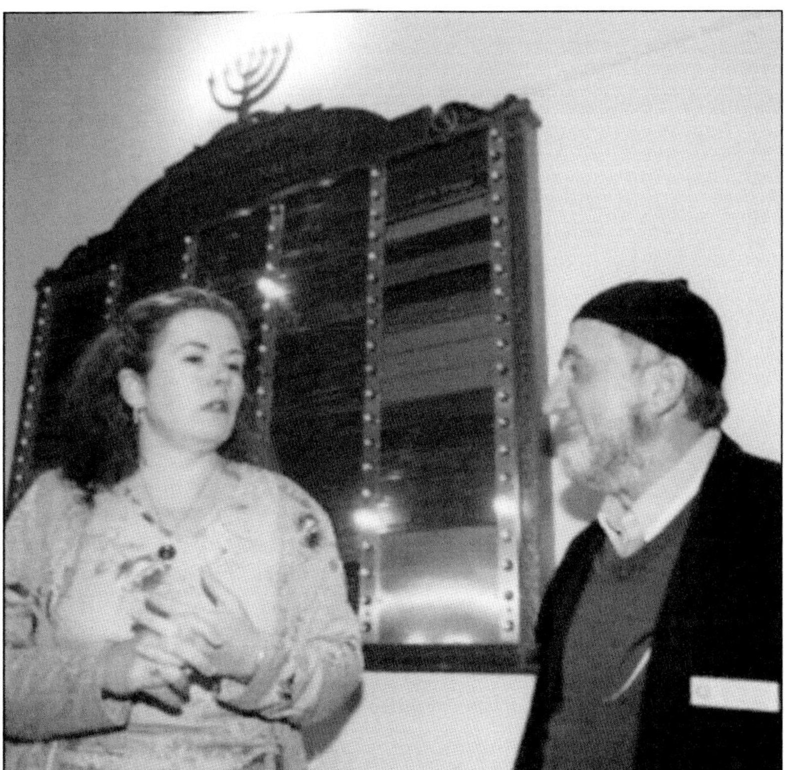

Bella Bogart (left), the CBI cantor and religious leader for several years in the early 2000s, is seen here just days after the 9-11 terrorist attacks on the United States, speaking with a local Muslim imam who was invited to the synagogue in an effort to foster understanding and peace between the two religious communities in Solano County. She was ordained a rabbi in early 2014 and lives in Benicia. (VTH.)

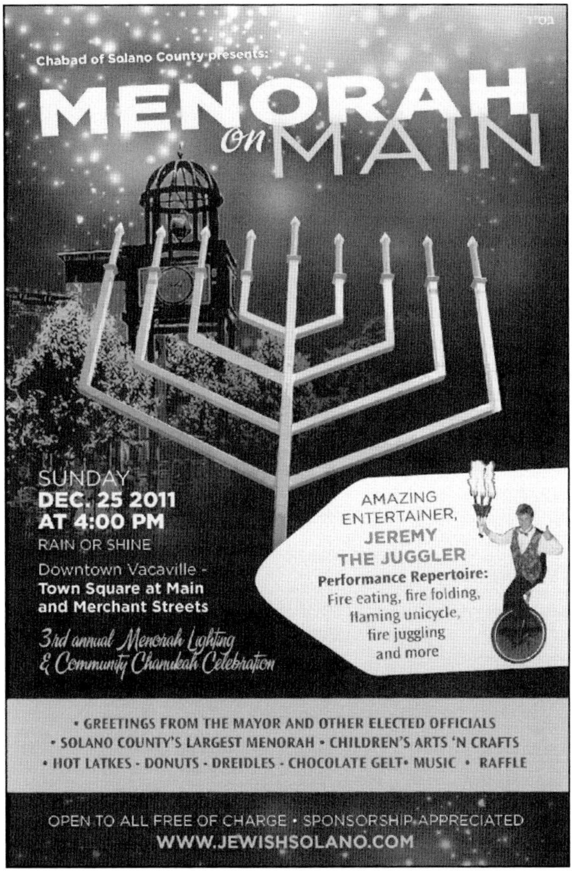

The Zakloses have been responsible for creating at least two popular ongoing community events—the public menorah lighting on Vacaville's Main Street and the annual Jelly Belly candy factory Hanukkah party. Both events have grown in attendance and popularity, drawing local and regional political representatives and attendees from across the region. Chabad's goal is finding and engaging as many Jews as possible, regardless of affiliation or lack thereof, particularly those living under the radar. One year, a torrential downpour did nothing to dampen the turnout at the Vacaville event. In 2013, the first night of Chanukah fell on Thanksgiving, and the Chabad event included a rare *upsherin*—a boy's first haircut at age three—providing a unique opportunity to include the larger community in this ancient tradition. (Both, Chabad.)

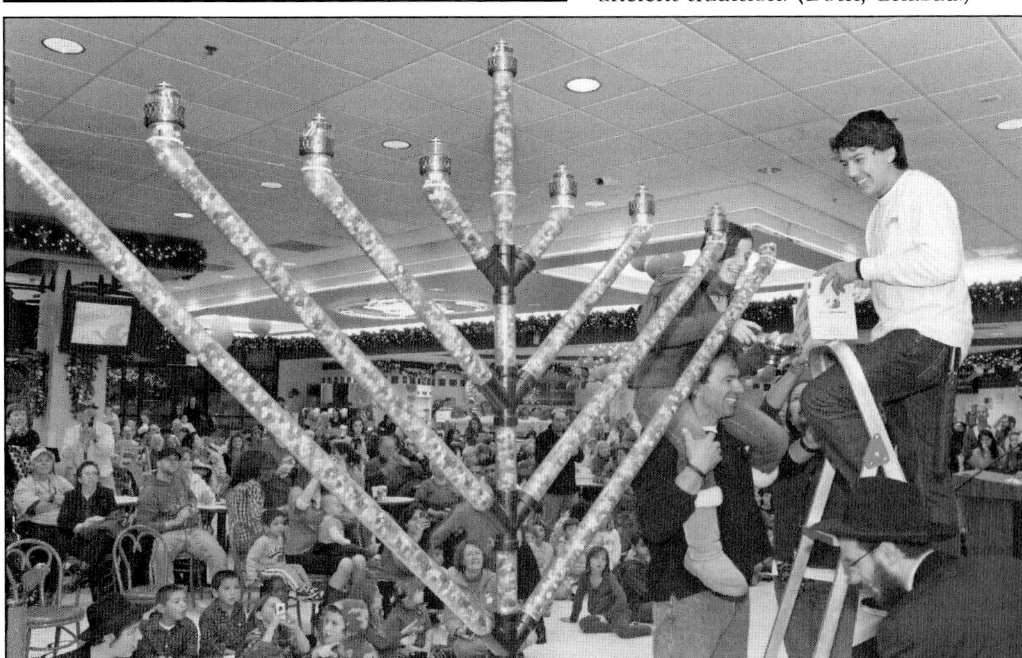

Vallejo's main library hosted an exhibit commemorating the 100-year history of Vallejo's Jewish community through pictures, print, and various cultural and religious artifacts. It was the brainchild of librarian Michael Senturia, a UC Berkeley music professor emeritus who also founded Vallejo's Lawyer in the Library program. He worked with Congregation B'nai Israel's Alisa Danyeur (below) and Arlene Rabin on the display "to illustrate how the Jewish community impacted Vallejo and Solano County." Danyeur, an animal lover and an animal foster parent, has served on the boards of the Humane Society of the North Bay, CBI, and the Solano-Napa Chapter of Hadassah. Arlene, a resident of the Glen Cove area of Vallejo, enjoyed hosting Torah study sessions in her home. (Right, of Jason Wiese; below, CBI.)

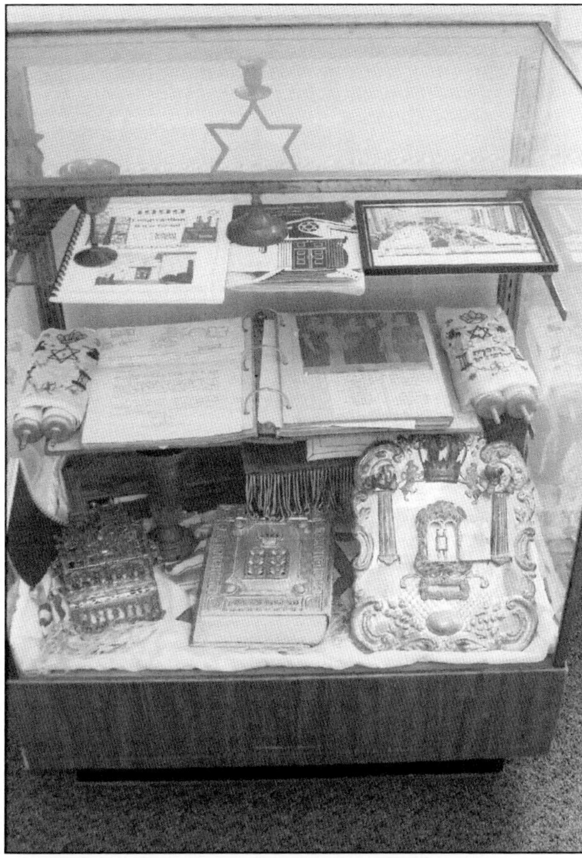

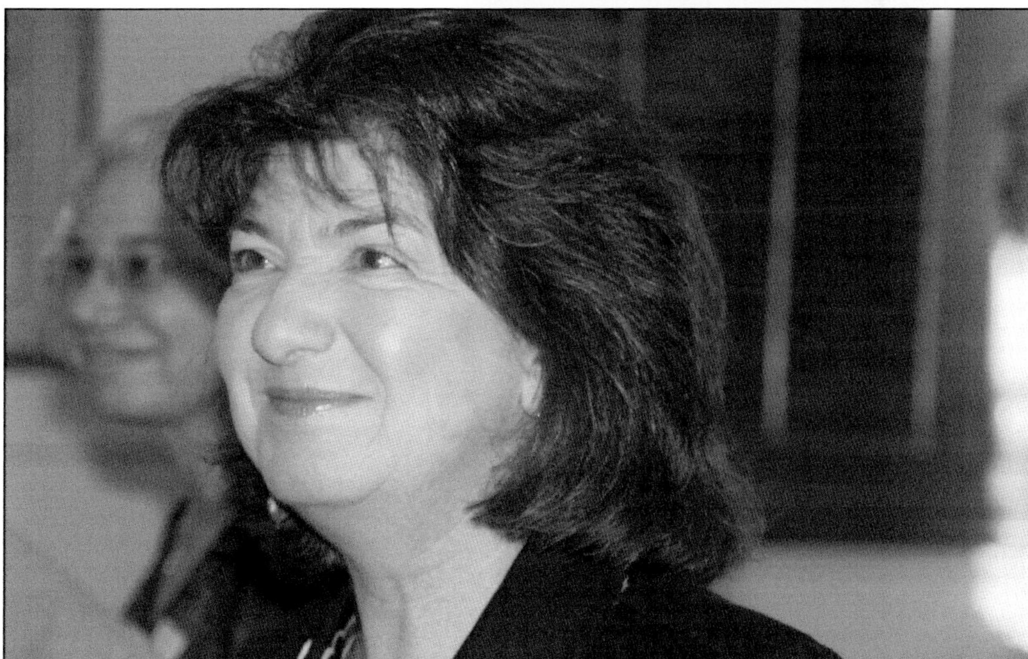

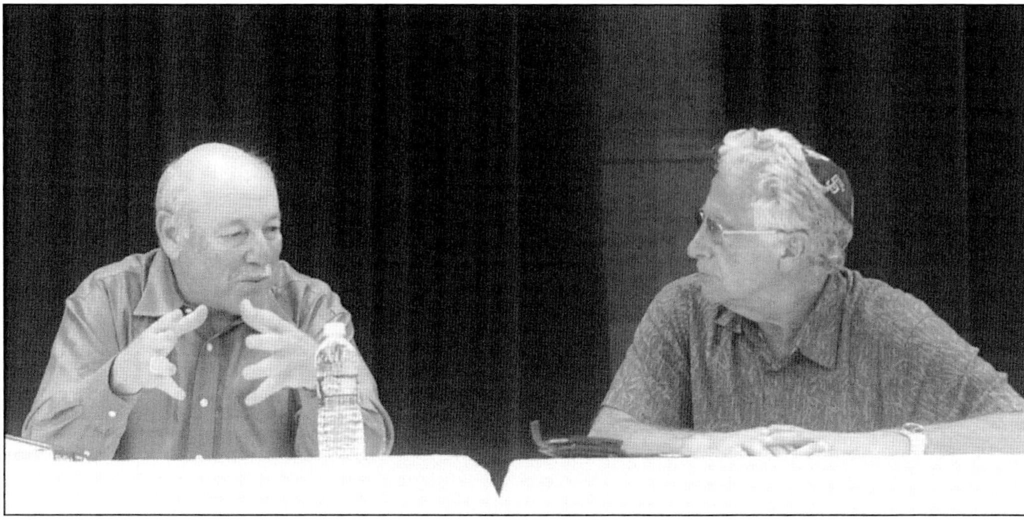

Judaism and baseball both overflow with rituals and create community, explained Jewish baseball maven and radio personality Marty Lurie (left) at a CBI event. Rabbi David White is also seen here, wearing a Giants *kippah*. Lurie, who had two of his children Bar Mitzvahed at CBI, wrote the baseball column "Batter Up" from 2004 to 2009 and hosted KNBR's Giants pre- and post-game weekend shows. (CBI.)

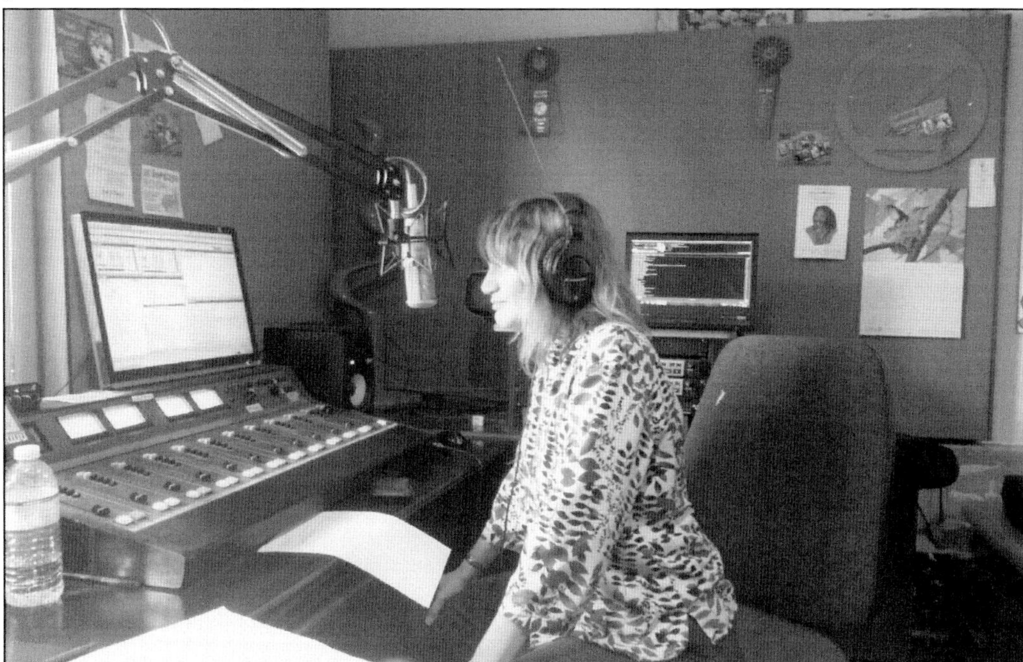

Rachel Raskin-Zrihen was approached during 2012's Unity Day celebration by OZCAT Radio station owner David Martin and asked to do a Jewish-themed program. She suggested the show to the Napa-Solano Chapter of Hadassah, where Rachel Lessem and Geri Kahn (pictured) volunteered to help produce such a show. Twice monthly, *Kol D'var*—Hebrew for "all things"—features any musical genre with any Jewish connection whatsoever, plus live and pre-recorded music and interviews on various topics of interest. (Courtesy of Geri Kahn.)

Jewish community member Sharon Petrellese competed in Benicia's camel races, riding the notorious Saddam. The event began as a fundraiser for the Benicia Historical Museum in 1997, building on the arsenal's history. In 1864, the US Army kept a camel herd at the warehouse now called the Benicia Camel Barn. In 2000, six dromedaries were brought from Nevada to the foot of First Street. (VTH.)

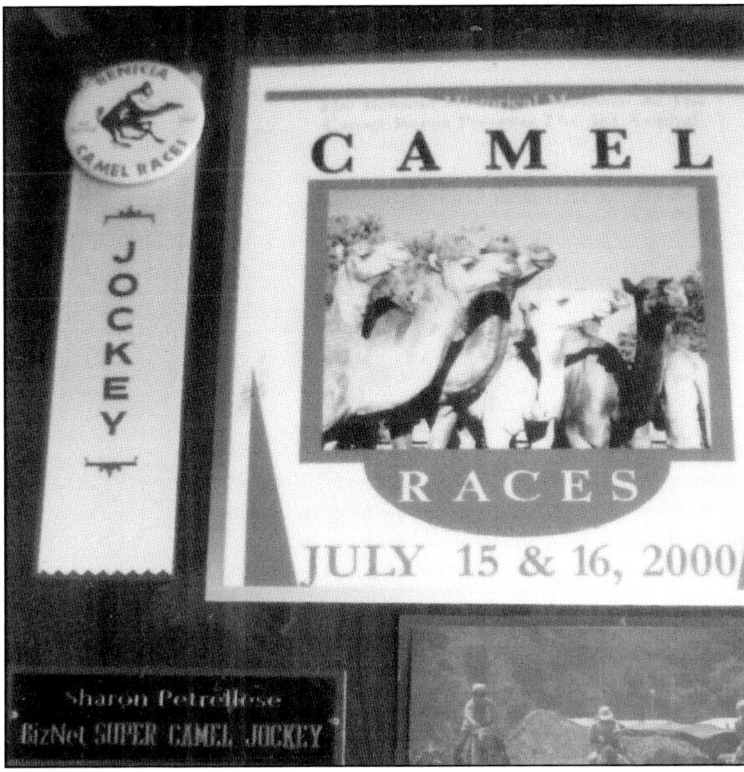

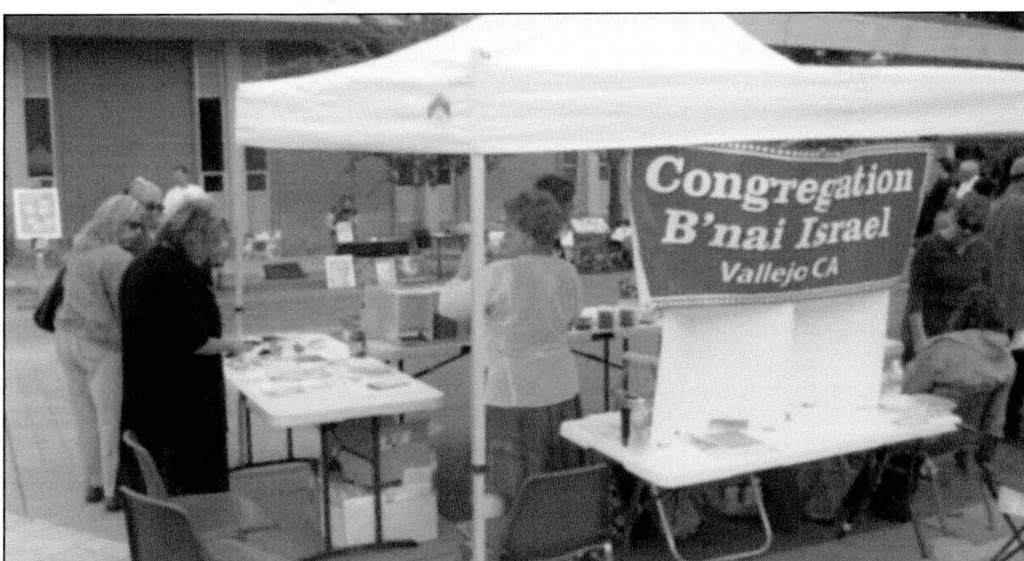

The civic group Vallejo Together, created in 2010 by independent filmmaker Maria Guevara in response to a rash of youth-related violence in the city, resurrected a long dormant Vallejo event called Unity Day. Its earlier incarnation was held on a Saturday, excluding the religious Jewish community. Upon learning this, Maria consulted with the group, the day was moved to a Sunday in September, and CBI and Hadassah have participated annually ever since. (Courtesy of the Zrihen family.)

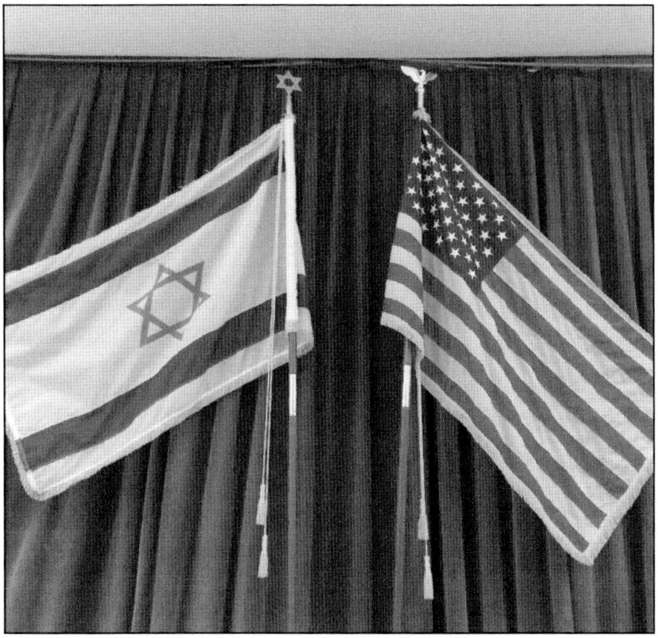

A dormant annual Israel Independence Day festival—which included Israeli food, music, and dancing, along with various vendors and displays—was restarted at CBI in 2011 by Melissa Edwards and Rachel Raskin-Zrihen. One year, Israel's regional deputy consul general to the United States, Gideon Lustig, served as the guest speaker. Friends of the IDF was featured one year, and, another year, the Indian Jewish comic Samson Koletkar provided the entertainment. (Courtesy of R. Zrihen.)

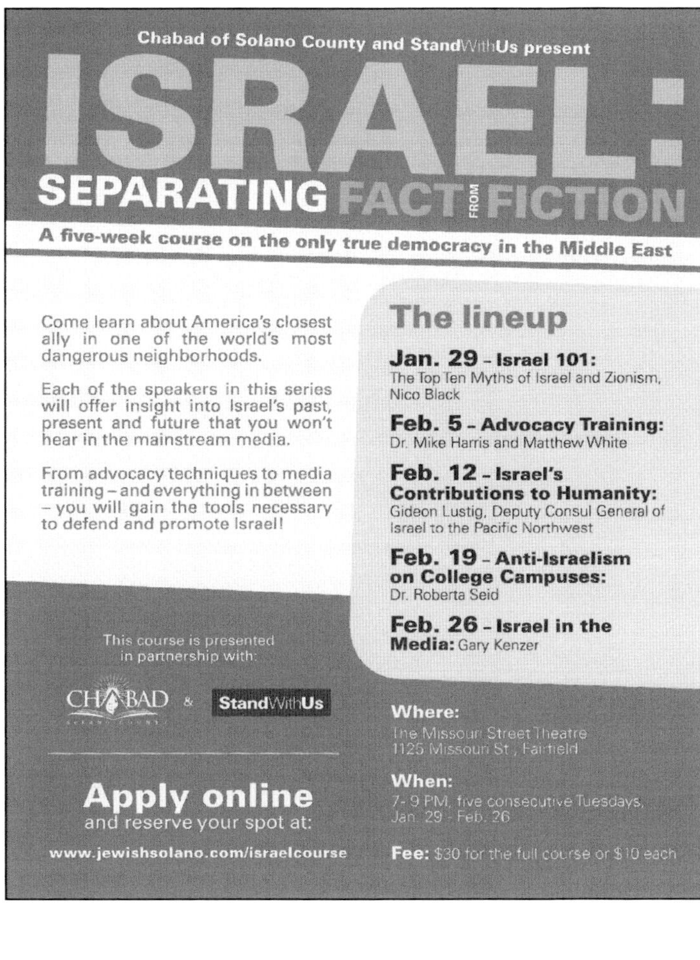

Concerned with growing anti-Semitism worldwide and in the United States, Chabad of Solano County and Rachel Raskin-Zrihen worked with the pro-Israel group Stand With Us to produce a public lecture series in 2013. Designed to arm participants with information for countering pro-Palestinian historical revisionism, lecture topics included the top 10 myths about Zionism, Israel's contributions to humanity, anti-Israelism on college campuses, and Israel in the media. (Chabad.)

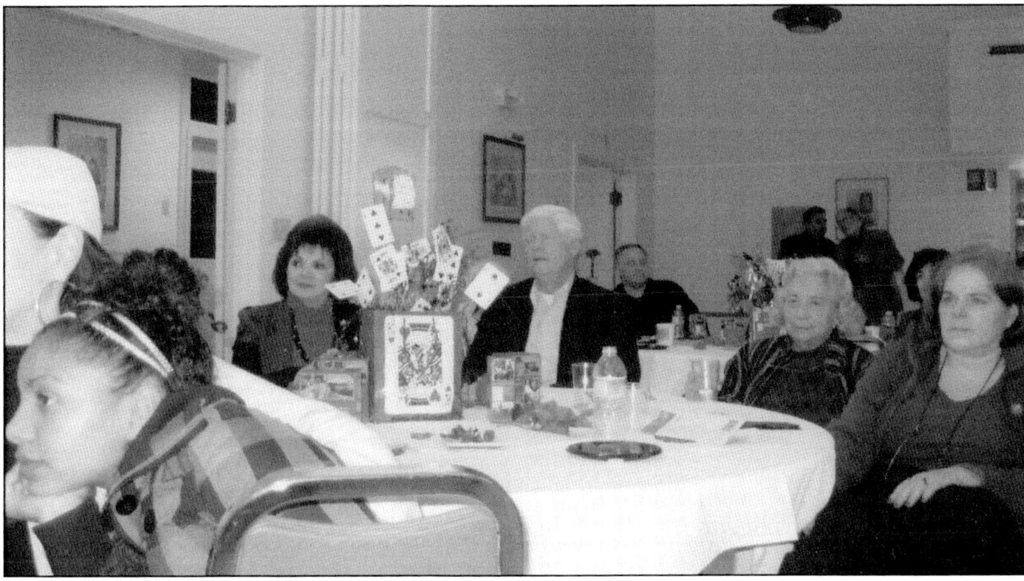

Established by Frieda and Seymour Marcuse around 1974, the 52/100 fundraiser became an annual event for the local Hadassah chapter. The idea was to sell 52 cards for $100 each and award prizes. Today, this fundraiser and dinner—organized by Nadine Goodban—attracts elected officials and community members, like Vallejo city councilman Robert McConnell and his wife, Paula, and Benicia's mayor, Elizabeth Patterson. (SDN.)

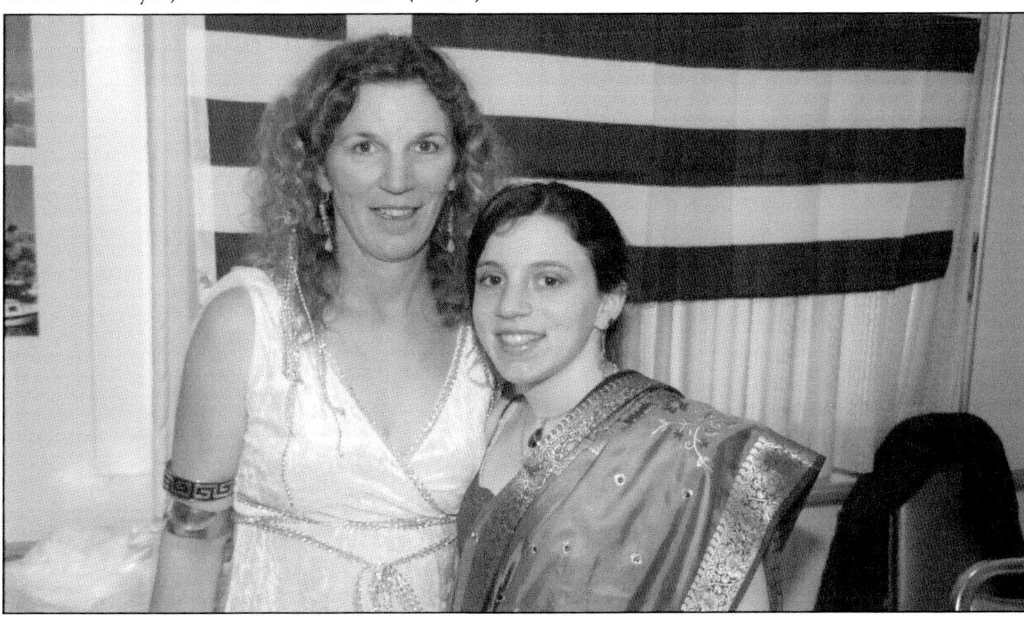

Above, Melissa Edwards and daughter Hannah Silverman participated in the 1994 International Food Night fundraiser produced by Yoram Rosenmann and Helene Falk for CBI. That year, cuisine from China, India, Japan, Korea, the Philippines, and Thailand was paired with Japanese, Polynesian, and Indian dancers. The next year, Mediterranean, Egyptian, French, Israeli, Greek, Italian, and Spanish food was accompanied by belly dancers, Mediterranean music, and Israeli dancing. Other years included foods from Africa, Mexico, Russia, and "around the USA," with each attracting more than 100 guests. (CBI.)

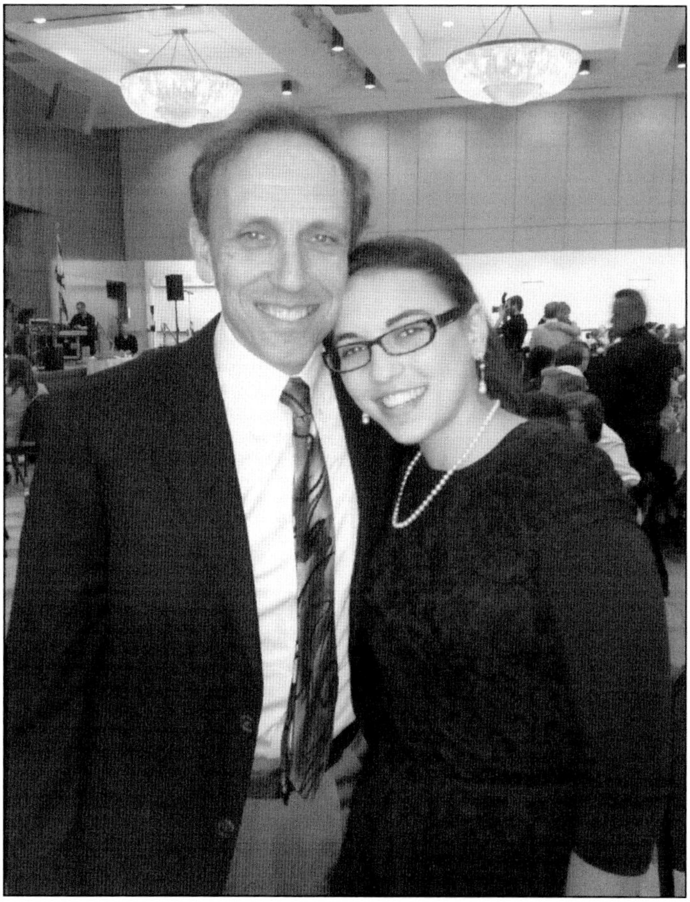

Vacaville High School's Carolyn Fine avoided making her graduation speech in person on Shavuot, pre-recording the speech and playing it as she stood by in obedience of Jewish law. Recognizing that being valedictorian was a "huge" honor, Carolyn walked to graduation and skipped being photographed, because it required electricity. Quoted in a newspaper article, she said that she would always remember graduation as the day she put her faith first. (Courtesy of the Fine family.)

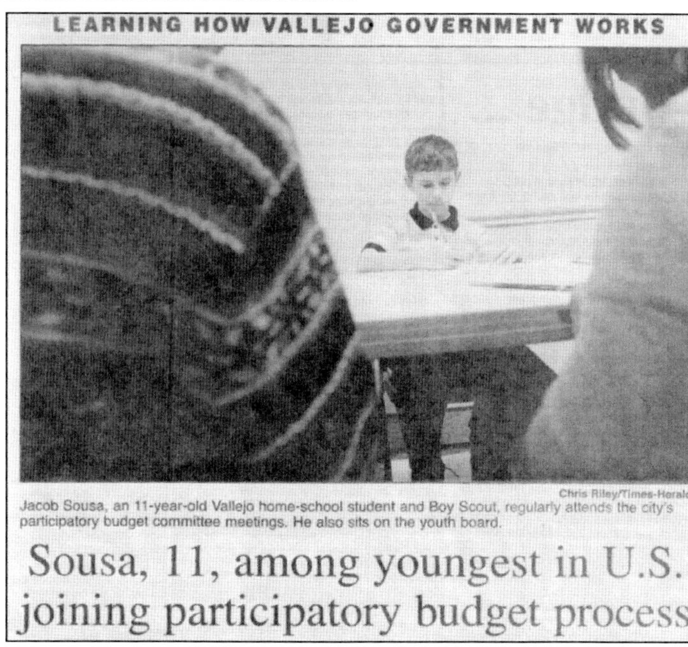

LEARNING HOW VALLEJO GOVERNMENT WORKS

Chris Riley/Times-Herald

Jacob Sousa, an 11-year-old Vallejo home-school student and Boy Scout, regularly attends the city's participatory budget committee meetings. He also sits on the youth board.

Sousa, 11, among youngest in U.S. joining participatory budget process

At age 11, Jacob Sousa became the youngest person in the United States to be involved in the participatory budgeting process after Vallejo entered into the process in 2013. Jacob has sponsored two fundraising booths for Alex's Lemonade Stand Foundation for Childhood Cancer. He made homemade lemonade and lemon sugar cookies, advertising the enterprise with flyers. His efforts made the paper in both years, at ages 9 and 11. He raised over $1,500. (VTH.)

Seven

CELEBRATIONS

שמחות (SIMCHOT)

סימכע (SIMCHA)

. . . Of a Jewish life, filled with commemorations

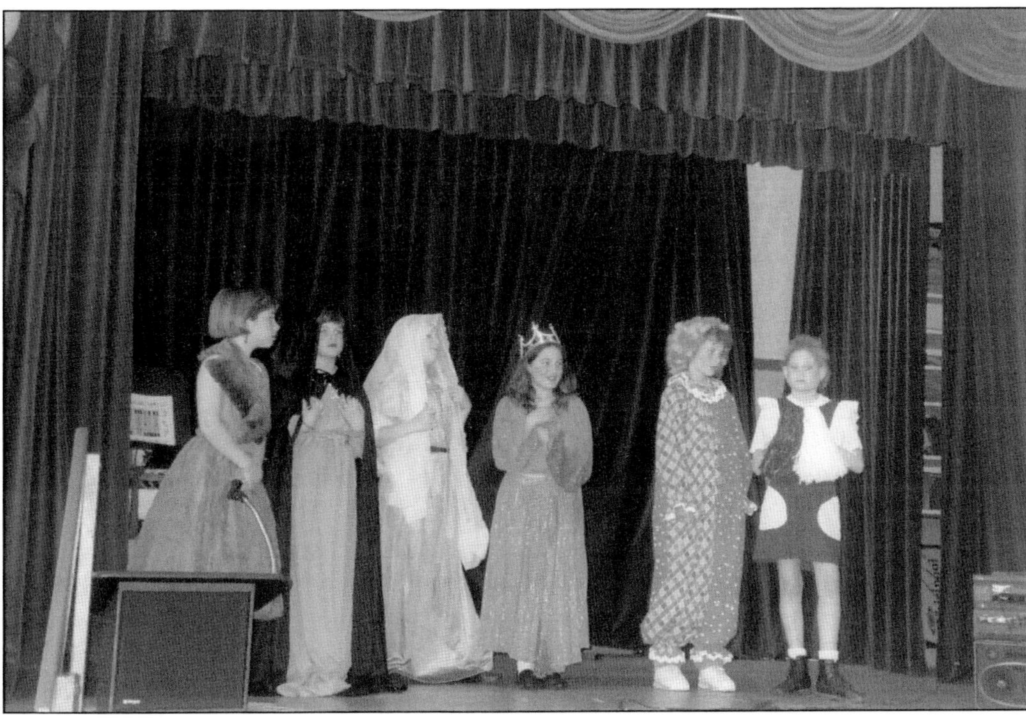

Hanukkah, Passover, Tu B'Shevat, and Shavuot are among the holidays that a Jewish community celebrates together, but they are not the only things honored. There are also life-cycle events like Brit Milah (circumcision), B'nai Mitzvot, confirmations, weddings, and even funerals. Pictured here is a Purim celebration from the early 1990s that featured, from left to right, Rachel Joseph, unidentified, Sarah Wiese, Alexandra Nurik, Katie Goudie, and Yael Rosenmann in costume on the CBI stage. (SDN.)

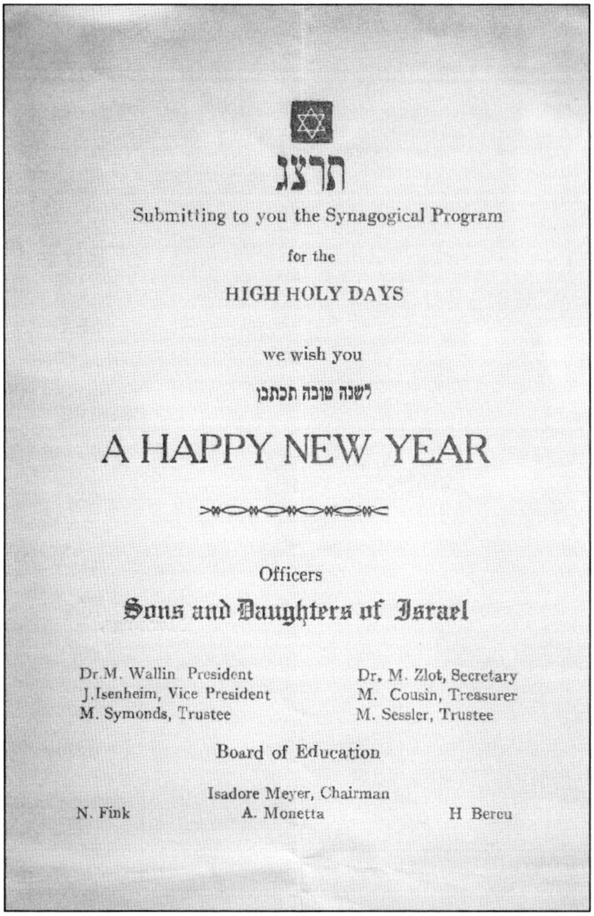

תרצג

Submitting to you the Synagogical Program

for the

HIGH HOLY DAYS

we wish you

לשנה טובה תכתבו

A HAPPY NEW YEAR

Officers

Sons and Daughters of Israel

Dr.M. Wallin President
J.Isenheim, Vice President
M. Symonds, Trustee

Dr. M. Zlot, Secretary
M. Cousin, Treasurer
M. Sessler, Trustee

Board of Education

Isadore Meyer, Chairman

N. Fink A. Monetta H Bercu

The first holiday of the Jewish calendar is the New Year, or Rosh Hashanah in Hebrew. Celebrations begin with sweet, round challahs (braided egg breads) and apples dipped in honey. Pictured at left is a program describing the Rosh Hashanah services held at Sons & Daughters of Israel in 1935. Named on the brochure are the officers of the congregation. Pictured below are congregation members dressed—along with the ark, podium covers and the rabbi's *kittel* (robe)—all in white as is customary among Ashkenazi Jews at Rosh Hashanah and Yom Kippur (Day of Atonement). Wearing white symbolizes purity, and most celebrants wear new garments symbolizing beginnings as they await the sounding of the shofar (ram's horn)—an ancient call to arouse the soul, proclaim liberty, and to look inward and upward. (Both, CBI.)

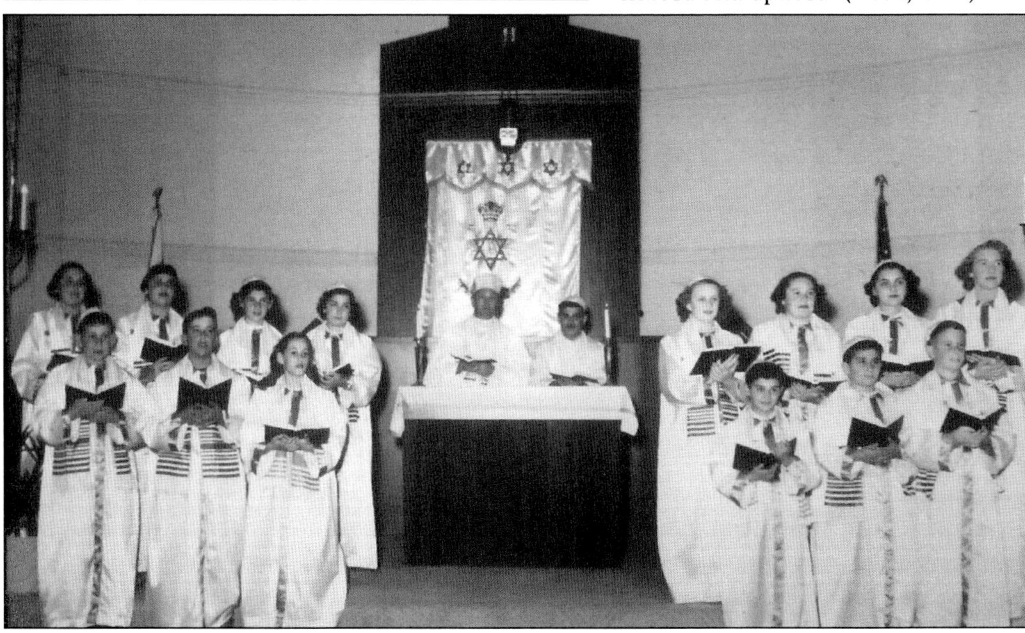

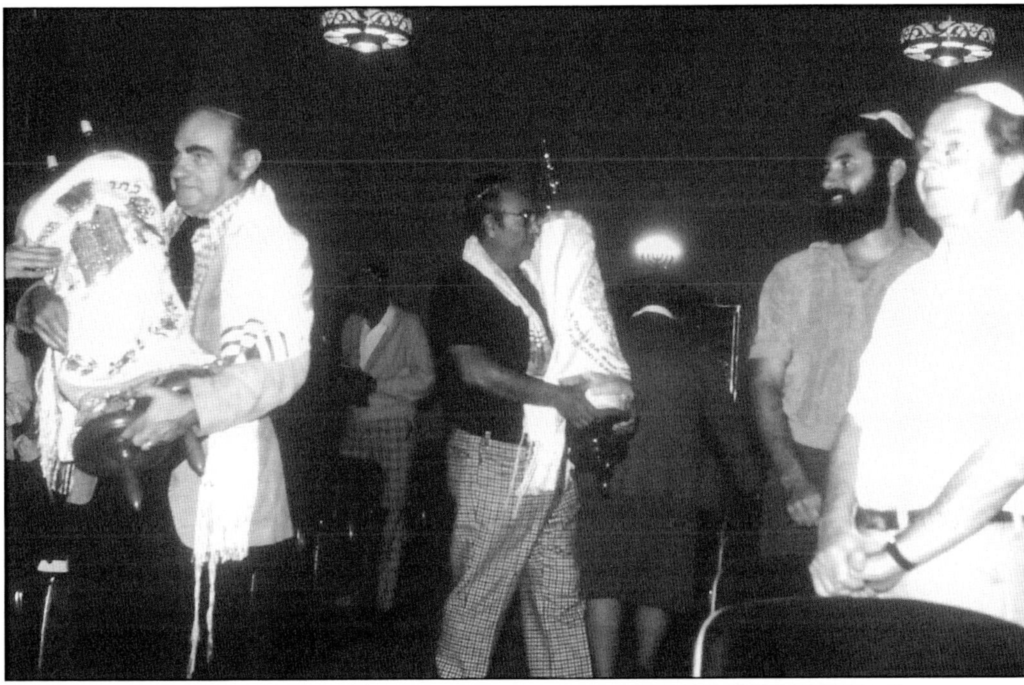

Following Yom Kippur is the Sukkot harvest holiday, which involves eating outside in a palm-frond or branch-covered hut. Biblical ancestors and other guests are traditionally invited. Following Sukkot is Simchat Torah, when Jews rejoice the annual completion of the Torah reading and the beginning of a new cycle. In the picture, Walter Bogner, Alan Rothman, and others are dancing with Torahs on this most joyous day of the year. (CBI.)

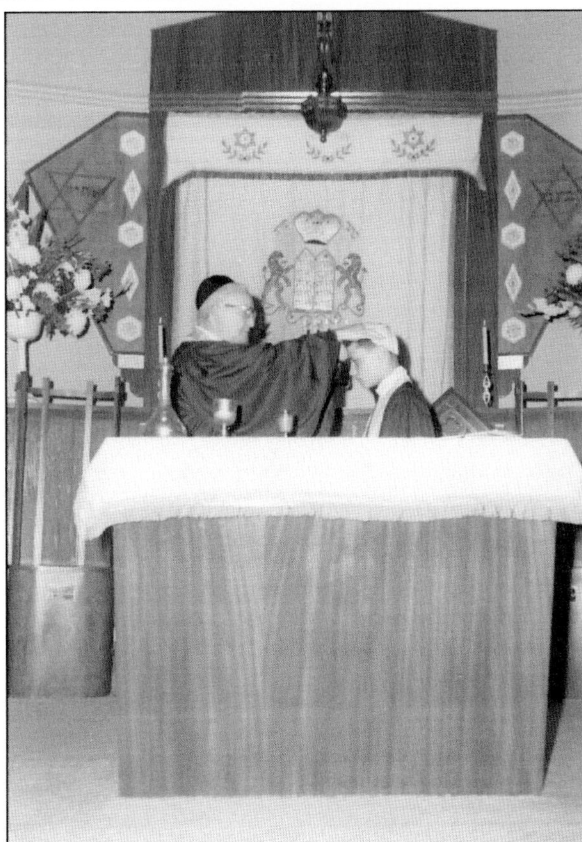

In a Jewish child's 12th or 13th year comes a traditional coming-of-age rite, the Bar or Bat Mitzvah. This ritual signifies that, religiously speaking, the child is now accountable for his or her actions. The young adult is called to the Torah to read the weekly portion and then explain it. Pictured here, Rabbi Sol Horowitz is saying a blessing over Bar Mitzvah boy Ralph Pierce. (Courtesy of Ralph Pierce.)

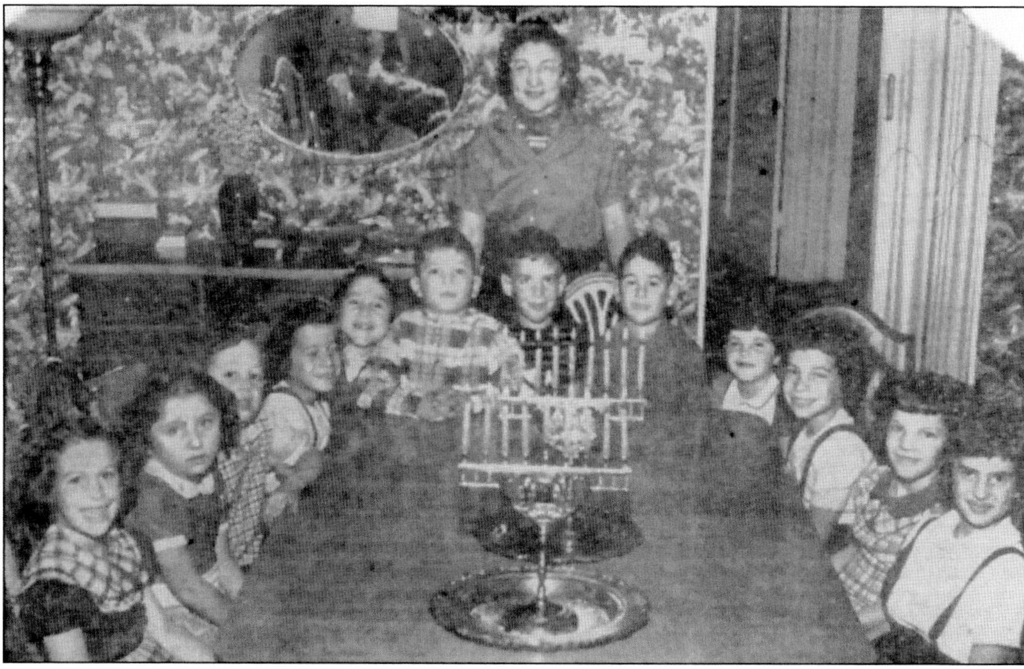

Chanukah, the festival of rededication that is also known as the Festival of Lights, commemorates the Maccabees' victory over the Assyrians, thus saving the right to be Jewish. Returning to Jerusalem, they discovered oil to relight the Nir Tamid (Everlasting Light), and miraculously, it lasted the eight days needed to get new oil. The photograph above depicts a children's program about the holiday in 1955, organized by Rebbetzin Jennie Horowitz. Pictured are children from the Rothman, Bogner, Garelick, Bonderow, Miller, Levine, Garber, Meyer, and Koppell families. In the photograph below, Rabbi David Kopstein—who led the congregation through much of the late 1980s and early 1990s—helps several of the congregation's children light the menorah for the seventh night of Chanukah in December 1988. From left to right, they are Steven Pierce, 4; Ross Meltzer, 10; Dov Rollins, 9; and Erin Fuchs, 7. (Both, CBI.)

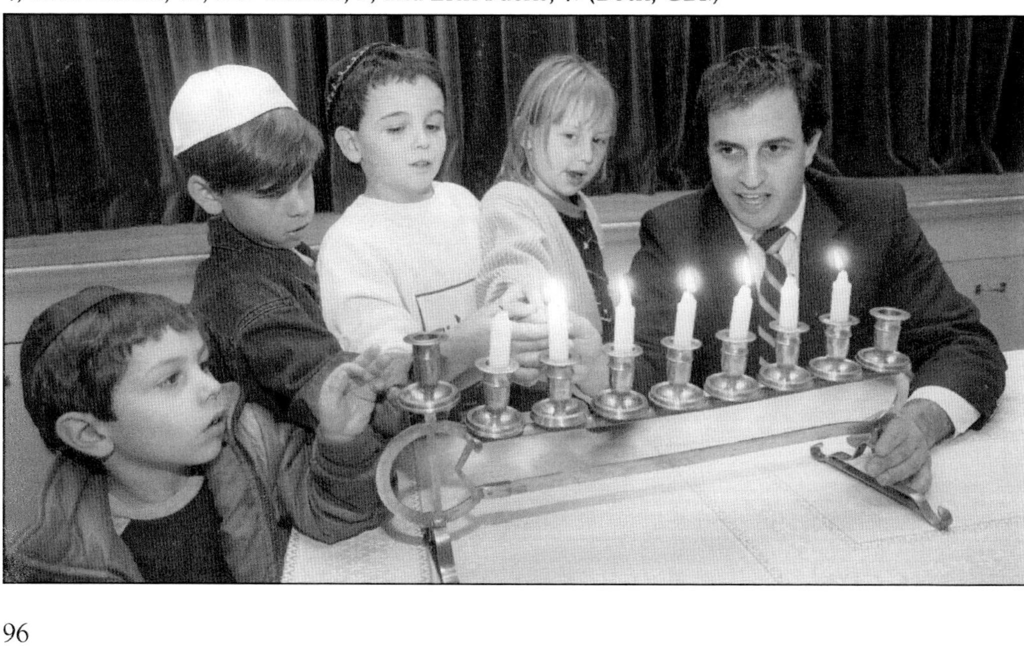

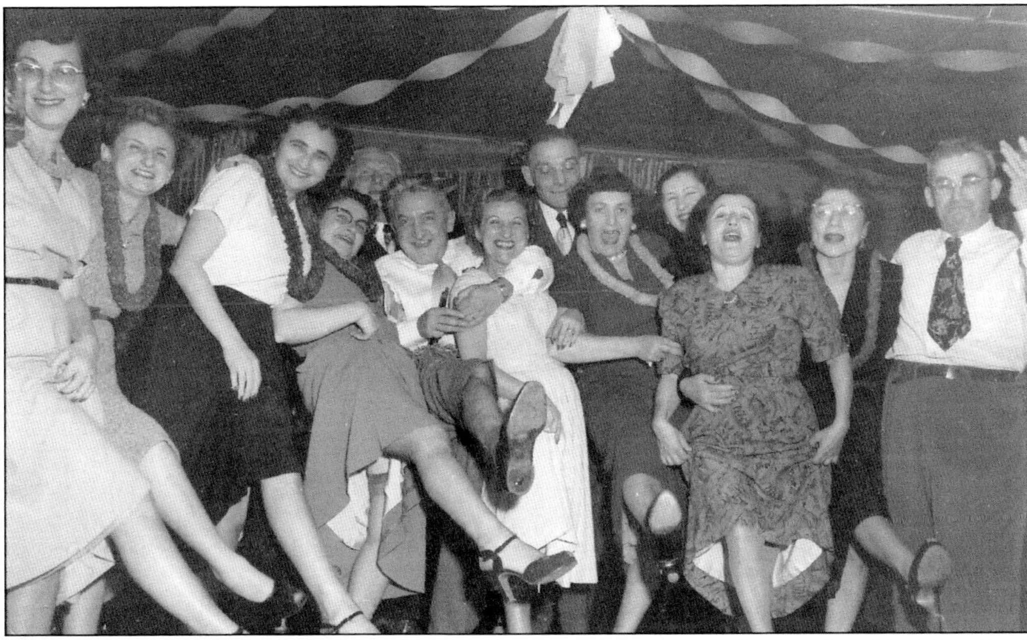

Along with Jewish holy days, the congregation also celebrates secular holidays like New Year's Eve. According to Bernie Monetta, this c. 1951 photograph shows "The Vallejo Gang kicking up their heels in revelry" during a New Year's Eve party. Community members often also gather to share in each other's life-cycle events. (Courtesy of Bernard Monetta.)

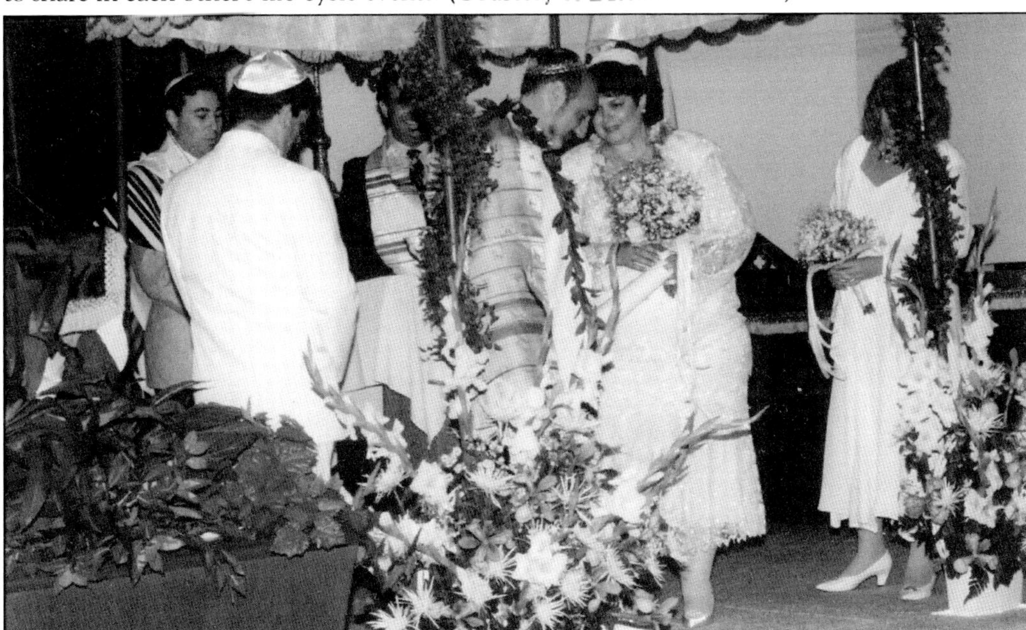

Weddings are very special occasions in Jewish life. The bride and groom stand with family members and honored guests along with a rabbi under a chuppah (canopy). Traditions include seven blessings, the signing of the *ketuba* (marriage contract), and the breaking of a glass at the ceremony's conclusion. Pictured is the wedding of Shari and Allen Salomon at Congregation B'nai Israel. (CBI.)

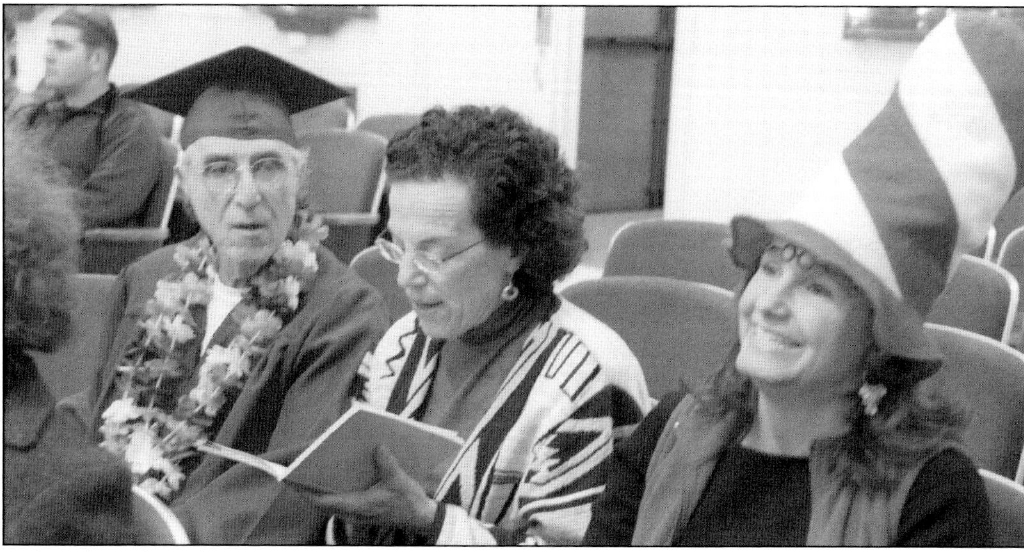

"That they should make them days of feasting and gladness, and of sending portions one to another, and gifts to the poor." So commands G-d in the Book of Esther (Megillah, Esther 9:22) on the holiday called Purim. With costumes and noisemakers to drown out the name of the villain Haman, Max Schleicher, Betsy Strauss, and Cindy Noonan are pictured above, from left to right, at the reading of the Gantze (Whole) Megillah. Purim services often include the performing of skits and parodies to tell this story, and celebrations follow with carnival games, the enjoying of *hamentashen* (triangular fruit-filled pastries), and the delivery of food baskets. Pictured below, Danny Zrihen, Courtney Harris, Dee ChristianScher, Rachel Levy, Melissa Edwards, Helene Falk, Josh Kreamer, and Hannah Groody, with others, attend a CBI Purim carnival. (Above, courtesy of Donna Plantz; below, courtesy of the Zrihen family.)

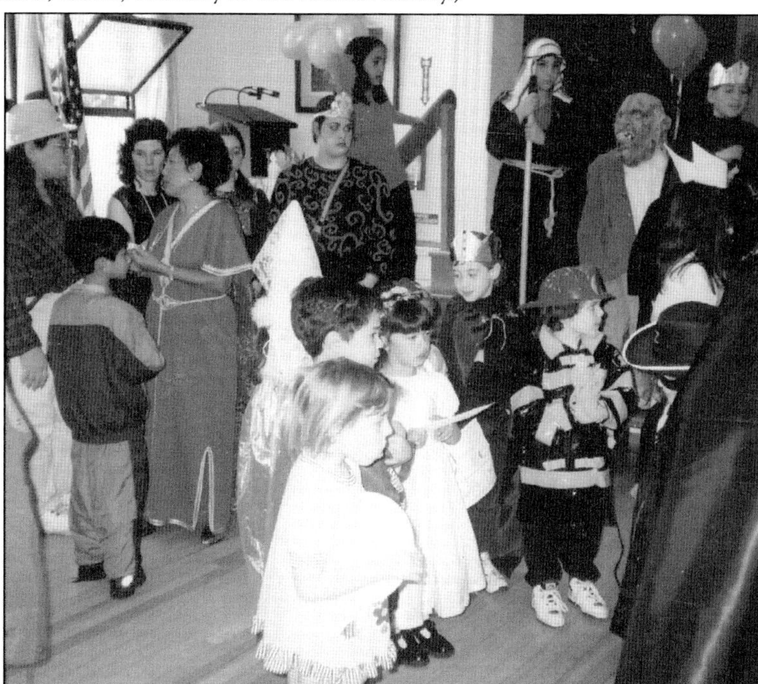

The Jewish community went all out to celebrate the Nebraska Street property's mortgage redemption on April 4, 1965, holding a formal dinner. The first building, at 512 York Street, was purchased in 1920 and its mortgage redeemed in 1925. Twenty years later, the Nebraska Street property was purchased. Groundbreaking ceremonies were held in 1947, and the building was dedicated in 1948. In 1958, the social hall and school building were added. (CBI.)

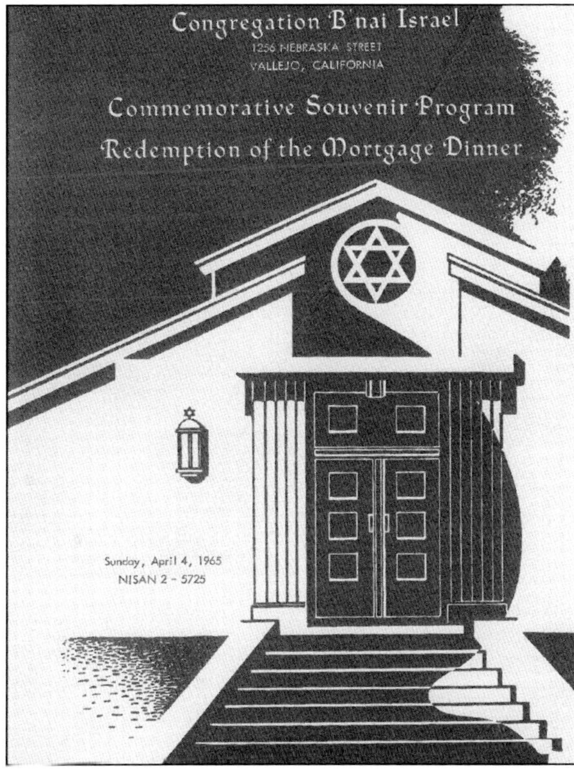

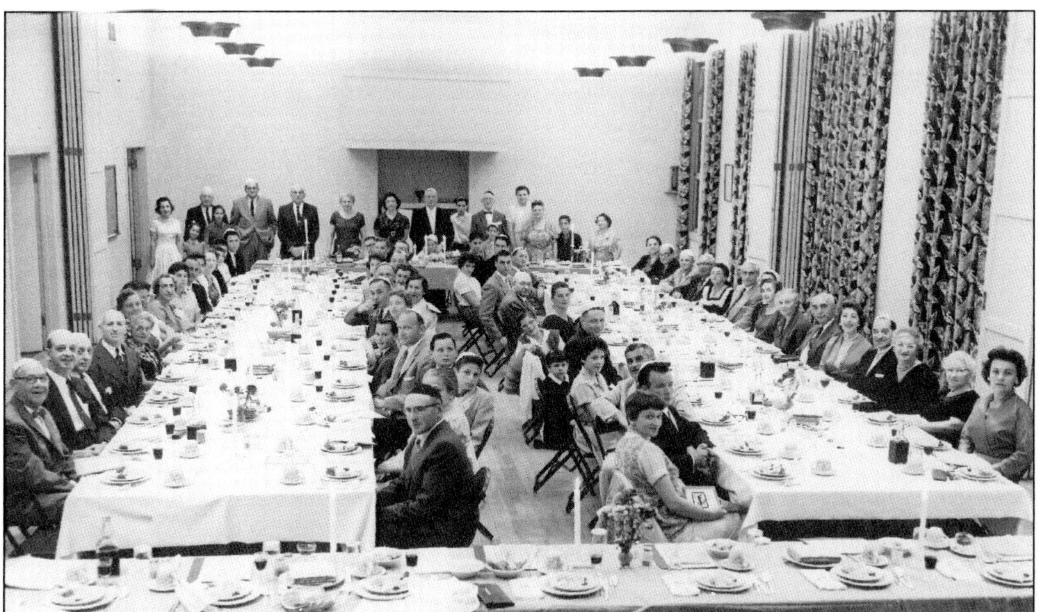

At least 60 people attended this community Passover Seder, held in the CBI social hall in the early 1950s. Passover is the spring holiday of freedom and renewal. The Seder is a special meal during which the story of the Hebrews' Exodus from slavery in Egypt and the Jewish nation's birth under Moses' leadership is retold annually. "Next year in Jerusalem," are the last words said at every Seder. (CBI.)

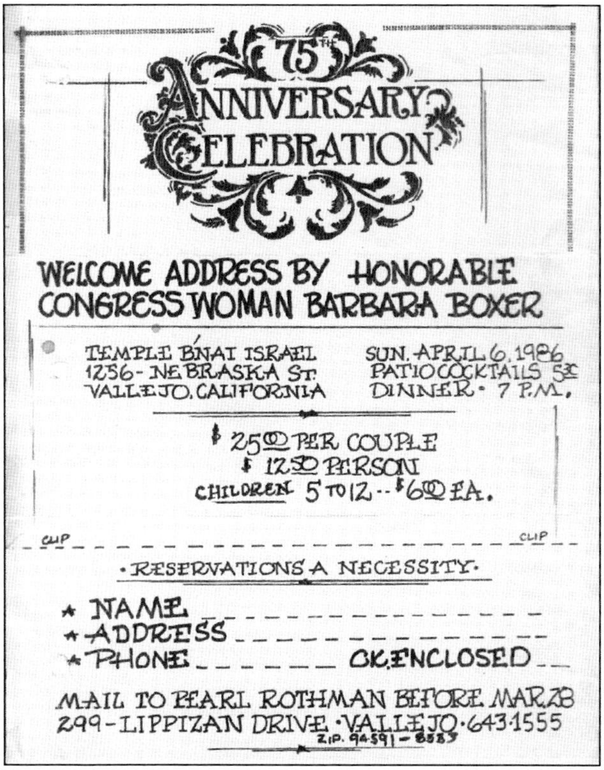

75th ANNIVERSARY CELEBRATION

WELCOME ADDRESS BY HONORABLE CONGRESSWOMAN BARBARA BOXER

TEMPLE B'NAI ISRAEL
1236- NEBRASKA ST.
VALLEJO, CALIFORNIA

SUN. APRIL 6, 1986
PATIO COCKTAILS 5:30
DINNER - 7 P.M.

$25.00 PER COUPLE
$12.50 PERSON
CHILDREN 5 TO 12 -- $6.00 EA.

CLIP - CLIP

· RESERVATIONS A NECESSITY ·

* NAME ______________
* ADDRESS ______________
* PHONE ________ CK. ENCLOSED ___

MAIL TO PEARL ROTHMAN BEFORE MAR 28
299 - LIPPIZAN DRIVE · VALLEJO · 643-1555
ZIP. 94591 - 8583

On April 6, 1986, members of Congregation B'nai Israel gathered to celebrate the 75th anniversary of the organization. Manny Gorland was the president, and MC Harry Gray introduced Rabbi Leo Abrami, who gave the invocation. Irving Scott led the Pledge of Allegiance and Ha Tikvah before Rep. Barbara Boxer gave the keynote address. (VTH.)

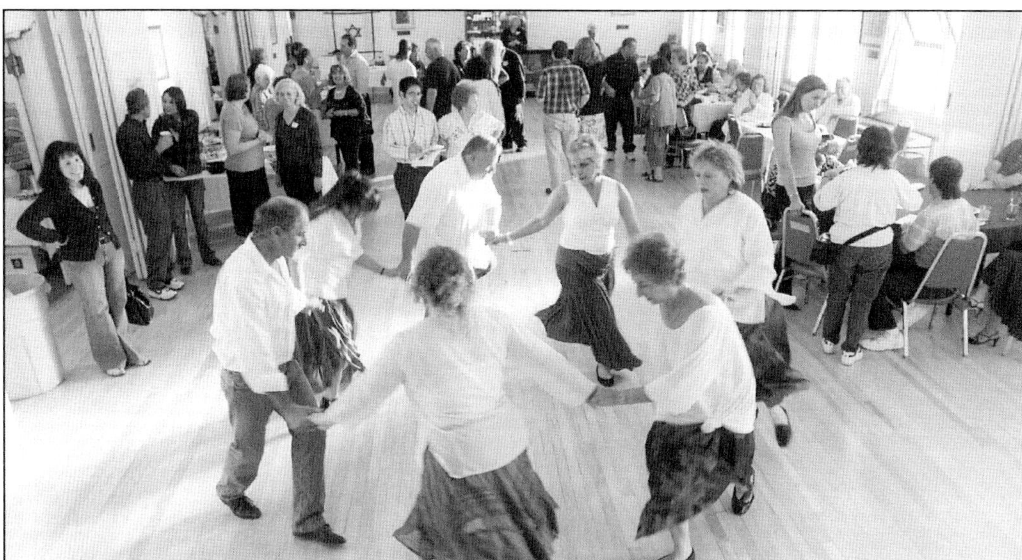

During the 60th anniversary of the congregation's founding, Danny Jacob, Jessica Pechner, Ralph and Fahni Pierce, Rachel Lessem, Nadine Goodban, and Rachel Zrihen gave a demonstration of Israeli folk dancing. Copresidents in 2008, Vicki Kemmerer and Gail Lamkins said that Solano County's Jewish pioneers had "the vision, the insight and the sheer determination" to provide "a religious home for generations." Dozens gathered to enjoy the exhibits, entertainment, and refreshments. (VTH.)

Eight

MILITARY AND WARTIME

צבא ומלחמות (TSAVA V'MILCHAMOT)

מיליטעריש און וואָרטיים (MYLYT'RYS UN VARTYYM)

. . . Heroes to be remembered

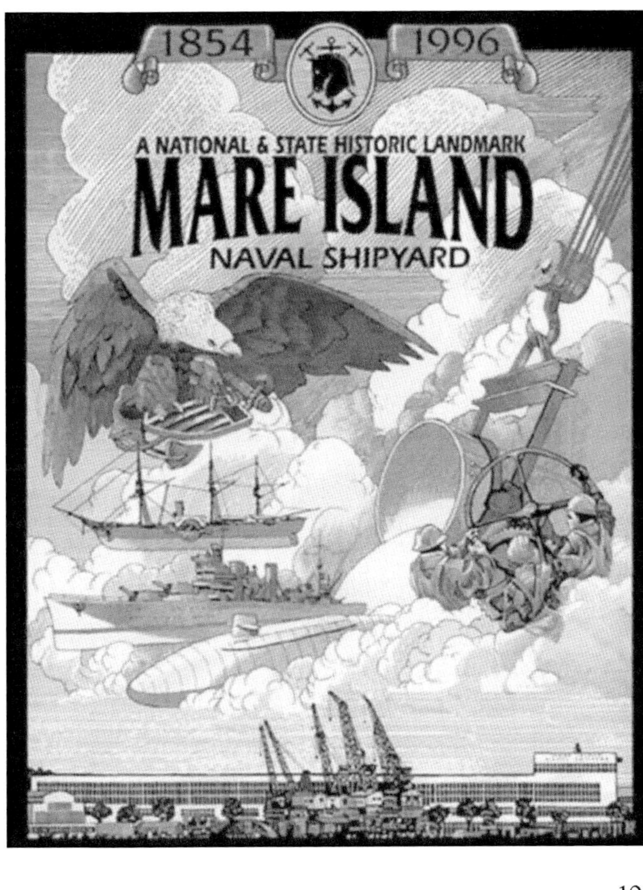

Solano County's Jews have struggled, lived, and died through all of America's conflicts since the Civil War. They suffered with their brethren through the Holocaust, joining the US military; celebrated the rebirth of the Jewish state; and watched with alarm as Israel was attacked by its Arab neighbors. Several Holocaust survivors have also called Solano County home. (VHM.)

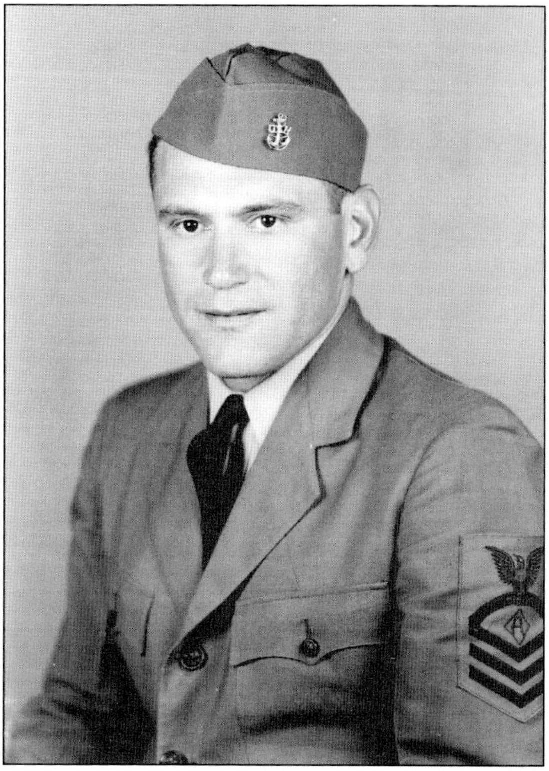

Seen here in uniform, Harry Gray—son of CBI's first rabbi—became a professor of history at Solano Community College and authored several books containing photographs of Jewish personalities, cemeteries, and institutions in California; programs and themes of western and Jewish historic interest; material on general Judaica; and the history of the western United States and the 1967 Arab-Israeli War. He also wrote, produced, and performed in several productions at CBI. (CBI.)

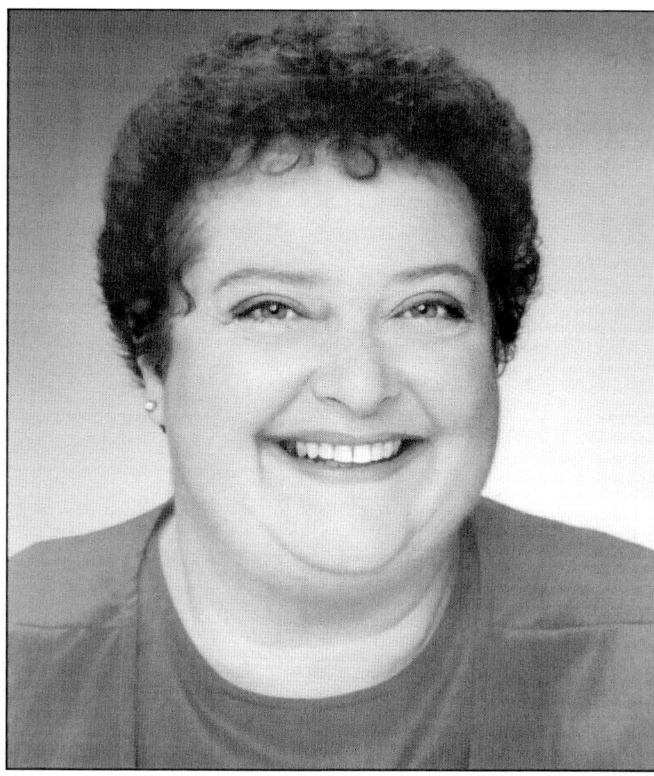

A lieutenant colonel, US Air Force dietician, actress, and comedienne, Bernice Kaylin served for more than 20 years. Until 1986, she was a medical inspector at Travis Air Force Base's David Grant Hospital, where she earned a Meritorious Service Medal. She later pursued a career in theater and stand-up comedy and became part of Chabad of Solano County. (Courtesy of B. Kaylin.)

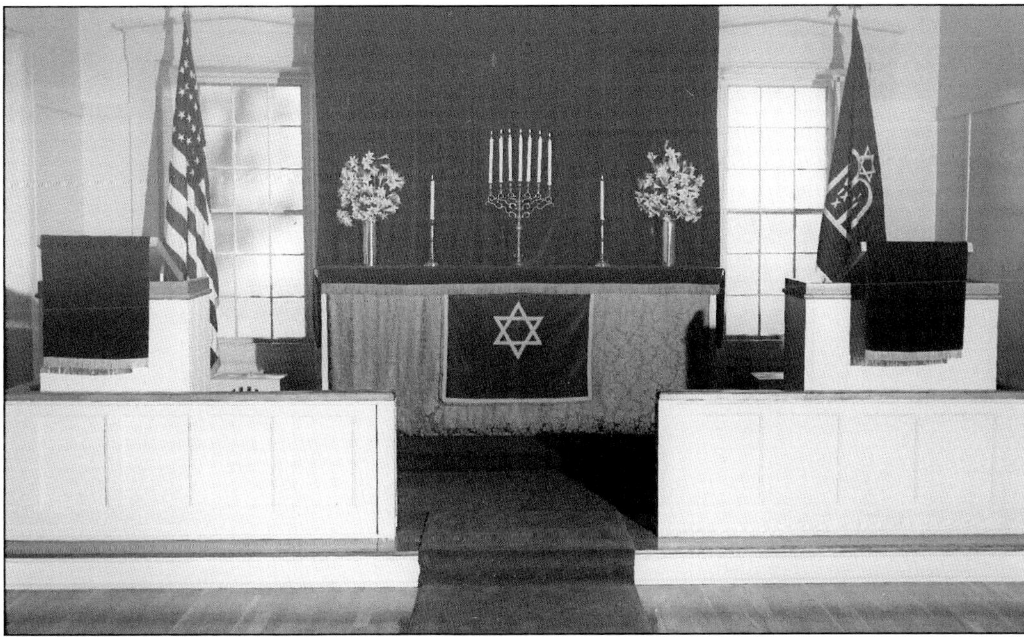

During World War II, one of the Benicia Arsenal's old stone buildings was turned into a chapel where Italian prisoners of war and California Youth Authority boys could attend services. In the "Little Chapel on the Hill," Catholic, Protestant, and Jewish services were held at different times. Shown in the photograph below are Jewish community members and military personal—some wearing the traditional tallith—holding the Torah. The Enduring Traditions program protects the free exercise of religion for Jews serving in the US armed forces. The US Department of Defense appointed the Aleph Institute to recruit and endorse rabbis to serve in the military as chaplains. Aleph supports the troops by sending packages to soldiers for every Jewish holiday, along with Hebrew and English books of Psalms. It also supplies spiritual and moral support. (Both, BHM.)

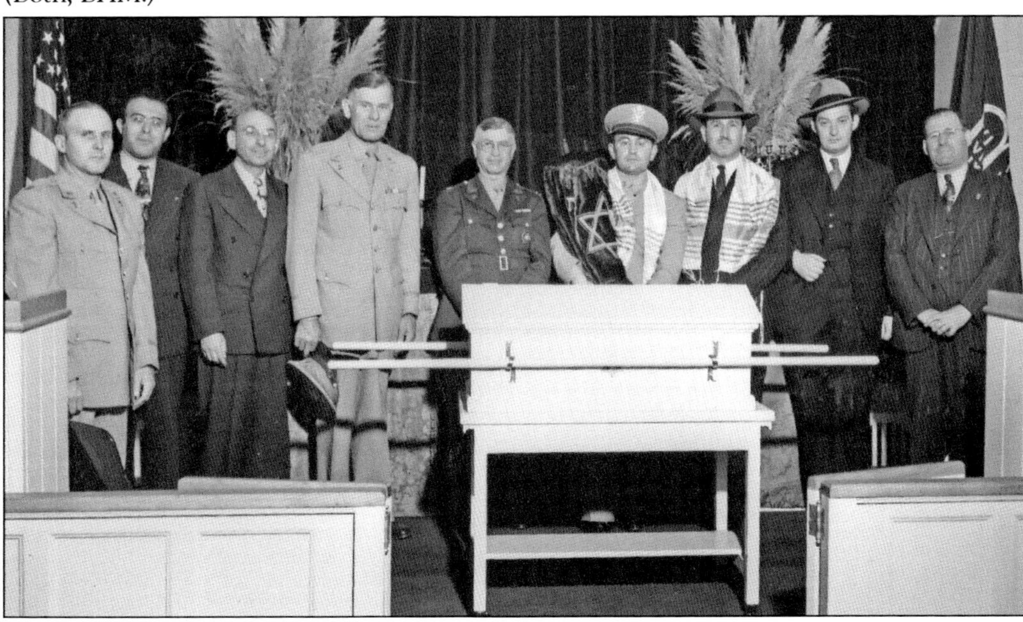

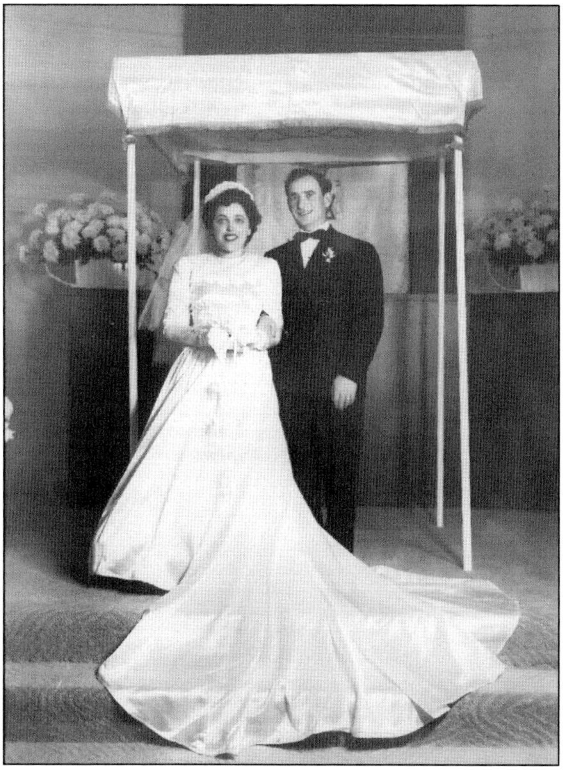

An Auschwitz survivor, tattooed 70173, Marty Rothman sued the I.G. Farben trust in 1954 for forcing him into slave labor during the Holocaust. After helping his US Army liberators hunt Nazi war criminals, he immigrated in 1946. He was working at 20th Century Fox when he was introduced to Pearl Pizante, a Vallejoan whom he married in 1948 in the new synagogue's first wedding. Pearl's parents were the first wed in the York Street temple. Often speaking at schools, Rothman said that his terrible Holocaust memories were tempered by his pride at Israel's founding and by his eldest daughter, Rita, volunteering for the Yom Kippur War. He and his brothers, Bernard and Alan, were among the survivors who returned to Germany in 1988 at the invitation of the mayor of their hometown of Hamburg. In 1979, Rothman headed the local Jewish War Veterans chapter. (Left, courtesy of P. Rothman; below, CBI.)

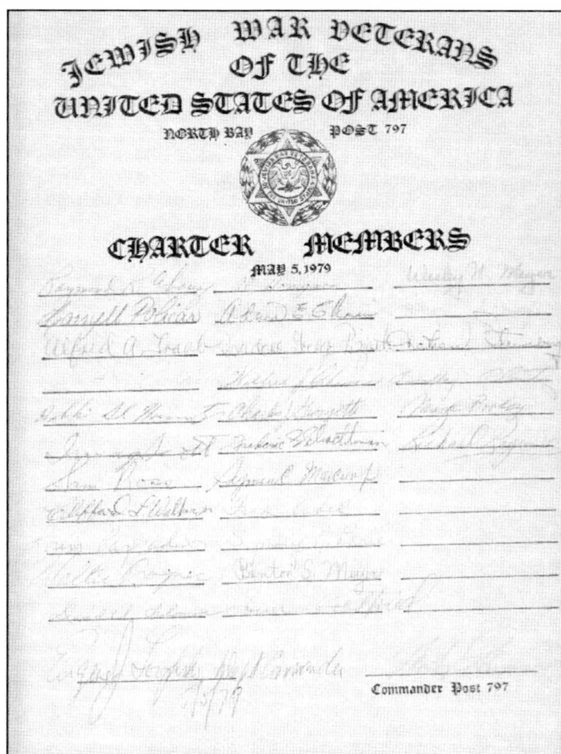

Jewish War Veterans of the United States of America

North Bay Post 797

Charter Members

May 5, 1979

Commander Post 797

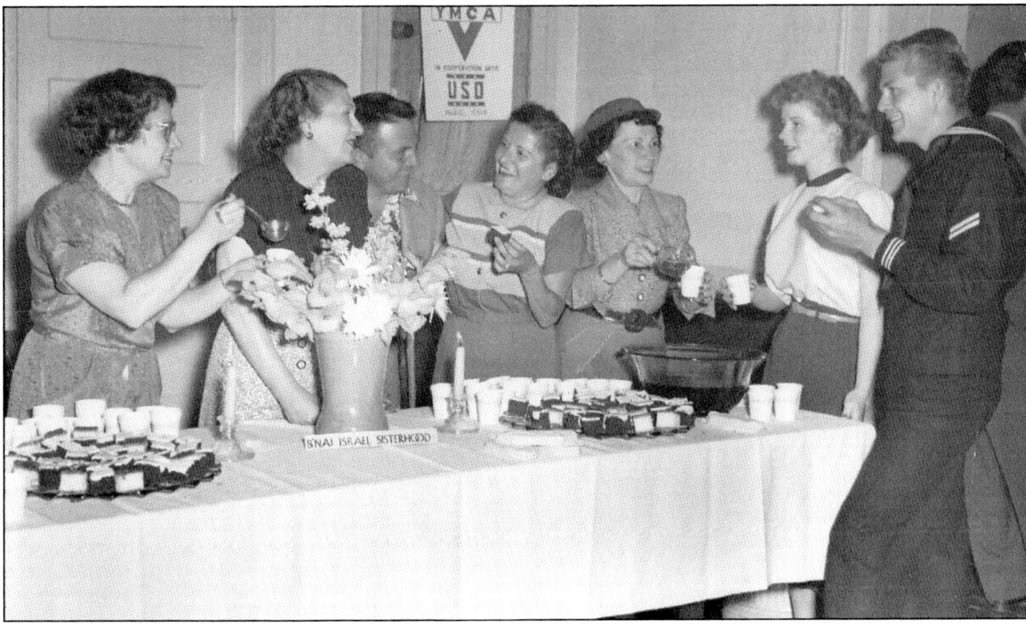

During World War II, Solano County's Jewish community was as dedicated to doing its part for the war effort as any one else. Here, several members of the B'nai Israel Sisterhood serve beverages to a sailor at Vallejo's USO. Pictured, from left to right, are Sylvia Weinberg, Mrs. Sidney Marks, Burt Sheehan, Kate Monetta, Mrs. Edward Woods, USO member Helen Fredricksen, and sailor Jack Rucker. (Courtesy of Bernard Monetta.)

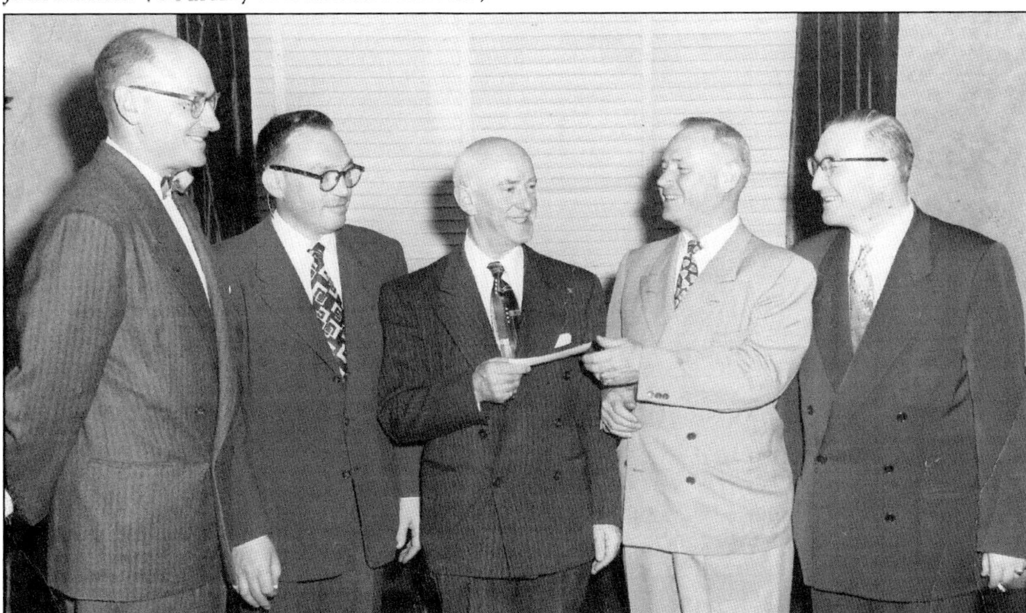

Pictured here, Isadore Meyer (center) is presenting a check to purchase Israel Bonds in 1952. In 1950, after the War of Independence—which devastated the new nation's economy—David Ben Gurion conceived the idea of creating bonds to help Israel. He turned to the Diaspora community for help. Dr. Morris Zlot, to the left of Meyer, encouraged the purchase of Israel Bonds during High Holiday services until his death in 1997. (CBI.)

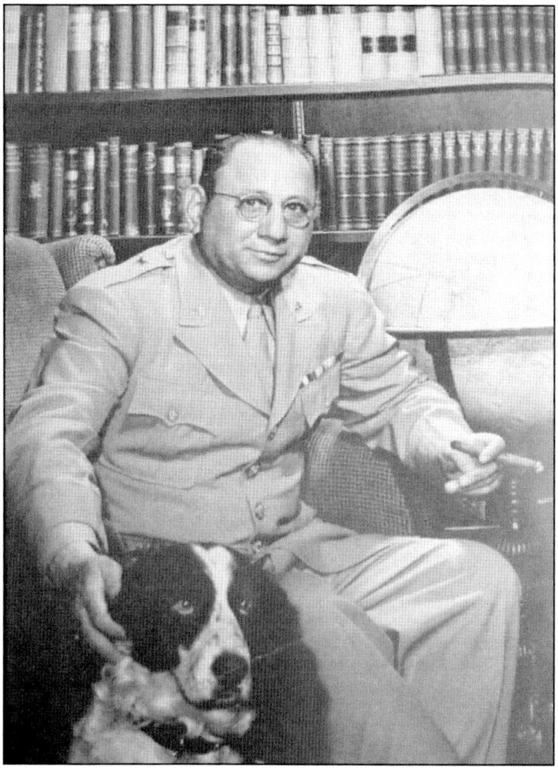

Col. Raphael Chavin (left) commanded the Benicia Arsenal from 1950 to 1953. When he first reported there, he read a Solano County Grand Jury statement by ex-Benicia city councilman Sol Rose that prompted Chavin to warn that the arsenal would close if vice wasn't addressed. It closed in 1964. When he retired, a dinner honoring Chavin was attended by arsenal employees and citizens of Vallejo and Benicia, who said "Colonel Chavin's military career has been marked with outstanding service," and "Industrialists and educators, as well as his civilian and military associates have marveled at his business and managerial ability which he has utilized to the utmost in all his military duties." During Chavin's tenure, Capt. Myron Meiselman (below) destroyed the three slot machines in the officer's mess after the federal government banned them. Also on the official Benicia Arsenal commanders list is Col. Alfred Mordecai, who served from 1899 to 1902. (Both, BHM.)

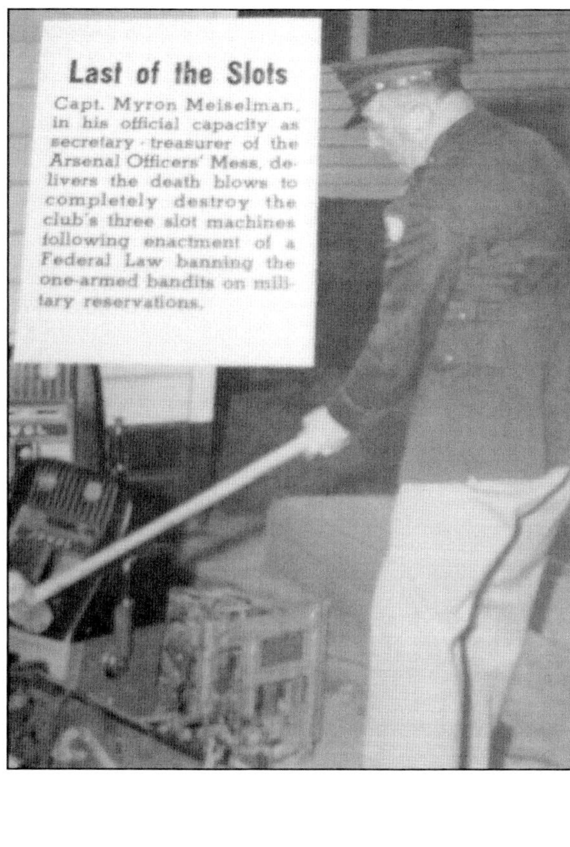

Last of the Slots

Capt. Myron Meiselman, in his official capacity as secretary - treasurer of the Arsenal Officers' Mess, delivers the death blows to completely destroy the club's three slot machines following enactment of a Federal Law banning the one-armed bandits on military reservations.

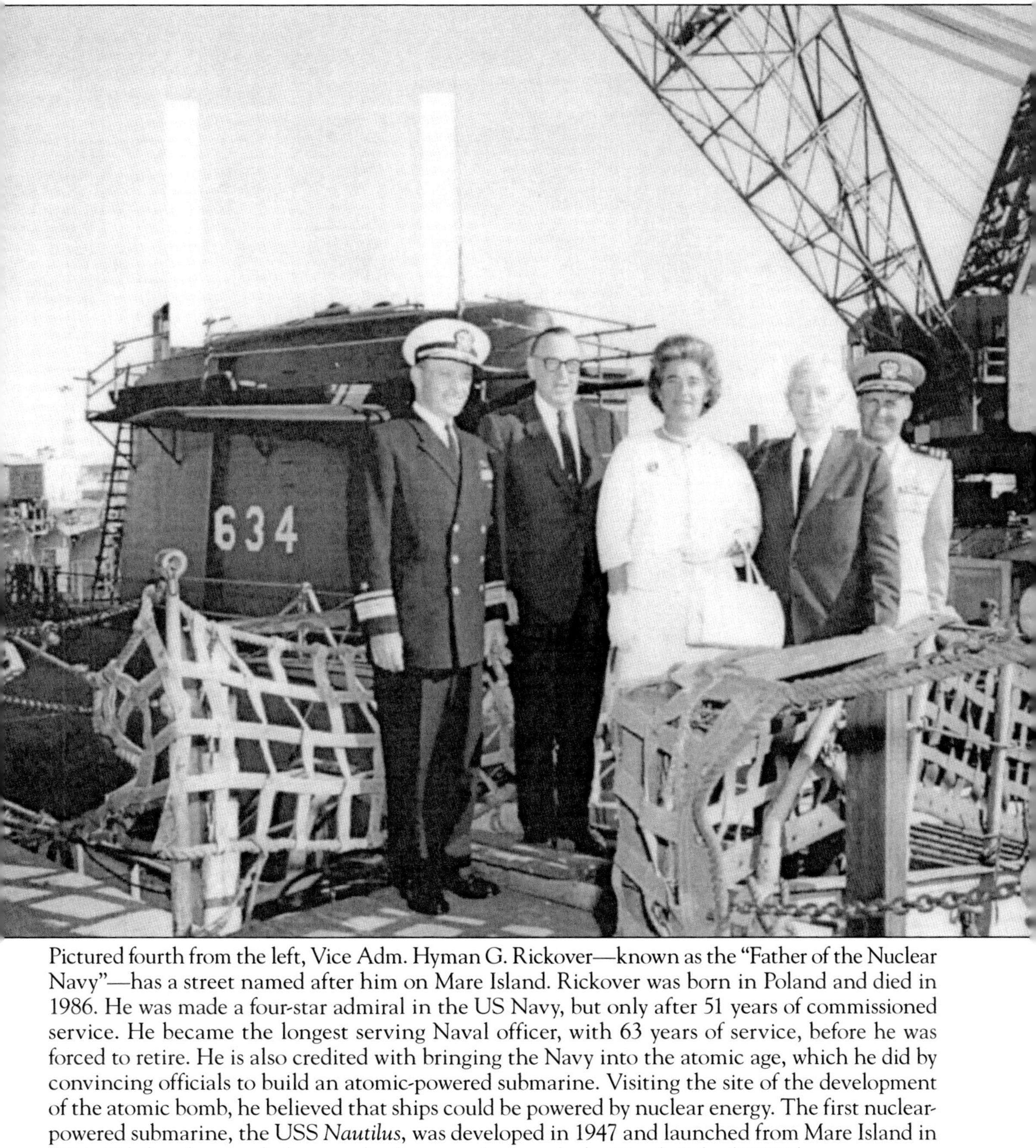

Pictured fourth from the left, Vice Adm. Hyman G. Rickover—known as the "Father of the Nuclear Navy"—has a street named after him on Mare Island. Rickover was born in Poland and died in 1986. He was made a four-star admiral in the US Navy, but only after 51 years of commissioned service. He became the longest serving Naval officer, with 63 years of service, before he was forced to retire. He is also credited with bringing the Navy into the atomic age, which he did by convincing officials to build an atomic-powered submarine. Visiting the site of the development of the atomic bomb, he believed that ships could be powered by nuclear energy. The first nuclear-powered submarine, the USS *Nautilus*, was developed in 1947 and launched from Mare Island in 1954. While submerged, she was the first vessel to reach the North Pole. (VHM.)

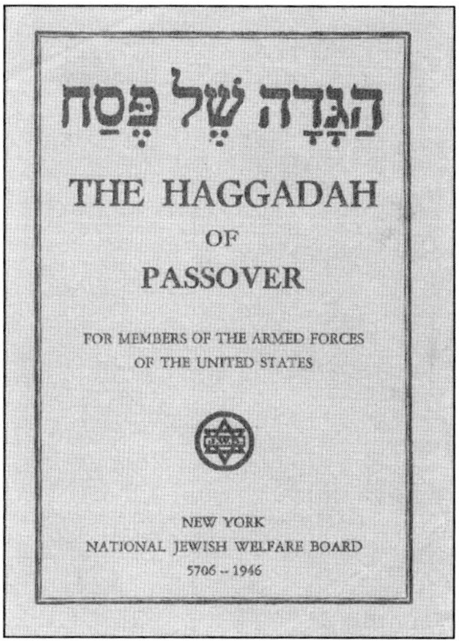

The US military has long tried to accommodate its members' religious needs, as evidenced by this Passover Haggadah, which contains the story and protocols for the Passover Seder and was printed by the National Jewish Welfare Board in 1946 for use by Jewish members of the US armed forces. It was likely used for those stationed at the Benicia Arsenal and on Mare Island. (VHM.)

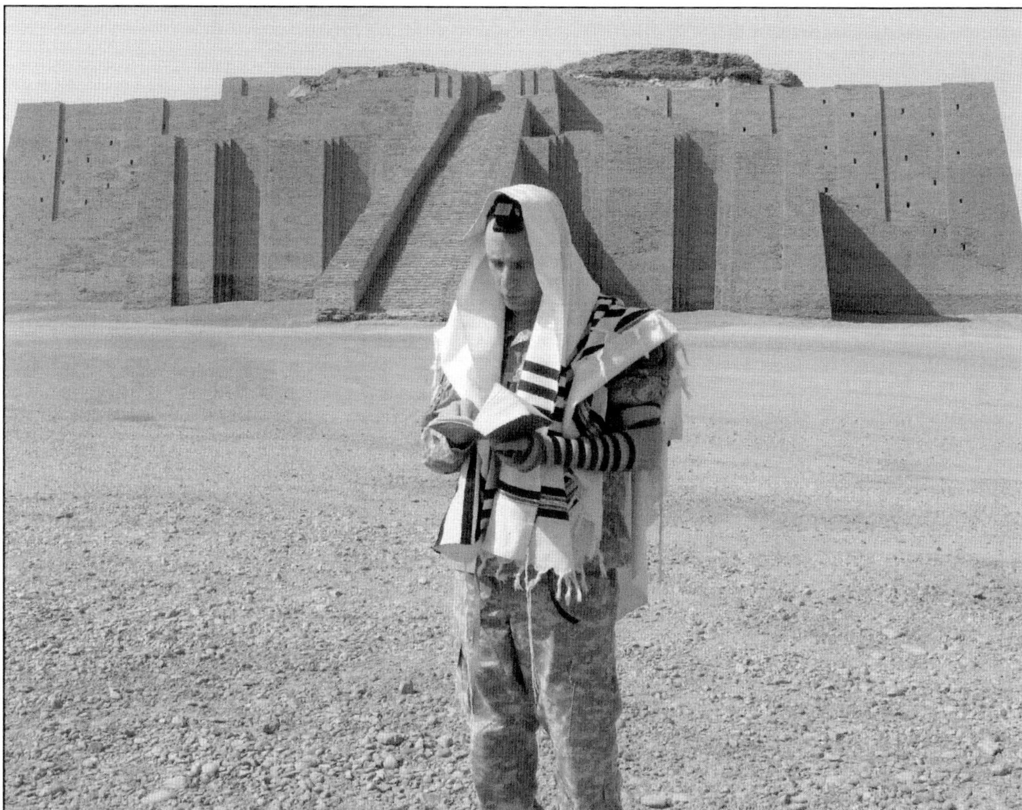

Mare Island was also where David Goldstrom—who eventually became one of the US military's Jewish chaplains—served in the Navy and later the Army. Having served in Iraq and Afghanistan, Goldstrom was concerned about the Scud missiles launched toward Israel in 1991 in retaliation for the US invasion of Saddam Hussein's Iraq, but as a military serviceman, he said that he knew what most people don't: "how incredibly powerful the US military really is." (Courtesy of D. Goldstrom.)

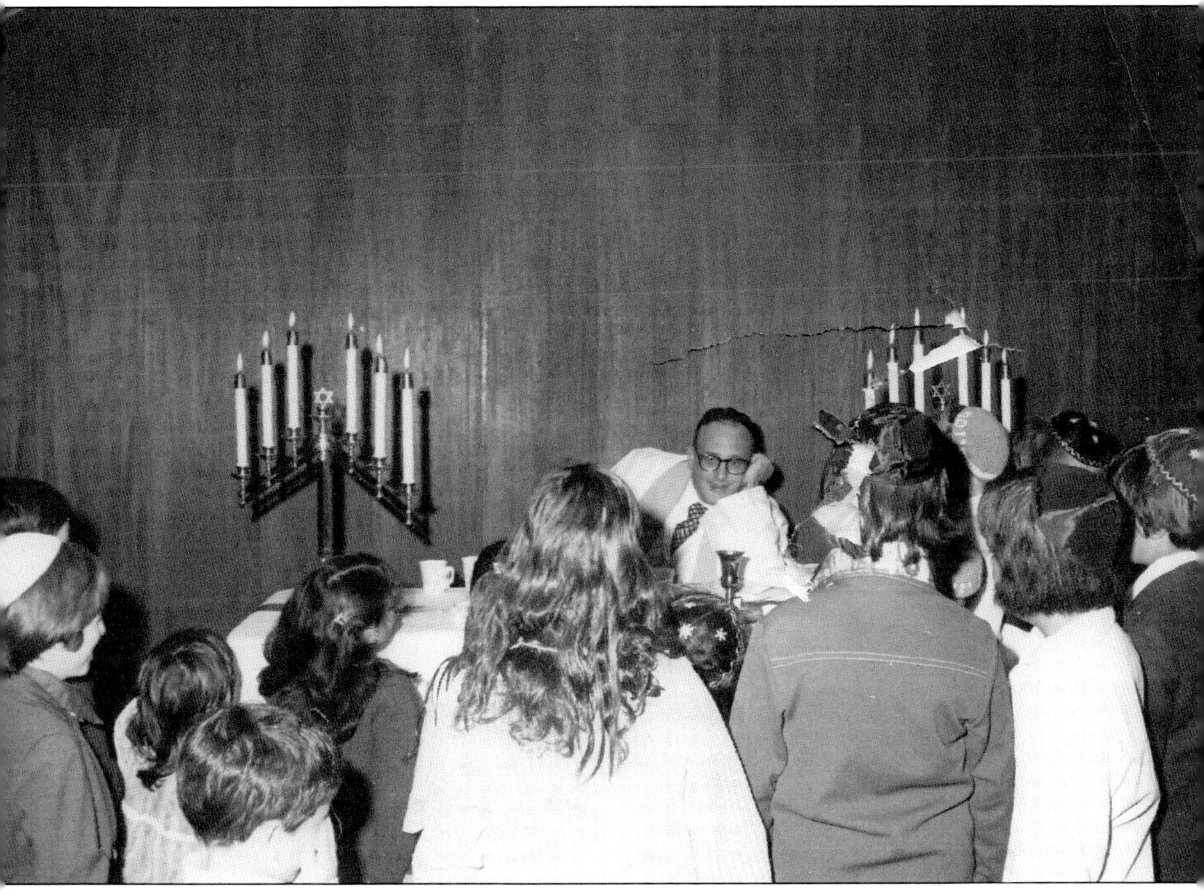

"A Jew was a gem," Chaplain Fred Lewin used to say of Solano—meaning that they were a rare and shining find. The Air Force was voluntary in the 1960s, and most Jews weren't volunteering. Orthodox rabbi Fred Lewin and his wife, Bluma, did volunteer, however, were in the military for 21 years, and were stationed at Travis Air Force Base from 1973 to 1976. The base made him kosher ovens out of barrels and provided the couple with new plates for the holidays. They had a Hebrew school and Friday evening Onegs (a Sabbath delight, usually including songs, a lecture, and refreshments). Like today, kosher food was not readily available, so it was brought in for them. The rabbi and his son always wore yarmulkes, though it was not popular at the time. As a chaplain at the Vacaville prison, Lewin was asked to pray in Jesus' name, and his refusal to do so made some people uncomfortable. Rabbi and Rebbetzin Lewin retired to, and live in, Baltimore. (Courtesy of the Lewin family.)

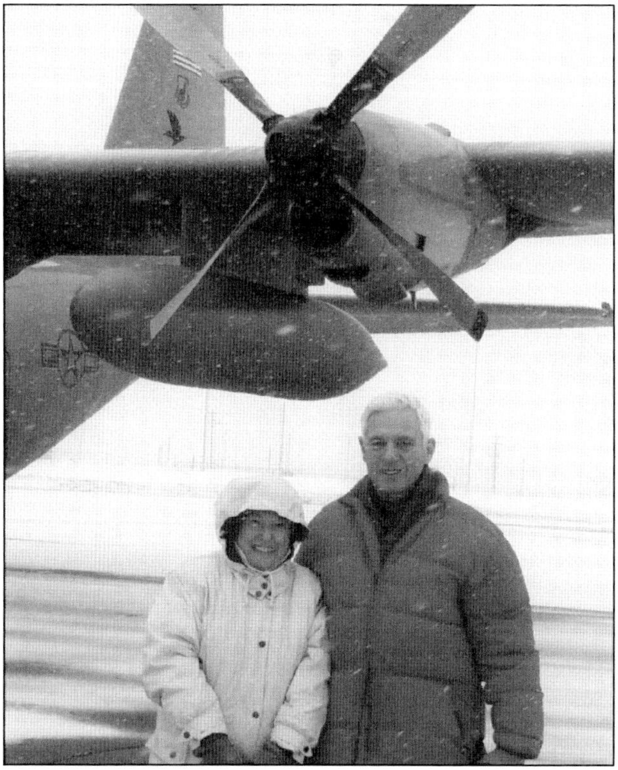

Col. Jim Waldman is a third-generation American Jew whose grandparents, the Fredrichs, fled Russia to escape army conscription and changed their name to the less conspicuous "Waldman" before coming to America. Jim married Ann Blake in 1958 and spent 25 years as a US Air Force pilot. In 1976, he transferred to Travis Air Force Base as a full colonel. The family lived in Vacaville and was active in the Jewish community. (Courtesy of Ann Waldman.)

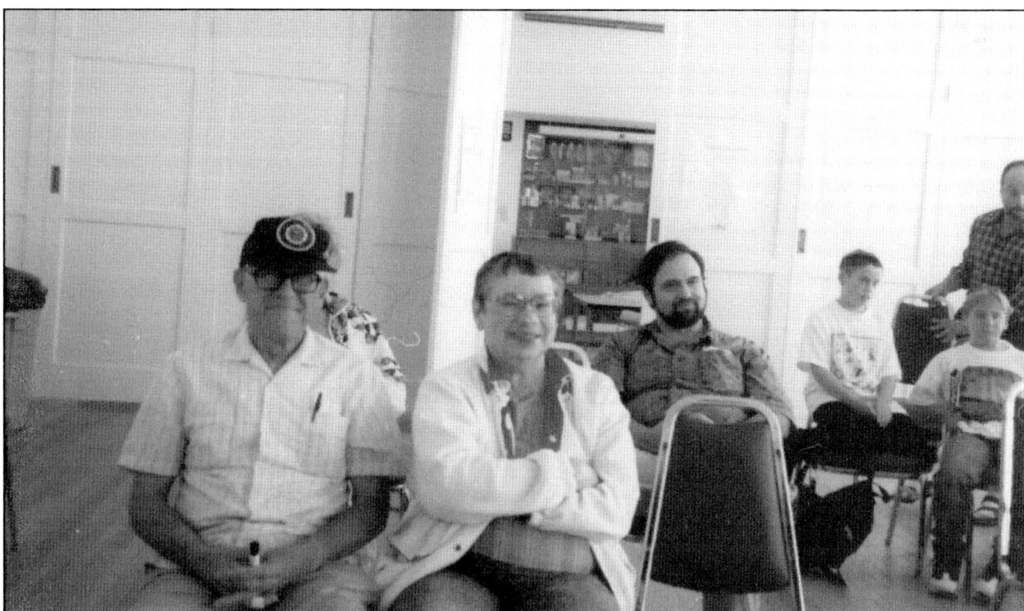

Phil Edelman came to the Travis Air Force Base from Los Angeles with his wife, Celia, in the late 1950s. This sweet, inspiring man was an MP and an Air Force colonel. Rabbi David White said that he modeled the best of Judaism—celebrating family, friends, and community in everything he did. He never kvetched (complained) but only kvelled (rejoiced) about everything. Phil also taught the community about *teshuva* (making amends) and keeping life balanced every day. (SDN.)

Nine

Troubles

צרות (Tzarot)

צוריס (Tsuris)

. . . Taken along with the good times

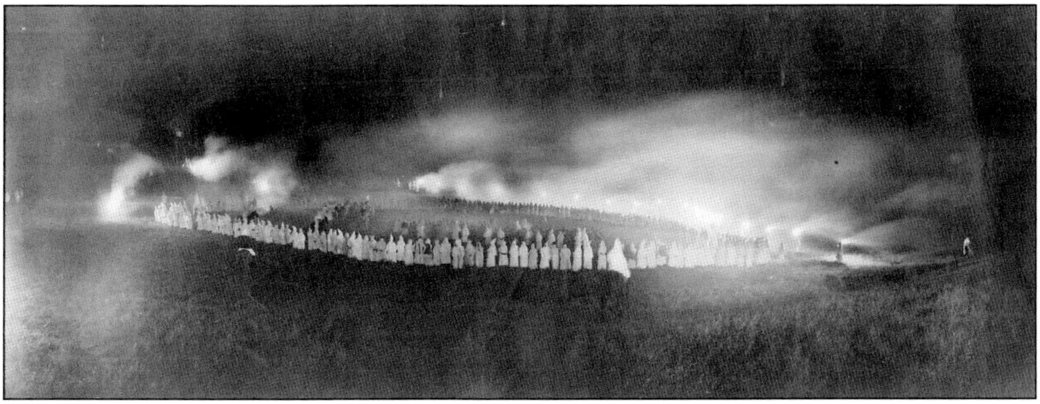

Even in 2014, there are some community members who prefer to keep their Jewish ethnicity a secret and declined inclusion in this book. At least one expressed concern about backlash from the Ku Klux Klan, which seems a valid fear, judging from this photograph of a Solano County Klan gathering—likely taken several decades ago. Nevertheless, the authors chose to present Solano County's Jews, warts and all, including the following negatives. (VHM.)

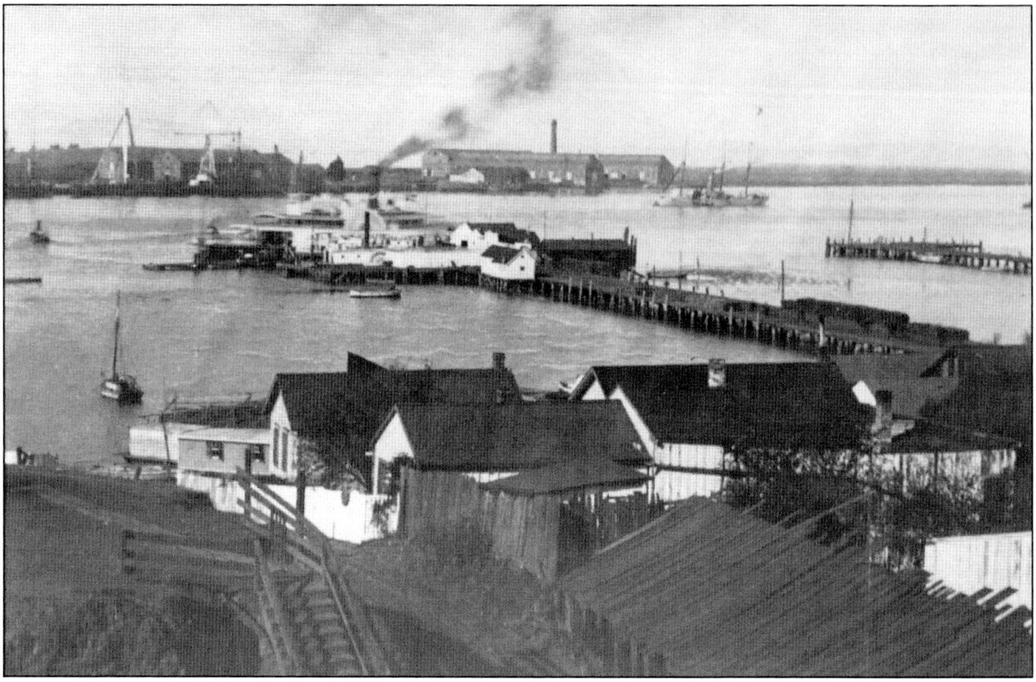

Jacob Blum barely survived the worst disaster in Suisun City history in 1864, when the boiler of the steamship *Sophia McLane* (sometimes seen as the *Sophie McLean*) exploded at Suisun Wharf, killing 10 and injuring 12 others. Blum had been invited on the ship's run to San Francisco by Capt. Henry P. Hulbert, but boiler explosions often came without warning on steamships like the one seen here in South Vallejo. Blum lived another 14 years. (VHM.)

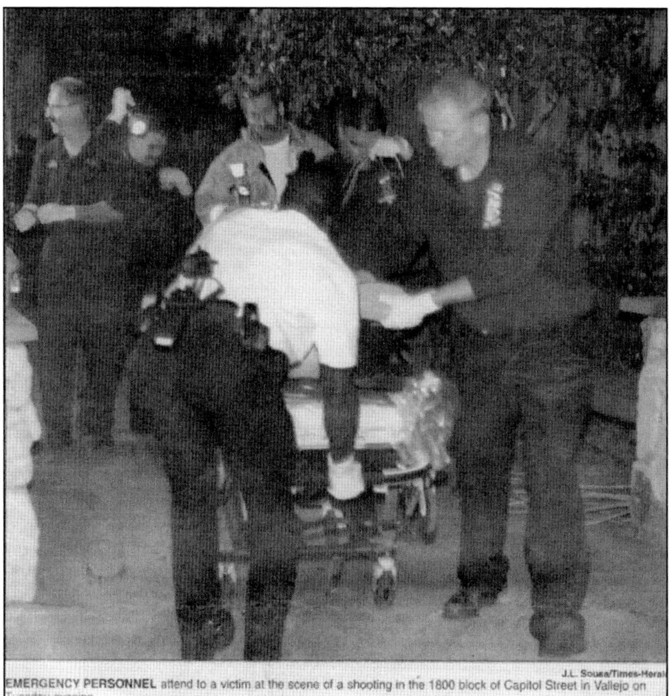

Psychologist Dr. Ira Polonsky—who had served the area for 30 years—was shot and killed in his Capitol Street office in November 2005 at age 64. Authorities said that the suspect was a stocky 30- to 40-year-old man with red hair, freckles, and blue eyes, who had been wearing a ski mask and combat fatigues. Despite roadside billboards advertising the $50,000 reward offered by Gov. Arnold Schwarzenegger, the Oakland resident's killer was still free in 2014—possibly due to a long legal battle to access patient files. (VTH.)

A Benicia pool hall and saloon owner, city councilman Sol Rose made a citizen's arrest of the police chief in 1949 and was afterwards "recalled for conducting himself since his election in a manner detrimental to the city of Benicia," according to the *Times-Herald*. The chief spent about an hour in his own jail for not arresting the assistant chief after a scuffle with Rose at the police station. The chief sued Rose for making him an object of ridicule in the press. Called a "five ring circus" and "the wildest election day in city history" by the *Times-Herald*, Benicia's first recall drew its heaviest voter turnout ever. Again a councilman in 1955, Rose demanded the ouster of a police chief and a judge after a prostitute sued Rose over an alleged un-repaid loan. That year, Rose told police that two men in trench coats were threatening the lives of his family. (Both, VTH.)

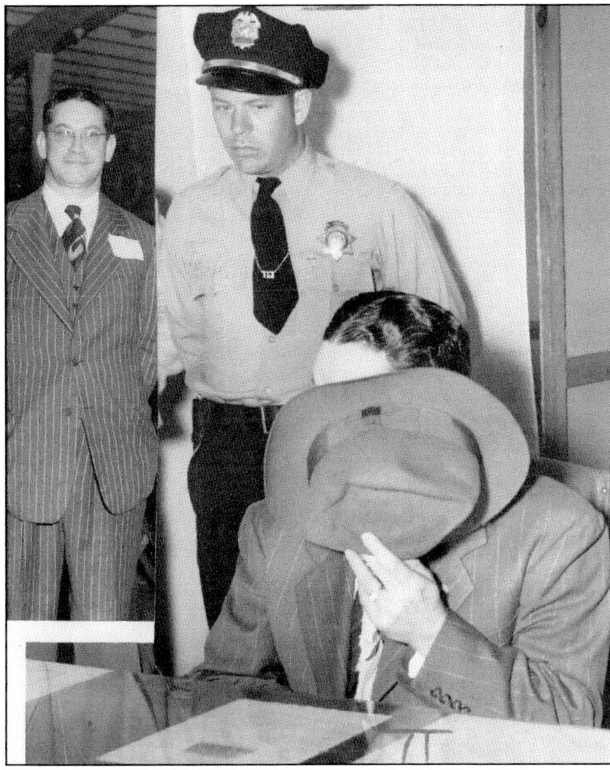

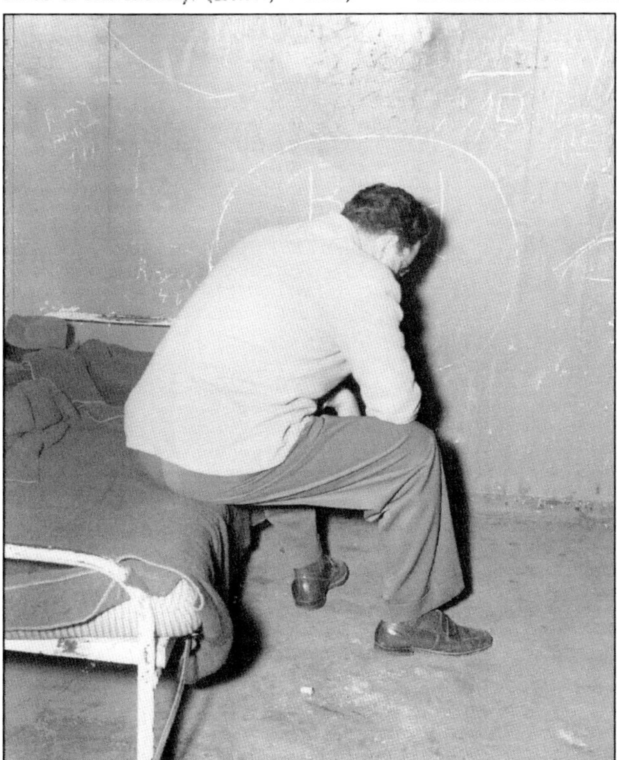

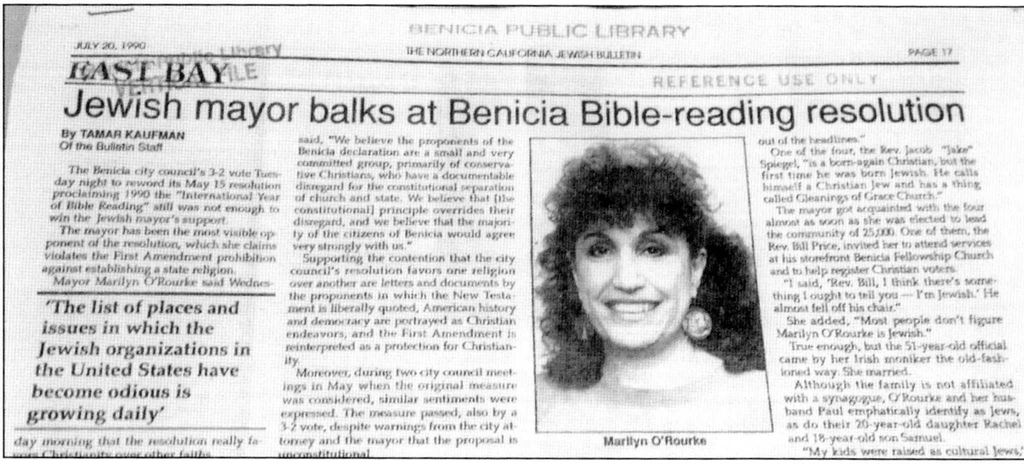

JULY 20, 1990 — THE NORTHERN CALIFORNIA JEWISH BULLETIN — PAGE 17

EAST BAY

Jewish mayor balks at Benicia Bible-reading resolution

By TAMAR KAUFMAN
Of the Bulletin Staff

The Benicia city council's 3-2 vote Tuesday night to reword its May 15 resolution proclaiming 1990 the "International Year of Bible Reading" still was not enough to win the Jewish mayor's support.

The mayor has been the most visible opponent of the resolution, which she claims violates the First Amendment prohibition against establishing a state religion.

Mayor Marilyn O'Rourke said Wednesday morning that the resolution really favors Christianity over other faiths ... said, "We believe the proponents of the Benicia declaration are a small and very committed group, primarily of conservative Christians, who have a documentable disregard for the constitutional separation of church and state. We believe that [the constitutional] principle overrides their disregard, and we believe that the majority of the citizens of Benicia would agree very strongly with us."

'The list of places and issues in which the Jewish organizations in the United States have become odious is growing daily'

Supporting the contention that the city council's resolution favors one religion over another are letters and documents by the proponents in which the New Testament is liberally quoted, American history and democracy are portrayed as Christian endeavors, and the First Amendment is reinterpreted as a protection for Christianity.

Moreover, during two city council meetings in May when the original measure was considered, similar sentiments were expressed. The measure passed, also by a 3-2 vote, despite warnings from the city attorney and the mayor that the proposal is unconstitutional.

Marilyn O'Rourke

... out of the headlines."

One of the four, the Rev. Jacob "Jake" Spiegel, "is a born-again Christian, but the first time he was born Jewish. He calls himself a Christian Jew and has a thing called Gleanings of Grace Church."

The mayor got acquainted with the four almost as soon as she was elected to lead the community of 25,000. One of them, the Rev. Bill Price, invited her to attend services at his storefront Benicia Fellowship Church and to help register Christian voters.

"I said, 'Rev. Bill, I think there's something I ought to tell you — I'm Jewish.' He almost fell off his chair."

She added, "Most people don't figure Marilyn O'Rourke is Jewish."

True enough, but the 51-year-old official came by her Irish moniker the old-fashioned way: She married.

Although the family is not affiliated with a synagogue, O'Rourke and her husband Paul emphatically identify as Jews, as do their 20-year-old daughter Rachel and 18-year-old son Samuel.

"My kids were raised as cultural Jews,"

Local and national media descended on Benicia when a group—including Benicia's mayor, Marilyn O'Rourke—questioned the constitutionality of a resolution proclaiming 1990 to be the Year of the Bible. O'Rourke refused to sign the proclamation, made by some evangelists and city council members, citing the separation of church and state. Civil rights organizations, like the American Jewish Congress, repeatedly became involved. The evangelists blamed her stance on her being Jewish. (Courtesy of *J Weekly*.)

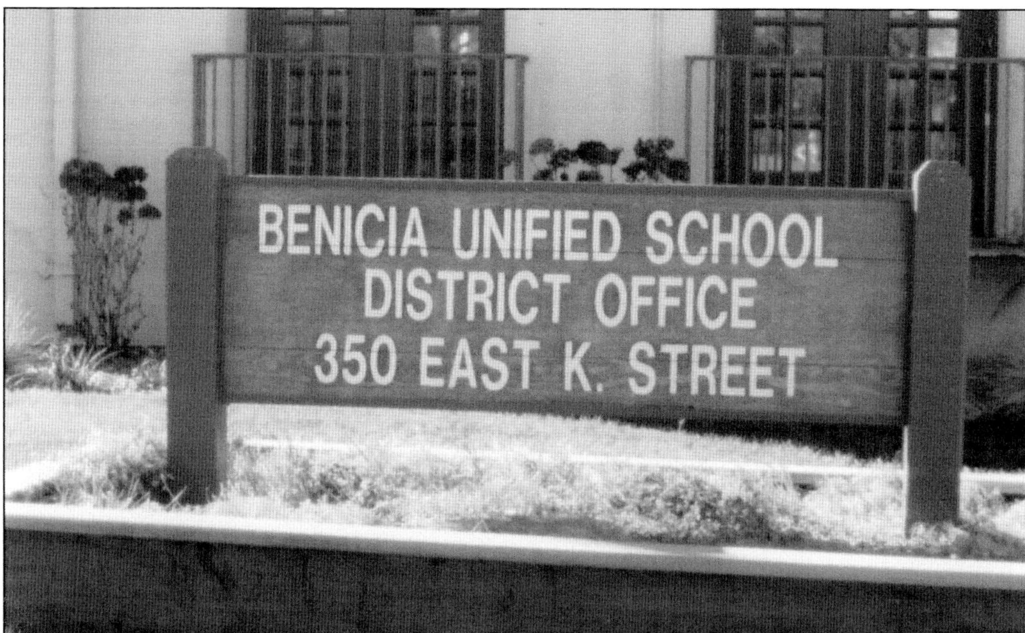

Benicia's Jewish students faced challenges later that year when, during the mandatory Christmas assembly, a teacher dressed her students for the nativity and read the first chapter from the book of Luke with the principal's knowledge. In 1994, civil rights organizations returned to address the scheduling of the first day of school on Rosh Hashanah. The union chief called local Jews "Little Hebrews" in a Catholic community before changing the date. Later, despite the school's having access to Jewish calendars, a prom was scheduled on Passover. (SDN.)

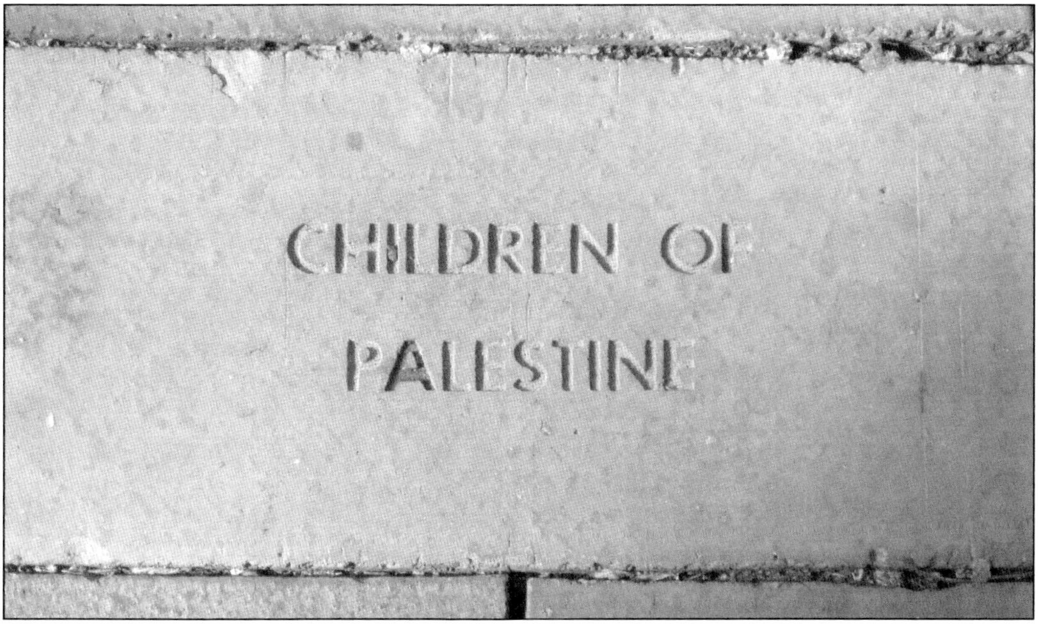

In the early 1990s, as a fundraiser for a new Benicia library building, bricks could be bought and named for individuals, families, nonprofits, or businesses. To have a brick to honor the "Children of Palestine," a Benicia resident took out a business license in that name. Benicia's Parks and Recreation Department denied a request to name a brick in honor of Israel, as it was not a family or business. (SDN.)

In 2008, Vallejo city officials created Unity Plaza near City Hall, which featured proverbs from various ethnic groups and nationalities etched into concrete but included no contributions from the city's Jewish community. A personal appeal by a newspaper columnist—who noted it couldn't be for lack of appropriate sayings from which to choose—went unheeded, as officials insisted that being Jewish is strictly a religion. They also declined to include anything from Israel—a nationality also represented in Vallejo. (SDN.)

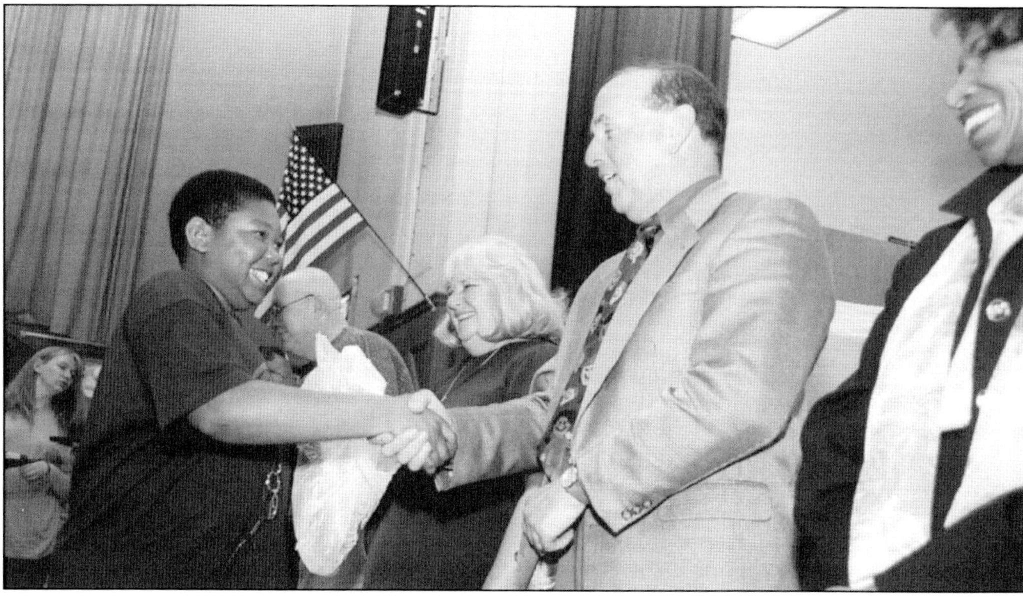

Vallejo's Steve Goldstone became school district superintendent in 1995 and was ousted at age 61 in 2000 in a highly controversial move by a newly elected school board. He then served as interim superintendent for the Berkeley and Fairfield-Suisun school districts before, in 2002, becoming the founding dean of Touro University's teachers college. He was also a school board and district consultant and a support teacher leader in the Nevada Department of Education before retiring. (VTH.)

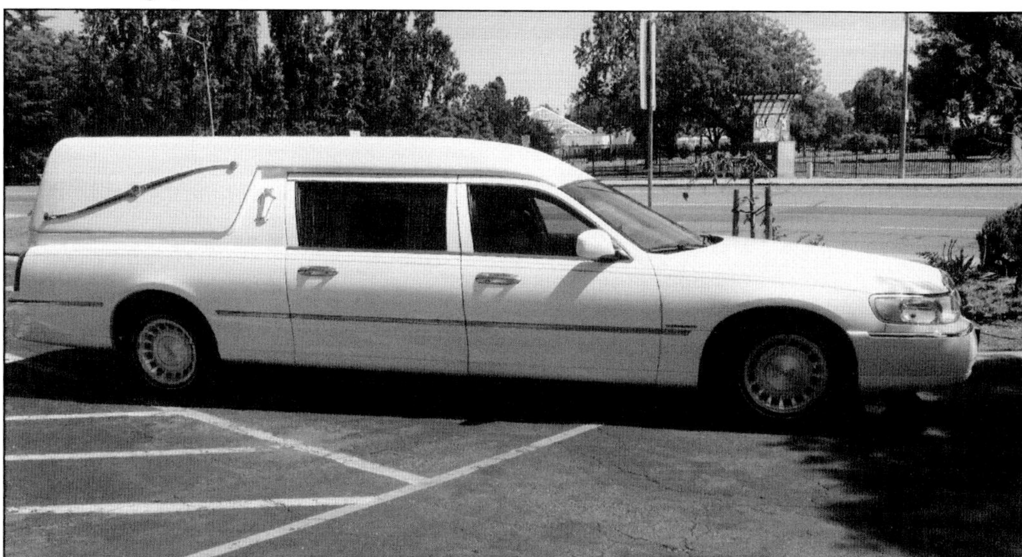

After trying for four years to build a Jewish mortuary business in Vallejo, Dan Mandel made headlines when his hearse—containing the body of a recently deceased Holocaust survivor—caught fire on the freeway in 2010. The spectacle was caught on video and widely viewed. Perhaps ahead of his time, Mandel had created a mobile funeral home and began live web streaming of his funerals so that those who could not attend services in person could still be present. (Courtesy of R. Lessem.)

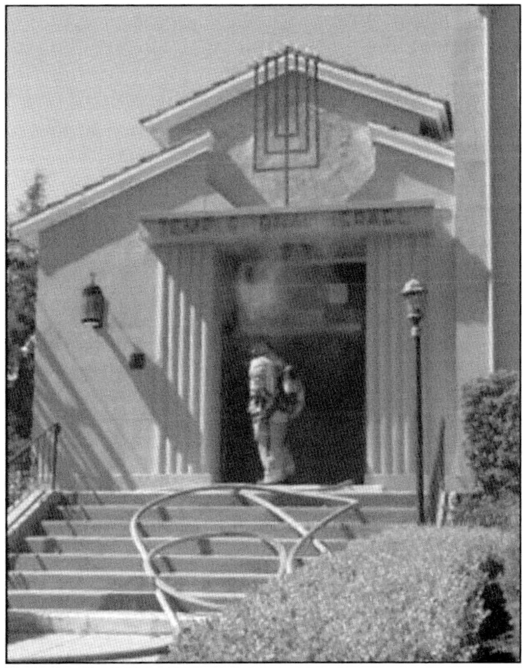

Vallejo firefighters battled a two-alarm arson fire in Solano County's only synagogue on June 17, 2004. The fire had been started in the temple's sanctuary, but there was other damage as well—including some items being stolen and the rabbi's office being ransacked. Though police determined that the arson was not a hate crime, many had doubts. Firefighters returning from another call noticed the smoke and sprang into action. In the fire's aftermath, services were held in the temple's social hall and parking lot, with attendants coming from miles around to show their support and donations and encouragement pouring in from around the regional population and several churches of various denominations. In June 2005, a swastika was found painted by hand—in egg—on CBI's door. Local police deemed this act to be a hate crime. (Both, VTH.)

Jewish congregation trying to bounce back from suspicious fire

No hate crime, police conclude

By MATTHIAS GAFNI
Times-Herald staff writer

Hours after police announced the fire at Vallejo's only Jewish synagogue was not a hate crime, members of the congregation met for weekly Shabbat, which because of smoke damage and lack of electricity was moved to the rear parking lot.

Congregation B'nai Israel's Rabbi David White led the prayer service from a folding table Friday, with about 60 people sitting in a circle of chairs around him, the smell of charred wood still present in the cold twilight air. The ceremonial wine and challah bread were served from a picnic table as darkness ended the ceremony at around 8:30 p.m.

White, joined by his own congregation and other

(See **FIRE,** A2)

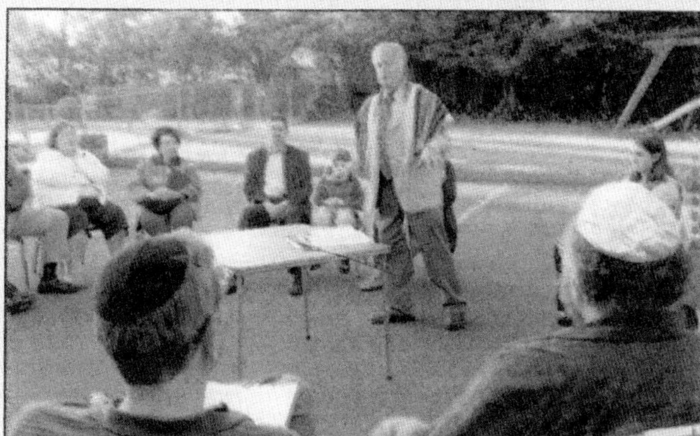

J.L. Sousa/Times-Herald

RABBI DAVID WHITE of Congregation B'nai Israel leads Shabbat services on Friday evening in the parking lot.

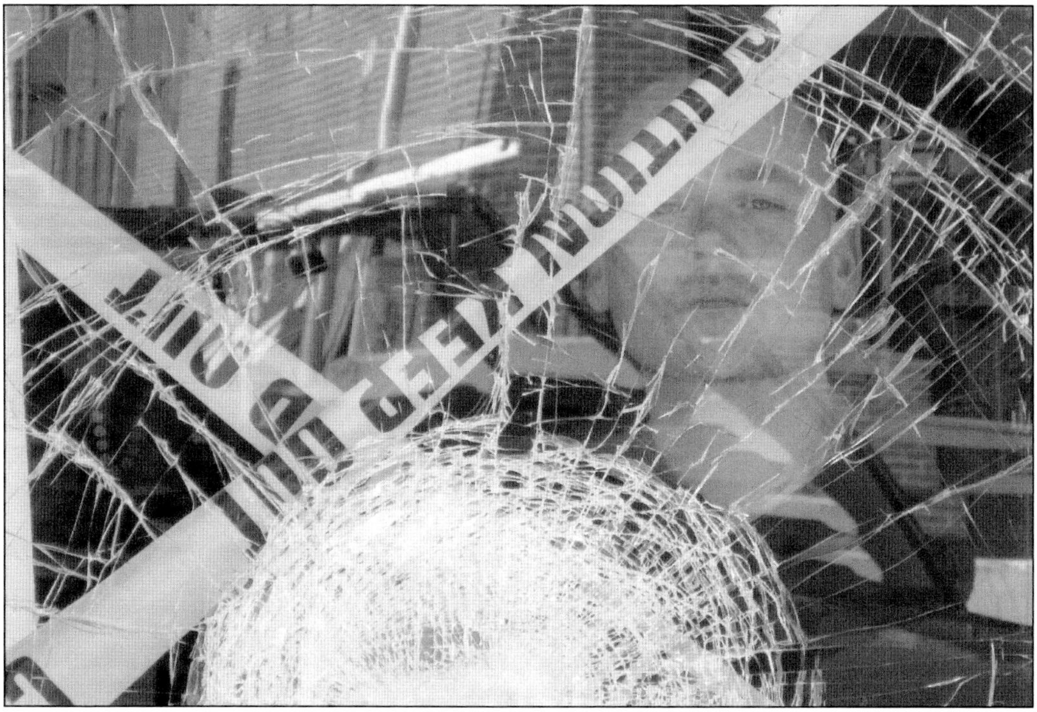

Having inherited the Victory Stores founded by his grandfather Al Ross, Ray Prather is shown here behind police tape and the damaged window of his Army/Navy surplus store. The security glass Prather installed after a series of "smash-and-grab" burglaries downtown was so effective that other businesses followed suit. Prather, along with business neighbor and friend Ken Ingersoll—of Gracie's Barbecue—helped to revive Vallejo's Independence Day fireworks, which had lost all corporate sponsors in the recession of the 2000s. (VTH.)

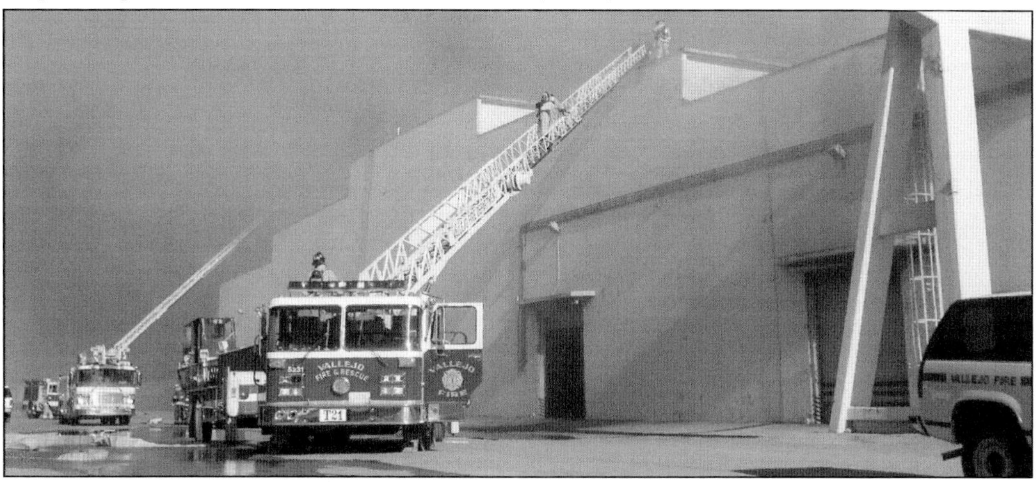

An eight-alarm arson fire destroyed Jack Krystal's Wines Central warehouse in October 2005. The Jewish immigrant and Bay Area resident had transformed the 1942 military fortress into a temperature-controlled storage facility for local boutique wines and gourmet foods. Millions of dollars worth of goods were lost in the blaze. Sausalito businessman Mark Anderson was convicted of setting the fire to cover the theft of his clients' wine and was sentenced to 27 years in prison. (VTH.)

Ten

Odds and Ends

תוספות (Tosafot)

אנדערע זאכן (Andereh Zachen)

. . . Including the kitchen sink

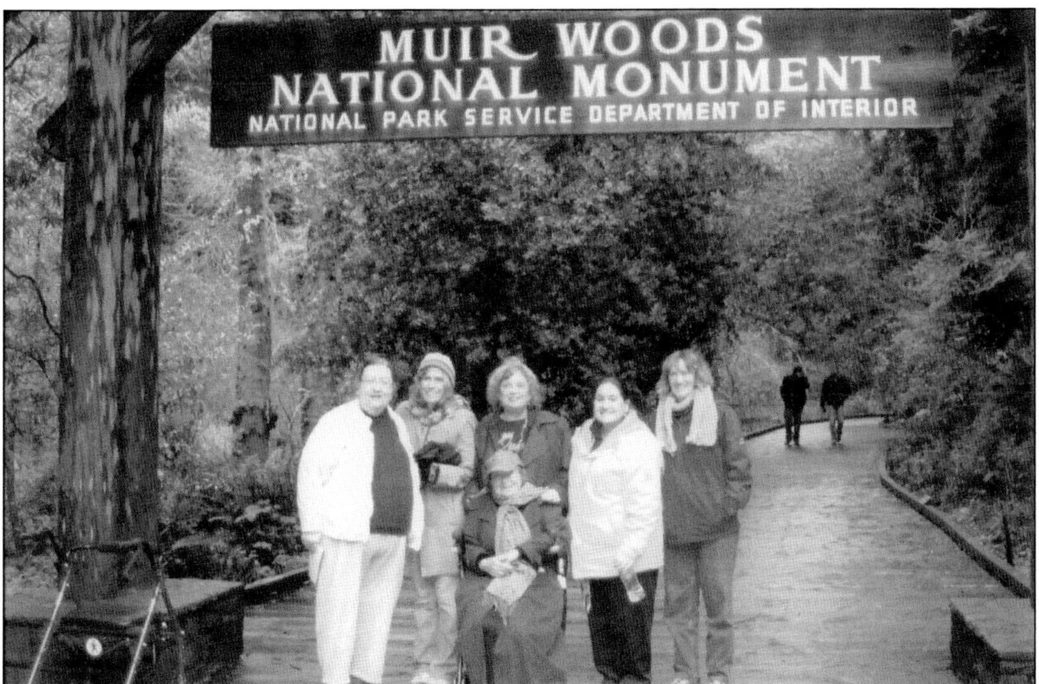

Hadassah's Solano-Napa chapter is a marriage of several regional chapters from Benicia, Fairfield, Napa, Vacaville, and Vallejo. Favorite activities for the group include the celebration of Tu B'Shevat, which often involves hikes or special Seders. Pictured here during a 2009 visit to Muir Woods are, from left to right, Mary Schwartz, Carol Levin, Rachel Lessem, Shoshana Deutscher-Nurik, Geri Kahn, and Molly Leavitt (seated). This miscellaneous chapter features other stories and photographs that didn't fit easily into previous chapters. (SDN.)

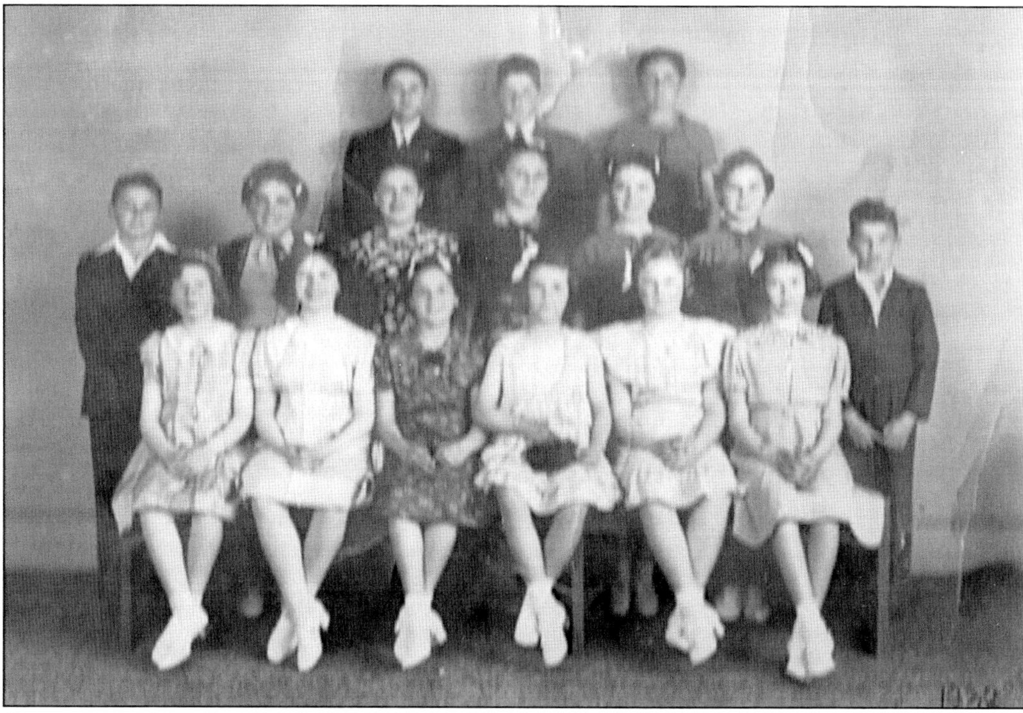

Congregation B'nai Israel, which Rabbi Kopstein once called "the synagogue center," has provided a wide range of activities over the years. These have included choirs, various classes for all ages, and both the youth choir and band pictured below. This group performed at CBI and at the Benicia Community Menorah Lighting. Seen here performing at the Veteran's Hall in Benicia, band members included—in no particular order—Jon Hobson, Chrissy and Sean Goldstein, Sarah Wiese, and Meghan Campbell. In the picture above, another CBI group—the Vallejo Juniors of 1938—included Fred Sessler, Robert Abriel, Bernie Laub, the Pizante and Abouaf cousins, Bernice Bregman, and Rosemary and Audrey Harris. (Above, courtesy of P. Rothman; below, SDN.)

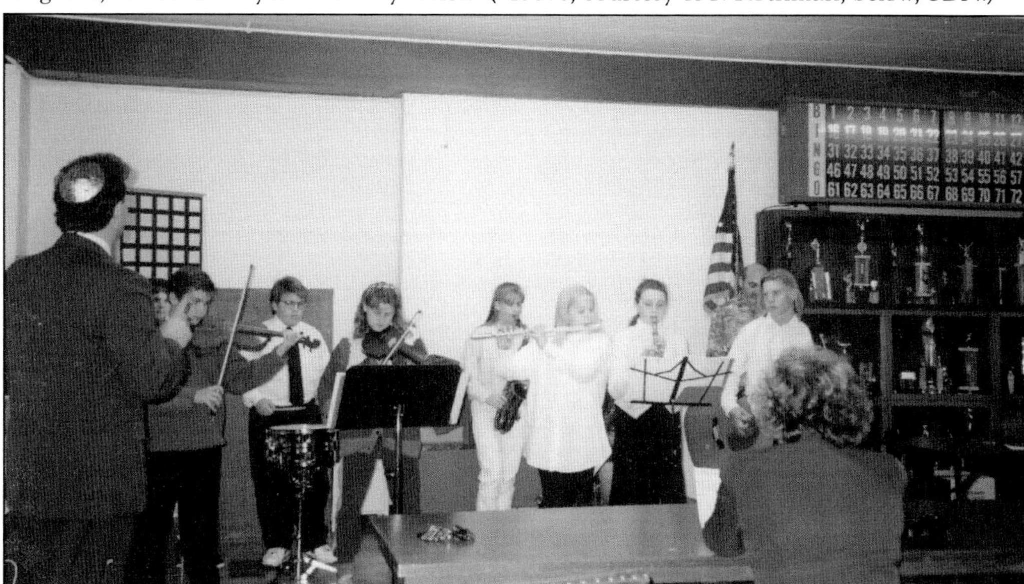

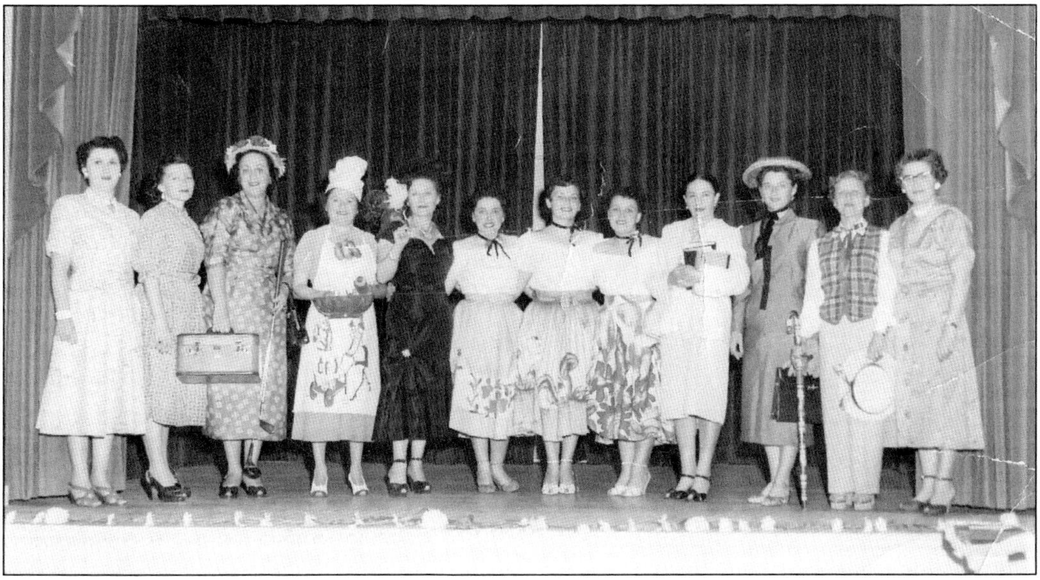

Formed at the same time as the Sons and Daughters of Israel was the Ladies Auxiliary, later known as Sisterhood. A crucial part of the congregation, the group played an important role in raising the funds to pay for the mortgage of the York Street temple, and it continues as an invaluable part of Congregation B'nai Israel in 2014. Pictured above, members of the CBI Sisterhood, including Helen Gray, Molly Leavitt, Ann Neparstek, Kate Monetta, Lena Feinberg, Pearl Rothman, Katie Policar, Kathryn Barsky, Sylvia Weinberg, Frieda Shankman, and Rebbetzin Jennie Horowitz, stand on the social hall stage in the mid-1950s, likely during one of the fundraising efforts that are the organization's main function. Pictured below is a Sisterhood reception honoring the 10th anniversary of the Horowitzes' tenure at CBI, featuring Rebbetzin Jennie Horowitz, Tamar Abouaf, Molly Leavitt, and others. (Both, CBI.)

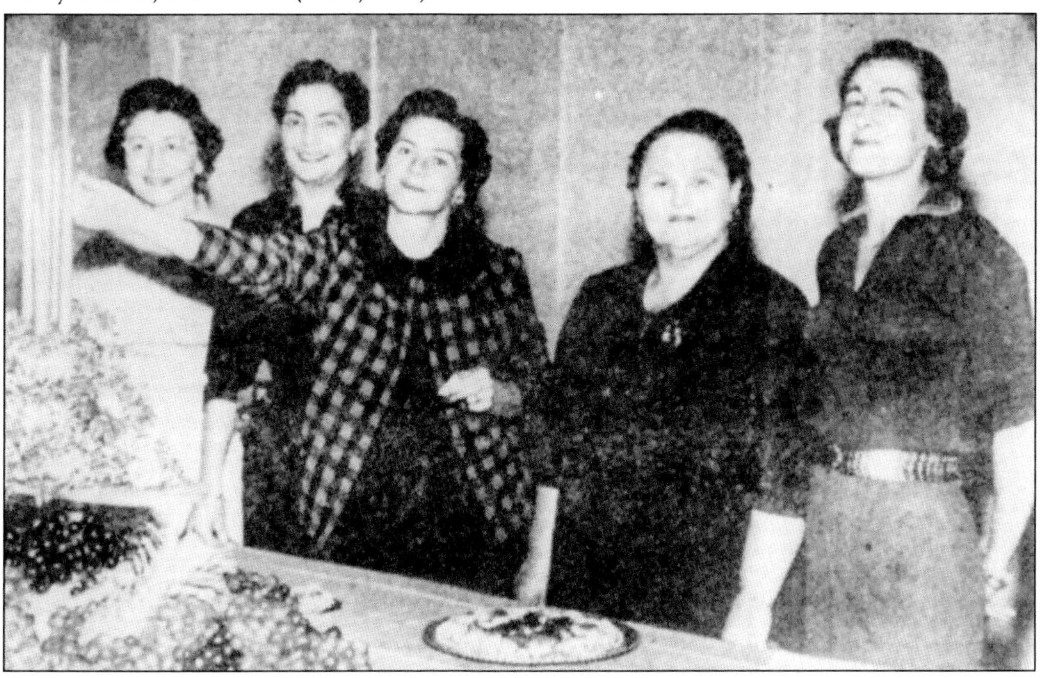

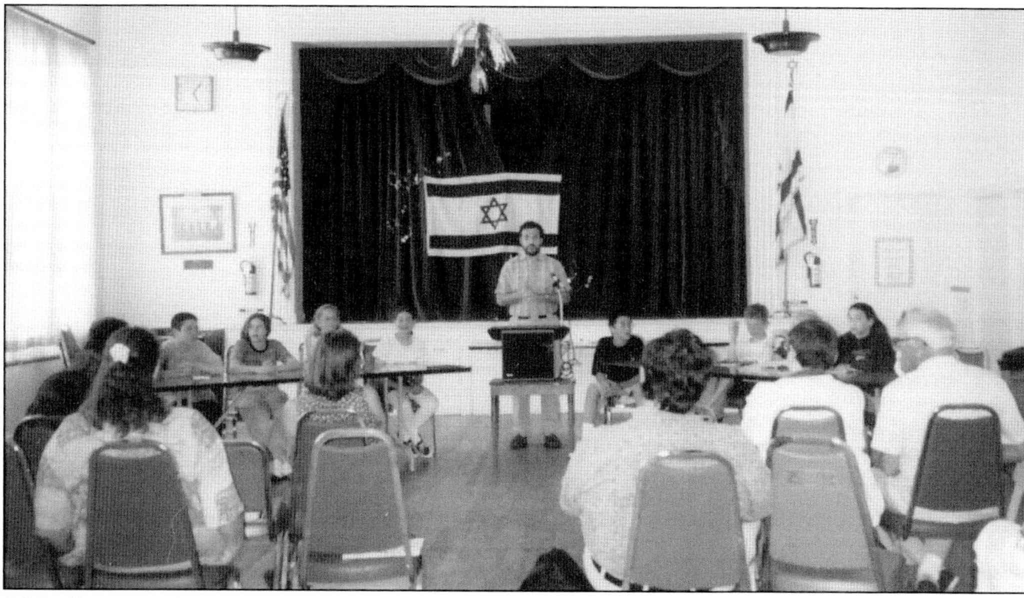

CBI offers a confirmation class in the hope that, after celebrating their B'nai Mitzvah, children will continue their Jewish education. In this photograph from the late 1990s, a year-end competition, in the form of a Jeopardy-style game, is being held to celebrate months of learning. Organized by Cantor Jim Heilborn and Rabbi David Kopstein, the young teenagers competed by displaying their Jewish knowledge. Participants included Toby Cantor, Nathan Reid, Rena Mendelowitz, Alexander Horowitz, Sarah Wiese, and Katie Goudie. (SDN.)

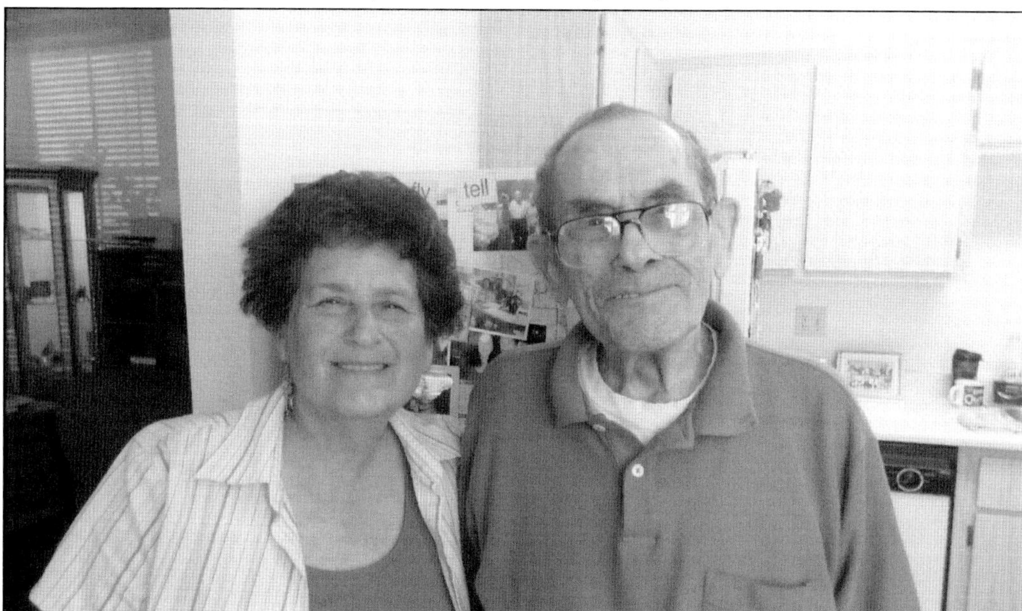

Bernie Freedman and Irene Sanders, father and sister of the *Times-Herald*'s Rich Freedman, came to California in 1947 and have lived in Vacaville since 2010. Both retired, Bernie and Irene spend time researching, writing, and lecturing on historical and human-interest subjects that include immigration and early American history. The American Legion medal that Bernie received in grade school for being the best history student has been symbolic of his life. (Courtesy of R. Lessem.)

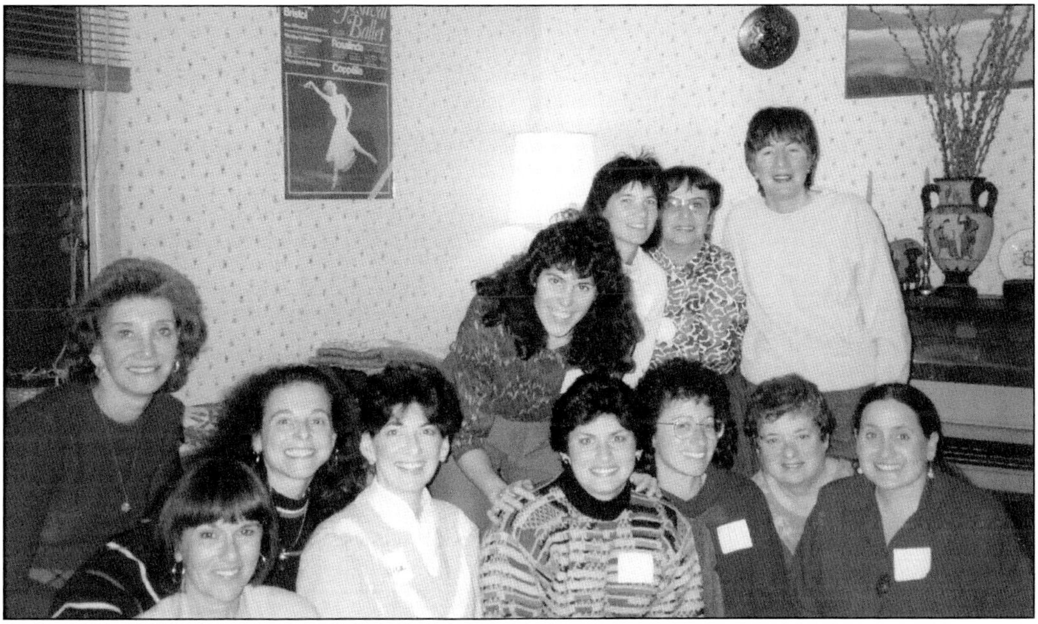

The Benicia-Solano Jewish Women's Network was organized in 1988 as a forum for women to meet regularly and discuss issues affecting their lives. Meetings were held in the homes of the members in Benicia, Vallejo, and Fairfield. A copy of this photograph was included among the artifacts buried in a time capsule at the Benicia Public Library, which is due to be opened in 2041. Shown here are Ronnie Horowitz, Susan Stern, Beverly Sherman, and others. (SDN.)

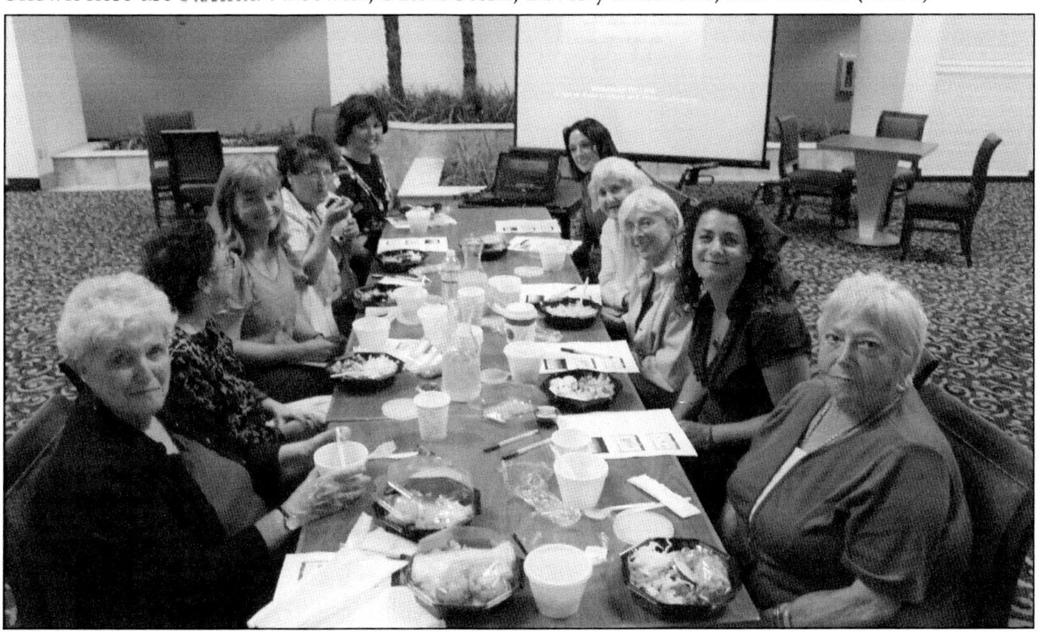

Rebbetzin Aidel Zaklos's Chabad Women's Circle is meant to "strengthen the pride of Jewish women in our history" by leading women of all backgrounds in a series of hands-on activities, discussions, and workshops and providing tasty noshes. Topics include the Torah, the Talmud, Kaballah, and women's issues. Shown here are Nina Cooper, Christine Richardson, Millie Henn, and others. (Chabad.)

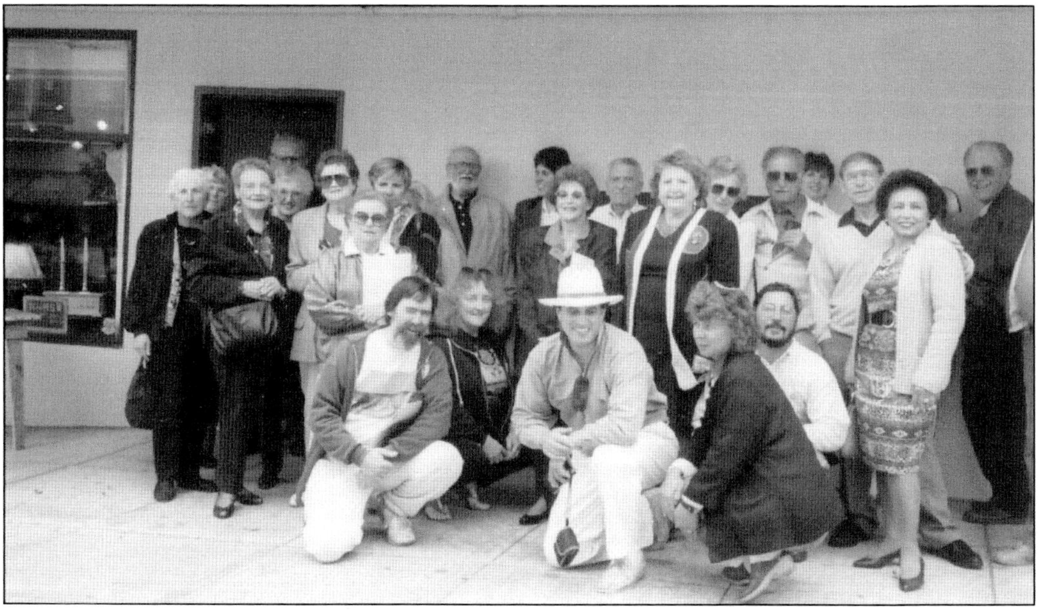

Members and friends of Congregation B'nai Israel went on educational trips with Rabbi David Kopstein. Some excursions were to Israel, while others explored the Jewish life and history of the Bay Area. Groups visited kosher wineries, synagogues, and *mikvahs* (ritual baths) in San Francisco and Berkeley and listened to stories from a Jewish chicken farmer from Petaluma. Participants seen above include the Grays, the Grosses, Debbie Williges, Fern Bernstein, the Walshes, the Schroders, Florence Bell, the Falks, the Balters, Jeffrey Nurik, and others. After visiting the mikvah, the group traveled to the Legion of Honor to view the Holocaust Memorial designed by George Segal. The sculpture, pictured below, is made of white painted bronze. (Both, SDN.)

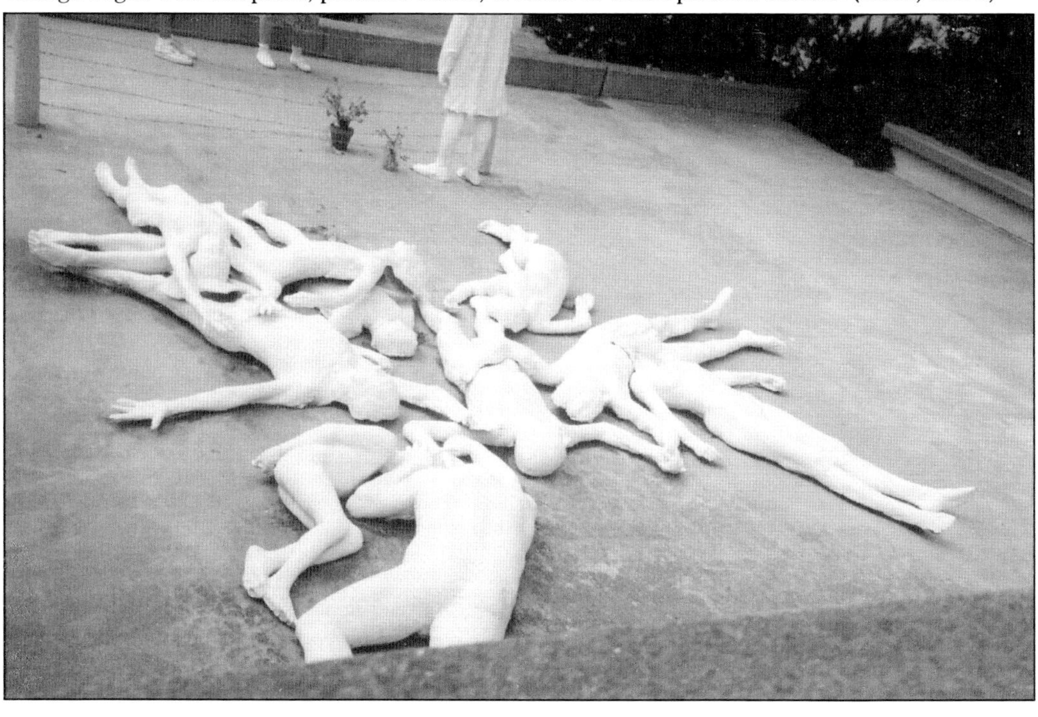

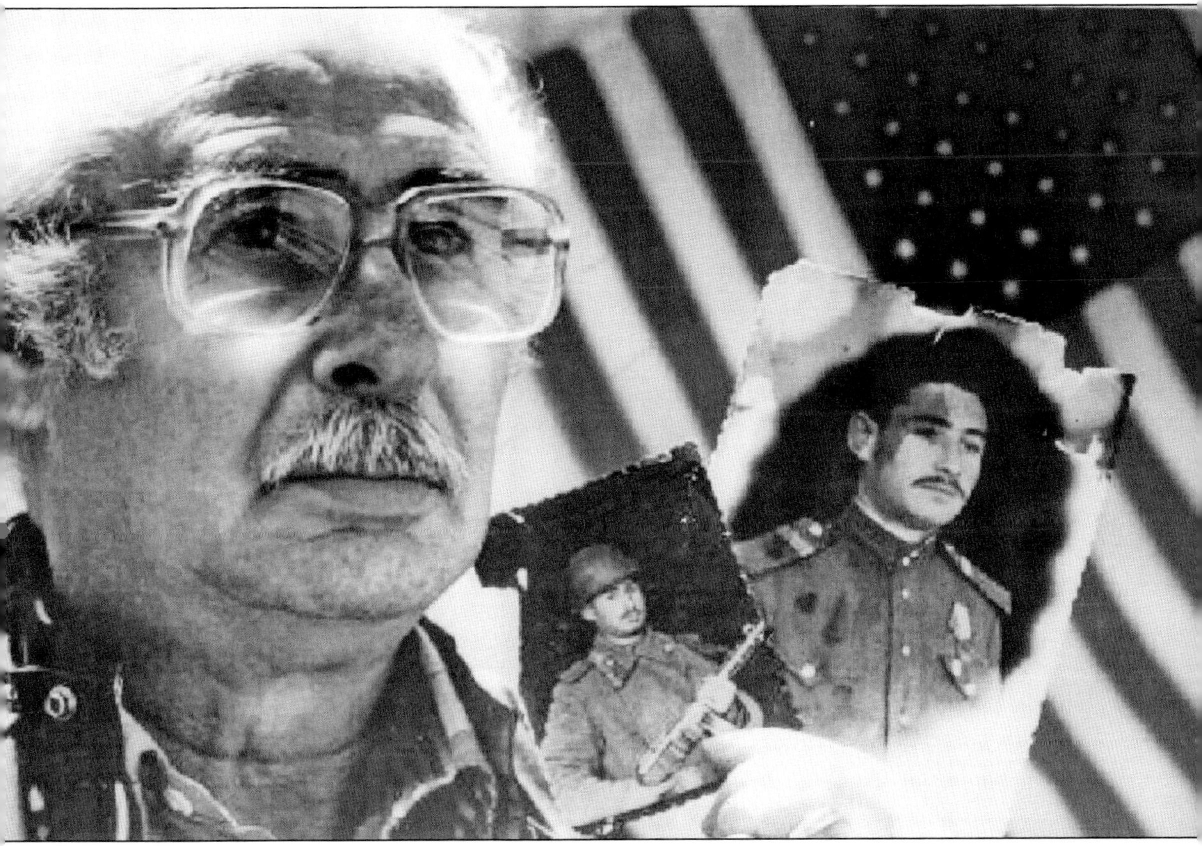

Among the first Russian Jews in a new wave of immigration to Solano County, Moses Mayzeles was a Holocaust survivor who died in 2003 at age 77. Born in Lvov, Mayzeles recounted his life hiding as a non-Jew in Nazi-occupied Poland before his capture and internment in a Russian prison after the war, where he was held until Russian premier Joseph Stalin's death. After surviving a decade as a Russian refusenik, Mayzeles was finally able to leave Russia with his wife and children in 1989. His testimony was recorded as part of Steven Spielberg's Shoah Project. He took English and computer lessons at age 70 and was possibly the first of Solano County's Russian immigrants to become a US citizen. (Courtesy of the Mayzeles family.)

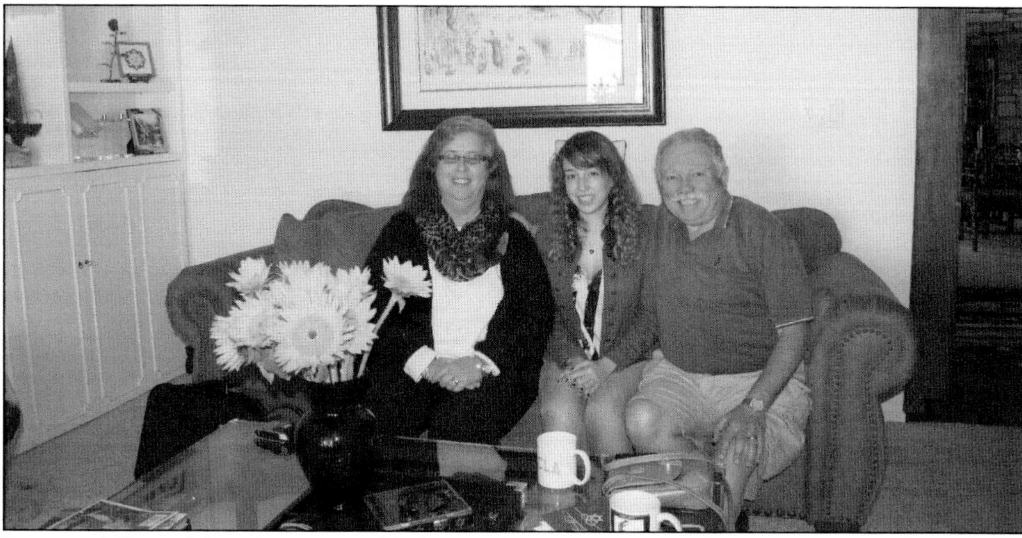

Ignat and Katya Mayzeles, pictured below with a load of Chanukah latkes, are among Solano County's Russian Jews—who came mostly from Ukraine between 1985 and 1995 and were sponsored by the Jewish Federation. In the relative safety of Solano County, these families began to openly embrace their Jewish heritage, which in the old country could only be practiced without reprisals behind drawn curtains. Though most were educated professionals in Russia, many had to begin again in minimum-wage jobs as they learned English. Jewish immigrants have also come to Solano County from other countries. These include the Nathan family, whose patriarch, Richard, and matriarch, Andree, escaped Egypt after the reestablishment of Israel made life difficult for Jews there. Their sons, Joe and Ron—who is seen above with his wife, Janet, and their daughter, Deanna—remain in Vallejo in 2014. Others have come from Morocco, Iraq, France, Israel, and elsewhere. (Above, courtesy of the Nathan family; below, VTH.)

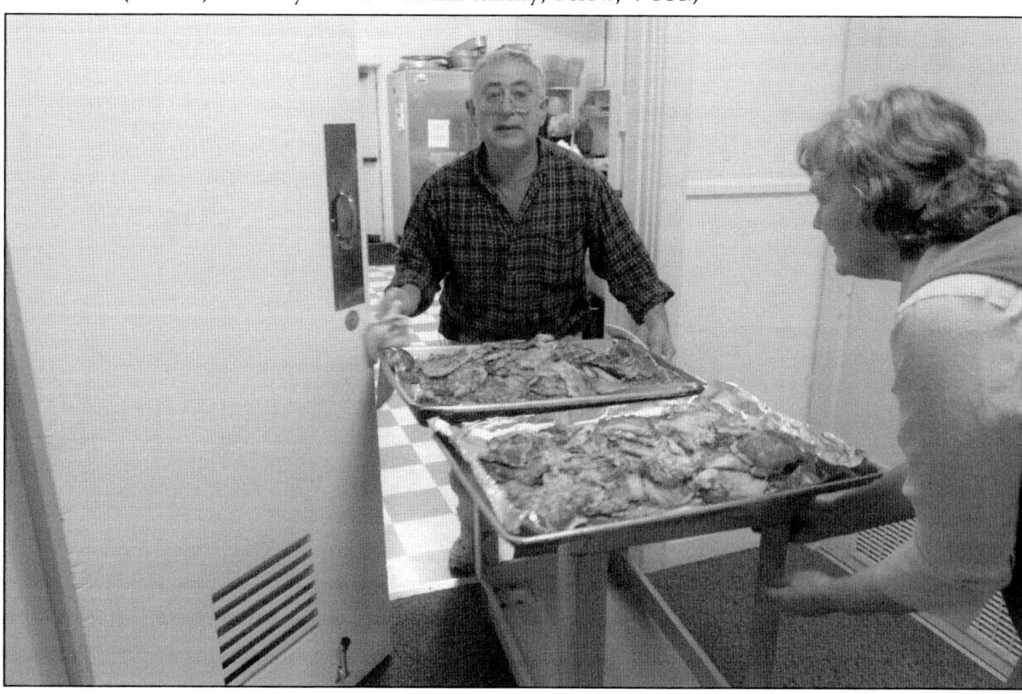

One of the few North American Jewish farmers, Aitan Mizrahi is a green and eco builder and an activist in the growing environmentally conscious food movement. Rachel Lessem's son, Aitan found this interest while in Solano County—where he taught Bar and Bat Mitzvah lessons—and later joined Connecticut's Isabella Freedman Center as a dairy manager and cheese maker. He identifies as a biblical Jew, growing his beard to symbolize his connection to his ancestors. (Courtesy of R. Lessem.)

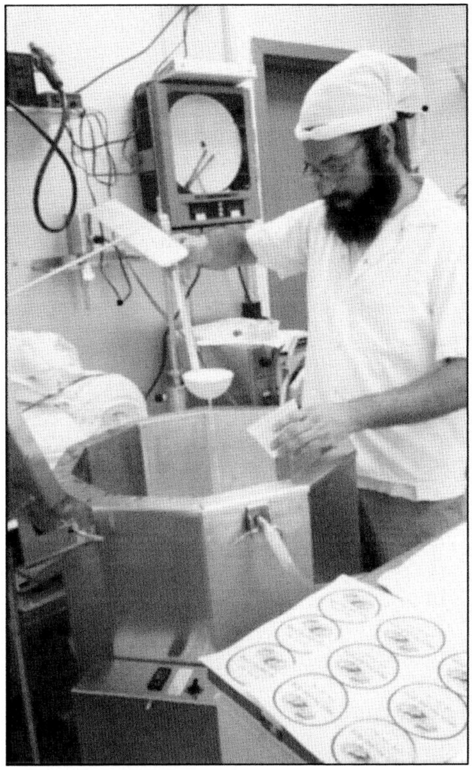

In 2004, Molly Leavitt, whose cousin Judy Baston works at the Jewish Library in San Francisco, had an idea to begin a women's book club with the intention of reading Jewish literature. Approaching local women, she created the Lively Ladies' Book Club. Pictured at a discussion are, from left to right, (on the floor) Susan Cohen-Grossman and Jan Levental; Rochelle Sklansky, Ellen Ingraham, Mimi Farone, Molly Leavitt, Shoshana Deutscher-Nurik, and Judith Lerner. (SDN.)

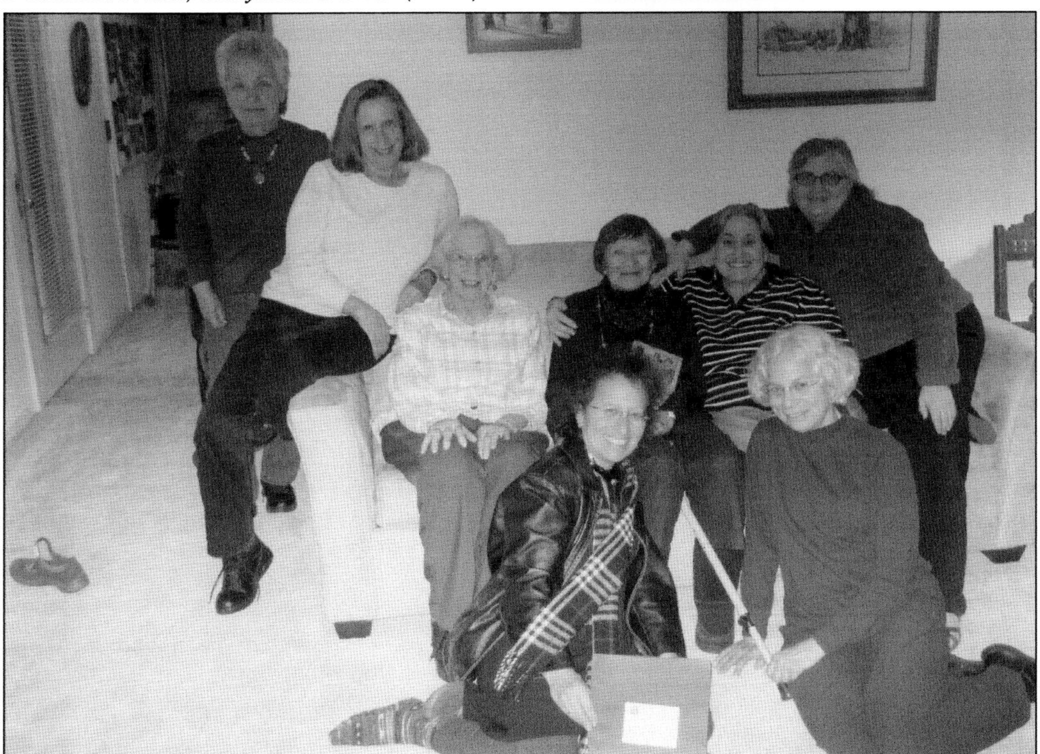